READING THE FIGHTS

READING THE FIGHTS

EDITED BY

JOYCE CAROL OATES
AND
DANIEL HALPERN

HENRY HOLT AND COMPANY

NEW YORK

Published by Henry Holt and Company, Inc.,
521 Fifth Avenue, New York, New York 10175.
Published in Canada by Fitzhenry & Whiteside Limited,
195 Allstate Parkway, Markham, Ontario L3R 4T8.

Library of Congress Cataloging-in-Publication Data
Reading the fights.
Includes bibliographical references.
1. Boxing—History.   2. Boxing—Matches.   I. Oates, Joyce Carol, 1938–
II. Halpern, Daniel, 1945–
GV1121.R4   1988   796.8′3   87–19248
ISBN 0-8050-0510-2

First Edition

Printed in the United States of America
10 9 8 7 6 5 4 3 2 1

ISBN 0-8050-0510-2

CONTENTS

viii   Contents

FOREWORD

The essays and photographs here assembled are all ways of "reading" the fights: variations of interpretation of that most controversial of sports in America in terms of its history, its tradition, its ideals, its practitioners. Theoretical analysis; closely transcribed accounts of such matches as Marciano-Moore, Frazier-Ali I, Leonard-Durán I, Bramble-Mancini II; personal recollections of a boxer's training; an interview with the near-legendary Cus D'Amato; an examination of the unstated role of race in boxing's drama, and of the "poetics" of *machismo*—*Reading the Fights* is a testament of the ongoing fascination writers have long felt for boxing, from the days of the English Prize Ring to the present time. It is for those of us who, like Hugh McIlvanney, believe that boxing, with even its myriad ambiguities, offers in its best moments a thrill "as pure and basic as a heartbeat."

—Joyce Carol Oates and Daniel Halpern

READING THE FIGHTS

Ronald Levao

READING THE FIGHTS

*Making Sense of
Professional Boxing*

Inhabitants of the boxing world have a highly developed instinct for paradox. Consider the case of Ferdie Pacheco. Not only does his nickname, the "Fight Doctor," mischievously pare down the traditional "Ringside Physician" as if to force an oxymoron, or worse, a sinister ambiguity (one who "doctors" or fixes fights), but his style of commentary—veering from enthusiasm to clinical detailing of injury to cries of concern to the blackest humor about hapless boxers—has produced a series of crazy juxtapositions on NBC's boxing telecasts.

Some of Pacheco's finest moments occurred while his network was grooming Frank "The Animal" Fletcher into a temporary contender. Despite Fletcher's violent floundering, he was in some ways a perfect television fighter. He punched in broad, sweeping arcs with legs wide spread, like Clayton Moore playing the Lone Ranger, so that no act of aggression could be missed by the viewer, or by his counterpunching opponent. Such recklessness, joined to a stout heart and a questionable chin, ensured that every bout would dramatize a struggle from the brink of disaster by a low-budget, but real-life, Indiana Jones. The sheer hyperbole of Fletcher's style inspired the Fight Doctor to flights of fancy during the fight—"first the Animal backs them up; then he eats them up"—and then at post-fight interviews, as in his unforgettable discussion with the battered and toothless fighter about the virtues of his new health food diet.

1

N. ALICIA BYERS

Fletcher's NBC miniseries was surely not boxing at its best; indeed, it often seemed dedicated to representing what boxing looks like through the eyes of its abolitionists: the brutal efforts of underprivileged youths to pound one another into senselessness. Yet any attempt to turn the Fletcher-Pacheco Odd Couple into victim and sadist runs aground on the facts of the case. Fletcher reveled in the violent melodrama of his profession, as did his mother, whose on-screen displays of maternal care included leading crowd chants of "Animal! Animal!" and racing around the ring apron to plead with her son to go more often to the body. Pacheco, for his part, is a persistent campaigner for medical reform; he was one of the first to urge Ali to retire in the mid-seventies when his reflexes and kidneys gave signs of darker things to come, and today shows so much solicitude at the sight of blood that some of the crustier observers have renamed him the "Fright Doctor."

What are we to make of such a spectacle? And if we can make

something of it, what of the broader questions that follow—questions about the problematic status of prizefighting itself in contemporary culture? More than any other sport, it both challenges and repels comment, review, and interpretation. Some of this urgency stems from the unique place boxing holds in modern discourse: it is the only major sport whose abolition is and will remain a continual source of controversy. Why does it arouse so much outrage and so much passionate defense? The low social and economic status of most of its participants seems to mark it as a sport of desperation and exploitation, yet even the most successful fighters, or those who ought to know better, have difficulty persuading themselves to retire. Even the blinded Ray Seales confesses that if offered a fight now, he would be tempted to accept. Spectators from all social levels, aware of its brutality and corruption, are likewise drawn to boxing with a fascination wholly unlike the spirit of campy, carnivalesque slumming that marks the recent boom in professional wrestling. There is, too, the mysterious appeal of boxing to masters of literary narrative, from Homer and Virgil to Hemingway and Mailer. Perhaps the spectacle's very marginality makes it irresistible: its violent action seems at once senseless and self-sufficient, beyond the reach of any possible translation, and yet demanding that something be said about it or made out of it. Boxing offers itself as something gratuitous yet fundamental, an especially vivid and candid enactment of all struggle, including one that joins participant and viewer: the struggle to make sense of action.

Evidence of that struggle is everywhere apparent at the fights. Fighters attempt to shape the course of events with their bodies and minds, reading their opponents and themselves for signs of strength and weakness. The impulse of narrative and critical analysis ripples outward from the ring: cornermen produce sixty-second synopses and projections between rounds; journalists scribble, type, or phone in ongoing reports from ringside (Dempsey's trip through the ropes onto a reporter's typewriter is one of the great moments in the history of narrative); and spectators in the highest bleachers argue about the significance of events they can barely see. Finally, there is the critical combat beyond the arena, on the editorial pages of *The Ring* magazine, *The New*

York Times, the *Journal of the American Medical Association,* and so on, between apologists and abolitionists. I want this essay to serve as a kind of commentary on the conflicting ways we look at, and try to talk about, boxing at the present time. My general strategy will be, in traditional pugilistic fashion, to start on the outside and work my way in. Much recent emphasis has been put on demystifying boxing, exposing its psychological, social, or economic motivations and its medical consequences. Like many followers of the fights, I find myself disturbed, illuminated, but finally dissatisfied by such revelations; inevitably I find myself implicated in polemic and schemes for reform. My primary purpose here, however, is to consider the difficulties boxing's appeal presents to any scanning, difficulties that are nonetheless valuable for sharpening our sensitivity to its strange attractiveness.

An axiom: there are few, if any, human institutions or activities that cannot be both praised enthusiastically and condemned as wasteful, vain, hypocritical, or cruel. This is true in part because of our ambivalence toward institutions in general, and in part because of the habit of rhetoricians, ancient and modern, of transforming the problem of ethical choice into virtuoso displays of praise and blame. And there is, too, a kind of sensibility that feels that it must take moral stands, that approval or disapproval, affirmation or denial, must be exercised throughout the entire range of its, and others', experience. The pull toward, and the difficulty of, making such judgments is exemplified by the abolitionist controversy.

The tenuousness of general affirmation—that is, praise extending beyond enthusiasm for local moments of the action—is clear enough. The first time I was introduced to a pair of padded gloves, I was also introduced to the phrase "manly art," an expression that now sounds more quaint than robust. The "sweet science" of Pierce Egan and A. J. Liebling now gets enough ironic use to make it, too, inaccessible unless accompanied by, at the very least, a knowing wink. Less easily dismissable are the claims of those who find in fashioning themselves as fighters a new sense of discipline, dedication, and concentration. The extraordinary, tragicomic tale of the reformed prison escapee, "Hector

Medina," exposed and arrested after a televised fight, proves the value of boxing for those with tremendous energies seeking outlet. But given the sometimes bleak results of ex-fighters' brain scans, the argument for character building is compromised by the danger of that character's accelerated erosion.

One of the final recourses for boxing's defenders is the appeal to economic opportunity. It was either the ring or crime, former champions like to tell interviewers. But the infrequency of financially successful boxing careers, even with the current proliferation of weight classes and split titles, suggests that we are dealing with the dreams of the underprivileged rather than any broadly realizable goal. The value of dreams, for individuals or for society, must not be underestimated, but neither should their susceptibility to exploitation. Financial opportunity, even for the best of fighters, often depends on a trickle-down economy dominated by managers and promoters expert at sealing up leaks. Nor does boxing draw its crowds and fill promoters' and network executives' pockets because the public is fascinated by the spectacle of young men improving their financial condition. Horatio Alger stories help only so much at the gate—Pinklon Thomas's evolution from heroin addict to heavyweight champ is the sort of drama that is good for the Nielsen ratings, but without his booming jab and crunching right, he would not be marketable. The Dr. Johnson of boxing, the late Nat Fleischer, used to dismiss abolitionists out of hand ("male grandmothers" was harrumph enough for him), but most current aficionados have found themselves with very little room in which to maneuver. They find themselves cornered, as it were, into conceding boxing's evils, advancing only to praise isolated moments within the ring. General commentary has become the property of condemning voices.

But if broad affirmation is in trouble, so too is categorical negation. Consider two opening shots in the AMA assault, the widely publicized editorials in the *Journal of the American Medical Association* by Drs. Maurice W. Van Allen and George Lundberg. They pull no punches: boxing is a "sin," a "throwback to uncivilized man," and as long as we don't probe too deeply into their supposition of some Other who managed to be more violent than civilized man, there is some force in their remarks. We know too

much about the consequences of a blow to the head not to need
to listen. The death of Deuk Koo Kim on national television reminded us of a terrible truth already established by the fate of
Ernie Schaaf, Jimmy Doyle, Benny Paret, and too many others.
Curiously, the sleepy, slurred speech of Muhammad Ali seems
to have inspired even wider outrage; Dr. Lundberg, editor of
JAMA, apparently joined the fray only after seeing Ali in a televised interview. Ali's case is, however, a complicated one, not
only because of the uncertain causes of Parkinson's syndrome,
but also because of Ali's odd emotional makeup. Media reports
powerfully juxtapose tapes of the youthful Ali, threatening Liston
or bantering about his greatness with Cosell, with tapes of sad,
recent interviews. But before accepting the before-and-after narrative as the final story, one should also listen to tapes of the
young Ali talking about his religion and his readiness to give up
everything for the Cause—even there one heard a distant, dreamy
monotone that prefigured a widening gap between sincerity and
joy. While it would be absurd to minimize the cumulative effect
of ring punishment on Ali (apologists claim he is merely bored
or depressed), one must not forget that Ali also suffers from an
acute loss of inspiration.

Moreover, because the AMA itself concedes that boxing "does
not seem any more dangerous than other sports currently accepted by society" (it is, in fact, ranked seventh), the question
left unanswered is: What makes this sport different from all others? Does the brain's delicate jelly spin and slosh any differently
within the cranium when hit by a 280-pound lineman than when
hit by a gloved fist? Van Allen attacks the trivializing attitude
toward brain injury of popular entertainment at large—cartoons,
TV detective shows, football—but in the case of boxing, he sup-
plements the medical with the moral: the *intention* behind boxing is evil. He is quite explicit about this: Prizefighters not only
risk injury but suffer a "basic degradation" by their performances,
as do all who are "expose[d]" to such a "show"; the physician
must eliminate boxing as a "public spectacle." If his terms sound
familiar, it is because they are a new edition of an old issue, the
most famous version of which comes down to us from the Puritan
attack on the sinful spectacle of English Renaissance theater.

The theater, too, was reviled as an abomination to a godly society for its power to attract rowdy crowds to witness the deformation of human identity. It is no coincidence that the Globe and other public, professional Elizabethan theaters were built either in the northern suburbs of London or south of the Thames in order to escape the Common Council's jurisdiction, even as early professional boxing in the United States sometimes mounted its spectacles in legal no-man's-land—on river barges, for example, or, in the case of the famous Fitzsimmons-Maher fight, just south of the border to avoid the Texas Rangers. For in both cases, human extremes are willingly and skillfully transformed into public entertainment.

What, however, has taken the place of an angry God to encourage one man to read into and moralize against the inner life of another? Almost universally, abolitionists appeal to social conscience and humanitarian concern. Van Allen reflects ironically on the way our society expresses a "near-hysterical concern for every conceivably deleterious factor in the environment" and whose "strident voices urge equality for all and promote and make capital support of equal rights," but will not put a halt to the "literal sacrifice of minority youth for the profit and delectation of self-styled sportsmen." Thunder on the Right meets oversimplification on the Left. Prize fights at English supper clubs or at Las Vegas and Atlantic City casinos (favorite spectacles in abolitionist polemic) may be unsavory, though more for what they show us about social inequity in general than what they tell us in particular about boxing; the fighters themselves welcome the payday. A visit to a more traditional fight club shows audience and fighter as part of one social group. The respect and affection between a crowd at, say, Stockton's Civic Auditorium and the veteran slugger Yaqui Lopez waving from ringside does not fit Van Allen's paradigm. Nor does Desmond Tutu's pointing to Joe Louis and Sugar Ray Robinson as his childhood inspirations—nor, more generally, does the fascination and admiration in black and Latin communities for Ali, Hagler, Durán, Arguello, Olivares, and many others. For Dr. Van Allen to admit the genuineness of such feeling, given his assumptions, would go beyond mere snobbishness and condescension; it would imply an equation between such communities and the sadistic, even the subhuman, an implication that may well lurk behind Van Allen's conjecture about why more fighters are not aware of progressive brain damage: They lack sufficient introspection to notice.

My point is not to question Van Allen's sincerity or the seriousness of the AMA's social and political concerns, however erratic they have seemed through the years. (Opinion in the medical community is, in fact, divided on the boxing issue, both on scientific and ethical grounds, as can be seen from subsequent letters to *JAMA*.) I am suggesting, rather, that some of the AMA attack, and a good deal of antiboxing polemic in general, is inspired less by a concern for the boxers themselves than by a discomfort about one's own role as an educated and prestigious member of a society where many, whether by necessity or choice, literally fight for a living. These attacks are vitiated by their singlemindedness and Olympian distance; their zeal is directed less against the exploitation of minority youth (I have yet to see alternative careers proposed for those who are to be deprived of their profession), than toward sanitizing and homogenizing American culture. And while voices of outrage usually get the most publicity, they are not always the most interesting. More valuable, and closer to the action, are calls for abolition that arise from a sympathy gone sour, voices such as Gerald Early's.

Early's "Three Notes Toward a Cultural Definition of Prizefighting" and "I Only Like It Better When the Pain Comes" (see pages 20 and 39) are valuable for their failure—despite the author's most strenuous attempts—to arrive at any definition at all. Early's "Notes" are, in fact, at their worst when they affect theoretical gestures to gain leverage on the subject: Boxing is blamed variously on racism, "male politics," primitive ritual, and the "Anglo-Saxon will to power." (More than a little bad faith shows through in the first essay, whose earlier title, "Hot Spicks Versus Cool Spades," Early tells us disingenuously, echoes the "vernacular of the average white," and more than a little absurdity in the second, in which Roberto Durán is transformed into "the mythical Anglo-Saxon male.") The essays are appealing nonetheless for their tensed juxtaposition of disdain and elation: Early calls boxing "vicious," "ghastly," and "ugly," yet confesses himself a "passionate lover of professional boxing." Even as he uses the confession to bolster his right—perhaps his "will"—to judge, Early gives expression to the schizophrenic reactions boxing elicits. In one paragraph he pities boxers as exploited victims of tawdry symbolism and in the next he extols Benny Leonard, Henry Armstrong, Joe Brown, et al., as "greats," as if such a term still had meaning. If boxing's "shoddy and cheerless brutality" is exposed in one place, it is the failure of big fights to deliver their promised drama that provokes a cry for the sport's "swift execution." Indeed, laments for the expense of spirit in the wasteful ring mingle repeatedly with outrage at spiritless fights: Ali's "suffocatingly passionless" victories over mediocre "White Hopes," or the Philadelphia middleweight Cyclone Hart's failure to show proper enthusiasm in his quest for a title shot.

The inconsistency of Early's focus is in some measure a consequence of his own background, as his essays describe it. A studious youth raised among poor Philadelphia blacks—though apparently of better means than they—he was drawn to the toughest street fighter: "He had a great deal of respect for my intelligence (even in those days I was known for being a bookish boy) which I thought surprising since virtually no one else did. It was an even exchange since I had a great deal of respect for the way he used his dukes." It is this dream of a lost reciprocity—when passionate, physical vigor and solitary, unappreciated intelligence existed on equal terms and could acknowledge and admire each other—that glimmers through Early's anger. The coy dips into the vernacular ("bookish," "dukes") betray a shy self-consciousness about such a memory; for now, having gone on to better things as a writer, he finds himself both an insider and an outsider, still an admirer but also a social critic. And he finds in the unsettling brutality of the prize ring a betrayal of that dream. Books and dukes coexist only in the local, studied metaphor of his essays: Ray Leonard's "Joycean dispassion" set against Durán's "romantic impulse of improvisation," for example. Yet other writers who dare seek their own figurative rapprochements with ring combat (Mailer, Liebling, reporters from *The Ring*) become targets for Early's jealous hostility. If, as Early intends to show us, "only a true lover of the sport can understand why the proles deserve a better fate," his essays also show the difficulty of coming to terms with an activity that may at one moment quicken the pulse and at another wrench the gut, one that may evoke, in the same observer, both passionate engagement and sullen rejection.

As we move still further into the culture of boxing, we may expect to find increasing sympathy for the fights, but we also find, in the fighters' own attitudes, continuing signs of a radical ambiguity. "There's nothing to love about being hit in the head," onetime WBA heavyweight champion Mike Weaver told a *New York Times* reporter. "There's nothing to love about feeling blood come out of your nose, or seeing it come out of somebody else's." Fighters routinely insist that they are only in it for the money, with defensive quips like Tex Cobb's, "It beats workin'." Yet boxing also evokes joy, not only in such notorious tough guys as Roberto Durán with his sinister grin and Charles Manson glare, but in "gentleman" boxers like Floyd Patterson who, in the waning days of a very long career, called boxing his "shot of LSD," and who now trains his adopted son as a boxer. Postures of hatred and contempt (Durán stunned a national audience when he boasted that his still unconscious foe, carried out of the ring on a stretcher, would be taken to the morgue if they fought again) coexist with those of love and respect. Bobby Chacon, stopped by Alexis Arguello, vowed to name his next child "Alexis," and did. Amy Levit, a former ballet student married to California boxer Ruben Solorio, told a documentary filmmaker that boxing was her husband's "identity." "It's how he expresses himself to people. It's how he feels love." Perhaps the most volatile attitude was Muhammad Ali's. Having announced his superiority to boxing the day after he won the heavyweight title in 1964, he continued to express his disdain, with hysterical assertions of his greatness, for the better part of two decades. Boxing is senseless, he would tell interviewers, a ludicrous spectacle of two grown men in shorts, jumping up and down while hitting each other; at the same time he was quite capable of promoting an upcoming fight as "the greatest sporting event in the history of the planet earth." To dismiss either position as mere sanctimony or salesmanship is to misread Ali's remarkable yet exemplary story: Few public figures have ever revealed so profoundly the compulsiveness of *homo ludens* and his appetite for serious play.

If there is any center to the mystery of boxing's appeal, it lies in that ancient paradox of serious play. Huizinga may have made the element of play in human culture a subject for academic scrutiny, but there are no activities in popular culture that make so agonizingly apparent as does boxing the unstable boundary between games and cold earnestness. Boxing, for this reason, assumes a special status among athletic events. Abolitionists routinely denigrate it as a "so-called sport" and they are in some ways right. We may just as properly call it a "metasport," because it exposes to the critical eye the deep structure and motivation of all athletics. Other sports "degenerate" into fights when rules and discipline break down—the swinging of hockey sticks, the emptying of benches after a bean ball—events that usually provoke indignation, videotape repeats on the evening news, and amused commentary on how few good blows were landed. Boxing orders and preserves the energies released at such moments, and it is for that reason that it is both the most primitive of contests and a match for any in the complexity of its strategies, counterstrategies, rituals, and traditions. Its strategies are relentlessly pragmatic, yet one is often surprised by the preponderance of means over ends. A great fighter takes pride in those means. After defeating Giulio Rinaldi at Madison Square Garden, Archie Moore complained of his foe: "His lack of finesse appalled me." The energies embodied by a fight may be pictured, to borrow an old figure, as surging within intersecting pyramids or gyres—variously nameable as skill and violence, play and earnestness, art and abomination—because we become aware that the blend is never stable, not from fight to fight, nor from round to round, nor even from minute to minute. The figure itself is unstable: where does one picture a skillfully executed foul, or a gracefully delivered knockout blow? It is, nonetheless, serviceable: As one side assumes prominence over the other, the fight takes shape as what the morning papers will call a "chess match" or a "pier-six brawl." There is, despite what Hollywood melodramas show us, a long-standing contingent that enjoys the former. Among the astounding tales fight buffs enjoy telling, dramatic knockouts rank no higher than Willie Pep's winning a round without tossing a single punch. Of course, even the most balletic fighter (unless he is throwing the fight) must eventually start throwing punches, yet the potential swing to brutality coexists not merely with athletic skill, but with a still further extreme—a joyous exhibitionism, and reveling in ornament. Though the "Ali shuffle" and the "bolo punch" were defended by their practitioners as having strategic value, they more truly show that the world of broken noses knows its own forms of the baroque, and that seedy gyms foster their own rococo.

But no great fight is unmixed. It is the area of intersection that is crucial, and in the most perfect fights—Louis-Conn I and Ali-Frazier I come immediately to mind—the pyramids of darkness and light, of violent struggle and the virtuoso's finesse, are most intimately joined. These are the forces played out on the physical stage—the raised white canvas is a blank and basic *platea*—which make it possible to see great fighters as great artists, however terrible their symbolic systems. It may be, and perhaps should be, difficult to accept the notion that a prizefighter's work merits the same kind of attention we lavish on an artist's, but once we begin attending to and describing what he does in the ring, it becomes increasingly difficult to refuse the expenditure. The fighter creates a style in a world of risk and opportunity. His disciplined body assumes the essential postures of the mind: aggressive and defensive, elusively graceful with its shifts of direction, or struggling with all its stylistic resources against a resistant but, until the very end, alterable reality. A great fighter redefines the possible.

Despite the melancholy image Muhammad Ali presents today, one cannot review his career without marveling at it. He forced us to reimagine the ways an athlete moves through time and space; even in his waning years, he waged a battle against stylistic norms. As a youth he held his hands too low, and yanked his head straight back from blows (an amateurish move, the traditionalists grumbled), yet he so accelerated the pace of heavyweight fighting that scarcely anyone could keep up with him. With extraordinary self-consciousness, Ali relished the difficulty his dancing around and back created not only for his opponent, but also for ringside cameramen trying to keep him in the frame. As he aged, he sought the opposite extreme in posture and pacing: Immobile along the ropes, head down and hands held high, he slowed the pace of major fights to an excruciating point, exhausting his foes, not by forcing them to keep up with him, but (consider this) by luring them into trying to force him to keep up with them. Ali was always the expert parodist, whether through his (and Bundini Brown's) cartoonlike nicknames for his opponents' styles ("The Rabbit," "The Octopus," "The Washerwoman"), or through his exaggerated mirrorings of his foe—his deliberately awkward rumbling around the ring, elbows swinging, against Bonavena, his outdaring Jerry Quarry in a game of chicken (who could drop his hands longer?). These moves gave Ali the illusion of omnipotence, even when he had to struggle, as he did against Bonavena, even when desperately hurt, as in the eleventh round against Frazier when, severely shaken by a hook, he did a campy, drunken dance, a comic's version of the staggering fighter. As he aged, he forced his opponents to parody themselves as eager young challengers working over the old man. If his aesthetic proved to be more dangerous than Ali at first imagined—his satiric impression of a punch-drunk fighter at a press conference for the first Frazier fight is horribly ironic today—he still insists it was worth it. Many would no doubt feel more comfortable if they could convince him that it wasn't.

Ali's loyalty to the profession that broke his jaw, slurred his speech, and possibly did worse, still hidden, damage is based in part on what he calls "my millions" and on his vision of future opportunities for the black man. But it also represents a performer's devotion to the medium through which he expressed genius, genius that might otherwise have remained unexpressed, perhaps inexpressible. He understands, too, that to ban the probable cause of his distress would be to render trivial the world's continued fascination with him. He became Ali by creating the Ali style. It is a style for which there are antecedents in Jimmy Slattery, Gene Tunney, Kid Gavilan, and others, but one which he fashioned into so distinct a form that one might say of the way he turned his head or countered over a jab what Coleridge said after reading the verses of a friend: "Had I met these lines running wild in the deserts of Arabia, I should have instantly screamed out 'Wordsworth!' " Ali's nuances and eccentricities provoked a world of observers to thunderous chants of recognition: "Ah-lee! Ah-lee!"

It is, finally, this mass fascination with the fighter's violent art that is most disturbing to the abolitionist. Why does it matter so much to so many? The answer, I have been suggesting, lies in the kinds of energies boxing makes explicit. When boxing brings to the surface the deepest impulses of sport, the immediacy of its revelations is registered in the conduct of its spectators. The image of the bloodthirsty crowd is accurate in part and inadequate in sum. At its worst, the crowd becomes vicious and vindictive; at its best, it is filled with the spirit of mimesis. The viewer rolls with the punches or mimics the blows he has seen or would invoke; boxing is the only sport I know in which the bodily motions of performer and spectator so exactly mirror each other. If the crowd hungers for a knockout, that, too, is a part of the mirroring transaction, but its appetite is less for carnage than for intensity, a state of heightened response that may be compromised by too brutal and one-sided a spectacle; cries of "Stop the fight" not uncommonly supplant cries for the kill. That intensity may, of course, take bizarre directions. A few years ago at a Yaqui Lopez fight I sat next to one ringsider who, after swearing threateningly and peeling off gambling stakes during the early rounds, apparently underwent a Saint Theresa-like ecstasy as his trailing hero rallied during the closing rounds: "Yaqui! Yaqui! Yaqui!" he moaned, eyes rolling up, rocking back and forth in his wooden seat. When the decision, a questionable one, went to Lopez over the smoother Jesse Burnett, I doubt that many mystics could have felt more transported.

More generally, the spectator's intensity is focused, fusing the passionate and the analytic. The skilled fighter does not lose his head in the heat of battle, and neither does the agitated fan. Even as he pays the most rapt attention to the action, he calculates the turns of strategy and advantage, recalling precedents and projecting consequences, scanning the subterfuges and tropes of style and action. It is this presence of both passion and analysis that draws so many different kinds of observers to the fights. Researchers have suggested that some personalities grow addicted to their own bodies' surges of adrenaline: they may become high-pressured businessmen or high-stakes gamblers. Casino owners and promoters in Las Vegas and Atlantic City have observed the type to their profit: Nothing draws the high rollers into town like a big fight. Less profitable for promoters, but no less conspicuous, is the attraction of men (and some women) of letters to the fights. Their fascination is, I think, generated by the same sort of fusion, though they are more accustomed to finding it in other forms. It was because of its apparent blend of passion and thought that Grierson and Eliot turned to metaphysical poetry as an aesthetic ideal—"passionate thinking is always apt to become metaphysical," Grierson wrote—and there is an analogous power to be found in the experience of a fight. "Though a quarrel in the streets is a thing to be hated," Keats mused in a letter to his brother and sister-in-law, "the energies displayed in it are fine." Sherwood Anderson saw in the fighter a metaphor for the artist's creative frenzy: "All of his nerves are on edge. I have watched painters at work who were like Dempsey about to enter the prize ring. One man I knew swore violently sometimes when he was painting. If you had interrupted him at such a time he might have hit you with his fist."

If we are reluctant or even repelled by the effort to direct such intuitions and analogies toward a fuller reading of boxing's appeal, one reason is boxing's spectacular failure to sustain an object commensurate with such intensity. Anyone involved in the fight game, whether as fan or professional, must expect to meet the most fundamental kinds of betrayal. Freddie Brown and Ray Arcel, trainers of another era, found a revival of their glory days in the great Roberto Durán until his "No más" return bout with Leonard shook them as deeply as any fighter Durán demolished in the ring. Government, universities, organized religion—all august institutions are liable to arrogance and cynicism, but the squalor of boxing corruption, the gratuitous brutality of its mismatches, the cynicism of its fixed fights, and the disastrous consequences for some of its victims, are as uncompromisingly visible as are its excitements. For all the self-serving hypocrisy that laces Howard Cosell's conversion to the abolitionist camp, the genuineness of his disgust is impressive: "I am worn out by it." Like Cosell, almost all who desert the sport do so not out of boredom, but out of sheer exhaustion. Every enthusiast who resists idealism or flippant fibbing (Cus D'Amato tried to blame congenital aneurisms for ring deaths; Angelo Dundee claims he has never seen a fixed fight) must find some way of negotiating between delight and dismay. Consider, for example, *Flash Gordon's Tonight's Boxing Program*, an insider's newsletter that swings wildly from devoted detailing of the smallest club cards to bitter (and sometimes paranoiac) exposés of a "racket which bursts at its seams with whores, slobs, and pimps." Conspiracy theories and the fixed fight are prominent in *Gordon*'s universe: the FBI, the crooked promoters, and the television networks are together a league of demons; notices of upcoming fights are punctuated with sixties-ish "wow!"s, even as they are scrutinized for mismatches and dives—*Gordon* signals these by changing the names of the participants: K. O. Pectate, Lew Sitania, Kenny Breathe, Willie Getup. The suspicious fight is, after all, not uncommon, and in a sport this tough no one wants to sound naive. Wise-guy humor, a peripheral atmospheric feature of many sports, becomes a necessity for so much of the fight crowd, both as a mode of accommodation and a means of forgiving.

But perhaps the greatest obstacle to a full and subtle reading of the fights is learned inhibition, a sense of decorum that requires us to cringe at the thought of overintellectualizing popular culture, particularly in aspects that seem lowbrow. "To 'read' boxing matches or pop festivals," one literary critic has complained, "yields . . . predictable results. Modern popular art is seen to be a 'bad dream' of high art." While such resistance may sensitize us to a discrepancy between our terms and the elements of culture we would probe, it also reflects on the intellectual's anxiety about his place in society, his cultivated and precarious distance. Fighters and those close to the action—trainers, managers, fight-beat correspondents—for all their jaded realism, feel no such squeamishness, and they revel in the subtleties of their trade. Watching a fight requires the observer to be alert to the rhythms and phrasings of the combinations, to the expectations they create and the improvisations that are born during moments of pressure. An alert reader of Ike Williams or Ray Robinson has more in common with an alert reader of Donne or Milton than with a dull reader of either. The fight itself encourages our keenest responses. Everything is done off the jab because the jab embodies attention, speculation, and penetration: "Weaver's jab is more *perceptive* than Dokes's," Angelo Dundee noted during their heavyweight fight last year. A live fight makes enormous demands on our own powers of perception. The decisive action of other sporting events is calculated to be as publicly visible as possible: A home run, a touchdown, or a basket can be witnessed from almost anywhere in the arena or stadium. The decisive moment of a fight may be more secretive—an uppercut delivered inside, or a subtle shift in strategy—and yet that event is perhaps the most highly concentrated moment of significance in any sport. A home run's greatest potency is four points; a team trailing by ten runs can hope only that the opposing pitching staff caves in, demoralized. But a single blow or combination may change a fight utterly, and there is no next inning to catch up. John Tate was leading roughly 13 to 1 when a left hook ended his reign as heavyweight champion.

Because so many major bouts are televised, complete with expert commentary (the CBS team of Clancy, Leonard, and Ryan is the best), one may forget how difficult it is to follow the action of a good fight. Even a closely observed fight is unpredictable, capable of changing direction, or making its main point unnoticed. Perhaps the greatest service Howard Cosell rendered to boxing fans, apart from championing Ali's cause during the latter's political exile, was his gross lapses of attention. His reliance on a priori scenarios that failed to fit the action (after the 1976 Olympics, every fight became a lesson in "lateral movement"), his miscalls of important shifts of action and decisive blows (review a tape sometime of the final rounds of Holmes against Leon Spinks or Cooney), his inability to grasp the nuances of style (he dismissed the prechampionship Hagler as a fraud, and was so bored by the now-revered Carlos Monzon that he spent half of one fight talking to race car driver Jackie Stewart) forced viewers to fend for themselves. Unlike his football shows, where fans could turn off the TV sound and substitute radio commentary, Cosell's boxing shows unwittingly reminded fans of the kind of concentration watching a good fight demands.

I began this piece by arguing that the fight crowd has a highly developed sense of paradox, and I want to end by stressing the double response that boxing requires. It evokes not a poised ambivalence, but a tensed juxtaposition of opposites, a fascinated engagement and an outpouring of terms and images that are indissolubly linked to an awareness of what that enthusiasm costs. The drive for medical and ethical reform is an essential appeal for decency and fairness toward boxing's workingman, the fighter, but everyone from fighter to network executive knows that the cost will always be high. The issue of abolition always returns to this: Who has the right to declare that cost too high? Who governs that economy?

If boxing survives, it will not be because of hoped-for reform, nor because of enormous television purses (as Cosell self-importantly declares), but because of the curious fact that it is harder to decry the violence of a skilled fighter than of a crude one, even if more actual damage is done by the former. A talentless fighter may be a sympathetic figure, but more often he becomes a source of displeasure, or of only fleeting interest; we can only wish he would find another line of work. Jack Dempsey's death evoked an outburst of praise for a "true hero," even from commentators who felt compelled to lament, in subordinate clauses, the source of his fame; Joe Louis's ability to fell an opponent with a blow traveling less than a foot remains a touchstone for athletic prowess of any kind. As a gifted fighter matures, his ring conduct becomes an increasingly complex assimilation of reality, and a confrontation of great fighters seems virtually a Thucydidean clash of cultures. Almost any scandal is forgotten in the wake of a great fight, whose transfiguring powers border on the magical. *The New York Times*, which in its editorials and sports columns has relentlessly demanded the abolition of boxing, reflected those powers as well as any publication after the Hagler-Hearns fight. George Vecsey's attacks on corruption and brutality gave way to

Dave Anderson's breathless adjectives: "thunderous," "tempes-
tuous," and "marvelous." The "perilous pace," the "sheer beauty
of brutality" not only "gloriously justified" Hagler's newly legal-
ized name ("Marvelous")—"He was as marvelous as a boxer can
be, perhaps as marvelous for eight minutes as any boxer has ever
been"—but justified, however temporarily, prizefighting itself:
"This was not just another third-round knockout, this was eight
marvelous minutes that will be remembered for what boxing is
supposed to be, but seldom is." Not even the voice of sophisticated
disillusionment could cancel out a quasi-erotic wonder at Hagler's
eight-minute revelation of glory. Anderson's enthusiasm was con-
tagious. A moving, if somewhat wishful, article on Ali appeared
soon after, invoking Ali's continuing good humor and playfulness
to suggest that he was as sharp as ever, only speaking more
slowly. *The Times*'s Sunday *Magazine*, which had run a neurological analysis of fighters' injuries and the nine levels of cerebral
concussion, complete with cutaway diagrams of the skull and
medical translations of boxing jargon (one of the neatest pieces
of linguistic imperialism one would ever care to read), ran Joyce
Carol Oates's meditative piece on boxing's dark fascination. This
turn, it must be emphasized, was not the result of boxing's cleaning house, of medical or ethical reform, or of a new editorial policy.
It came out of a great fight in which boxing once again revealed
most truly what it is: highly skilled and highly dangerous, a
keenly focused public exhibition of human will and intelligence
translated into articulate energy.

Gerald Early

THREE NOTES TOWARD A CULTURAL DEFINITION OF PRIZEFIGHTING

One must have a mind of winter
To regard . . .
And have been cold a long time
To behold . . .

WALLACE STEVENS, "THE SNOW MAN"

Note 1

In the eighties, as the sport of boxing spotlights the lighter weight divisions where the Latin fighters tend to congregate, a new variation on the old theme of race has emerged. The most important, that is, the most symbolic, battles are no longer, as in the old days of Jack Johnson, Joe Louis, and Ray Robinson, white versus black, nor, as in the sixties and seventies with Muhammad Ali, Joe Frazier, and Ken Norton, black versus black, but rather black versus Latin. No fight could more appropriately have opened the era of the eighties in boxing than the first Sugar Ray Leonard versus Roberto Durán bout for something called the World Boxing Council's welterweight championship.

No title fight of the seventies, with the exceptions of the Ali-Frazier clashes and, possibly, the Ali-Foreman tilt, received so much publicity as this one, or reached out so far beyond the confines of the sport's enthusiasts to excite the general public.

Yet no fight of this caliber in recent memory was more disappointing. To put it bluntly, it was a failure—perhaps a poignant signal of what our slouch to the end of the century will be. The fight was surely exciting; despite complaints from some quarters about Durán's mauling and wrestling tactics, hundreds of punches were thrown by each fighter and most of them landed. The fight was performed (the most apt verb that comes to mind) at a very brisk pace, and any true boxing aficionado, any dedicated devotee of what was called in 1824 "the sweet science of bruising," found more than enough in the bout to keep his interest and even to elicit his admiration.

But the fight was a failure to the general public, and even the cultural instincts—the cultural radar, if you will—of the boxing aficionados sensed it to be a failure, because it was not conclusive. The fight had excitement but no drama, tension but no true engagement; it ultimately gave the viewer the incredibly weird sense of experiencing a kind of rhythmless syncopation. At the end of fifteen rounds, the question of who was the best—the only relevant question in boxing and, indeed, in all sports—remained largely unanswered. Leonard and Durán seemed as if they had fought the entire fight underwater; once it was over, once they emerged from the deep, there was a lingering sense that they had never touched one another, a feeling that the fight just witnessed had never even taken place. The fight was so close that it became nearly a kind of pointless derring-do on the part of the fighters. To the public mind and to our cultural selves, it was important, to be sure, that one man come forth clearly as the best. Durán was chosen the winner almost as an afterthought.

Some said that this fight would be, metaphorically, the matador and the bull—in other words, the classy boxer against the slugger; old-timers talked about its similarity to the Jake LaMotta–Ray Robinson battles; others reminisced about Carmen Basilio and Ray Robinson or Sandy Sadler and Willie Pep; those of more recent memory said the fight was a scaled-down version of Ali versus Frazier. All of these fights were very big affairs, and all of them, except Ali-Frazier, were fights between men of different races. Even the Ali-Frazier fight had a deep and bitter intraracial contrast which I will mention shortly. So, in truth, the Durán-

Leonard fight was, quite properly, placed in this tradition. The fight was the mythical confrontation that was to apotheosize one particular minority as the underground male image of the American collective psyche. The fight was the super-cool nigger versus the hot-blooded greaseball. Here was the monumental encounter between the hot and the cool, between the classical order of technique and the romantic impulse of improvisation; the inner-city warriors went at each other for ownership of the night (one as Clark Kent in a Brooks Brothers suit, the other as Chanticleer in a sombrero).

There was Durán, whose style, like that of a jazz musician's, relies so much upon the inspiration of the moment that when he is uninterested in a fight he is worse than mediocre; and there was Leonard, so completely absorbed with the intricacies of his talents that with Joycean dispassion he seemed to watch the beautiful nuances his left jab made as it traveled its trajectory through the air. George Benton, once a world-class fighter, and now the trainer of such fighters as the up-and-coming featherweight, Rocky Lockridge, also seemed to be just such a combatant, enamored of the artistry of his style. One imagines that Leonard could overwhelm his opponents while not even realizing that they actually existed. Futhermore, Durán represented the old, perhaps dying, order of champions, the young kid who learned his art on the street and went straight into the pro ranks at the age of sixteen. Leonard was the product of A.A.U. meets and the extensive amateur programs in this country that threatened to make the old street-corner art of fighting obsolete (just as the old after-hours jam sessions among jazz musicians are a thing of the past. Now, young musicians learn jazz in the practice rooms of Juilliard).

The question arises why the first Leonard-Durán fight was the symbolic racial showdown of the Latin and the black or, to put it in the vernacular of the average white, between the nigger and the spick, as opposed to the fight between Wilfred Benitez, a Puerto Rican, and Leonard, in which Leonard won the title by a knockout in the fifteenth round. Benitez, who became junior welterweight champ at the age of seventeen by beating Antonio Cervantes and who became welterweight champ before he was twenty-one by beating Carlos Palomino, certainly had credentials that were as impressive as Durán's. Futhermore, while the book-makers made Benitez an underdog in his fight with Leonard, it must be remembered that Durán was also an underdog. The answer to our question is that Benitez is black. Moreover, he anglicized his first name from Wilfredo to Wilfred, an act for which most New York Latins, among whom Benitez was once considered a young, reckless god, will not forgive him. More important, Benitez does not fight in what we have come to think of as the Latin-macho style of, say, a Durán, or a Pipino Cuevas; Benitez is a slick, polished boxer, a counter-puncher who slips his opponents' blows very well. In short, there seemed to be no real racial contrast between Benitez and Leonard for the press to exploit and the public mind to latch upon.

And racial contrast is what the male politics of boxing is all about and it has a long history. Jack Johnson, the first black heavyweight champion, avoided fighting such talented blacks as Sam Langford, Joe Jeanette, and Sam McVey during his cham-pionship reign because the ticket-buying public—that is, at that time, the white public—was only interested in seeing him fight a "White Hope." Even with Joe Louis, certainly the most beloved of all black boxing champions during the 1930s and 1940s, his most important and most publicized fights were those against Max Schmeling, "Two-Ton" Tony Galento, Billy Conn, and the final bout of his career with Rocky Marciano, all of whom were white. Granted that Louis's fights with black fighters such as Ezzard Charles and Jersey Joe Walcott were certainly major con-tests, one has only to check the various record books and boxing annuals to discover that only Louis's matches with whites get the pictures. Ray Robinson, the great black welterweight and middleweight champion, also had his most important fights against white opponents: Jake LaMotta, Gene Fullmer, Paul Pender, Bobo Olson, Carmen Basilio, and, for the light heavyweight title, Joey Maxim.

The Patterson-Liston bout changed the racial emphasis and then the most publicized title bouts became intraracial instead of interracial. Most of Ali's important fights, unlike Louis's or Robinson's, were against blacks (e.g., Liston, Frazier, Norton,

Foreman, and Spinks). This, of course, was because there were very few white fighters left in the game. Just as the Patterson-Liston bout became in the public mind—and, now, *public* means both black and white collectively—a fight between a "punk" and a "bad nigger," the first Ali-Liston match became the "crazy nigger" versus the "bad nigger," and the first Ali-Frazier fight, an encounter so fraught with political overtones that many blacks cried in the streets the day after Ali lost, became the "politically hip" black versus the "homeboy." Ali never really needed to fight white men to create racial contrast for a bout since, with the help of the media, he was able to make over his principal opponents into whites by virtue of their politics or their lack of politics: Nearly every Ali opponent became a representative of the white establishment. Indeed, by the time of the Foreman fight, Ali had become a sort of Calvinist redeemer of the race and Foreman the pork-eating king of the unelect. (We must except Leon Spinks from this process. Spinks's ghetto image made Ali seem the bourgeois, overfed, conservative black. Remember, Ali never bragged, never acted the street corner clown role before the first Spinks fight. For the second fight, Ali became the old, wily pro, the "old head," and Spinks was the green amateur, the "young boy." The bout became a classic street corner lesson in humility for Spinks. Never try to beat an old head at anything, whether it is doing the dozens or doing the dukes.)

Remembering Ali's title fights against white opponents is almost a test to discover how much trivia the mind is unable to discard. During his first championship reign there were George Chuvalo, Henry Cooper, Brian London, and Karl Mildenberger (four forgettable and largely forgotten fights in chronological order, from March to September of 1966); and during his second reign there were Chuck Wepner, Joe Bugner, Pierre Coopman, Richard Dunn, and Alfredo Evangelista. Between the two reigns there were Bugner, Rudi Lubbers, Jerry Quarry, Jurgen Blin, and Chuvalo. These fights were uninteresting not only because Ali usually did not fight at his best against these opponents, but because they were so suffocatingly passionless.

Black fighters captured Ali's easily distracted attention not only because they were better than the corps of white fighters he faced, but quite simply because they were black and because they were rivals for the attention of white America. And after all, Ali, since winning the gold medal at the 1960 Olympics, wanted the attention of white America, not even its adoration, though to a large degree he got that as well, but its attention was what he, and perhaps secretly in their hearts, most blacks craved. He wanted to make himself so important that whites could not ignore him, to bring the black psyche out from the underground and onto the stage, the very proscenium, of the white consciousness. And he felt that he could do this better than other blacks. Ironically, Ali, while playing the role of the militant Muslim, denigrated his black opponents in ways that one would have expected only from a racist white, or a black ill at ease with his collective identity. He called them "stupid," and "ugly," he said that they "couldn't talk," and that they should not be allowed "to represent the race." In short, Ali's black opponents became symbolically that marauding mass of lower-class tricksters and berserkers who made whites flee the cities in fear, and Ali, a roguish combination of Reverend Ike and Ellison's Rinehart, a sort of jive-time, jive-assed shaman, was the middle-class, brown-skinned black who kept them at bay. If on the part of these opponents there was jealousy and envy against Ali, the "crab in the basket" mentality of the poor, then, on the part of Ali, there was honest abhorrence of blacks who traditionally made things "hard for the race." In some ways, Ali was as much of a striver as a hardworking, light-skinned hero from a Charles Chesnutt or Jessie Fauset novel.

Since the retirement of Ali no other black fighter has been able to make an effective contrast between himself and another black fighter. If two black fighters are in the ring the white public generally ignores it and the black public, while on a local level supporting such endeavors of black club fighters and novices, tends to feel a bit uneasy when the fight is for higher stakes, obviously thinking that "two brothers shouldn't be beating up each other for entertainment." In effect, the Leonard-Benitez fight was two black men slugging it out. In truth, racial contrast eases the painful realization that boxing is a sort of vicious exploitation of simply being male; racial contrast gives boxing matches symbolism, a tawdry, cheap, sensational significance which the sportswriter may understate but never leaves unsaid. So, with an insufficient white presence in boxing, and lack of general public interest in most black-versus-black fights, the only racial contrast that can be manipulated is black versus Latin. But the Latin must be of a certain sort.

So enter Roberto Durán, the man who, despite or perhaps because of his Indian heritage, looks both so classically and so uniquely Latin, the man with the relentless and uncompromising style—with fifty-five knockouts in seventy fights—who was champion of the lightweights for six and one-half years and who exterminated the division's opposition with a degree of fury and disdain that endeared him to the television networks when they decided to recognize the existence of boxing below the heavyweight division. (We will not speak here about the level of Durán's competition while he was champion. Nor will we comment on the distinct possibility that Durán's considerable talents may be vastly overrated. Suffice it to say that it is doubtful that such mediocre fighters as Lou Bizarro, Vilomar Fernandez, and Edwin Viruet would have lasted until the 13th, 14th, or 15th rounds if they had been against such lightweight greats as Benny Leonard, Henry Armstrong, Joe Brown, Carlos Ortiz, Joe Gans, or Ike Williams.) Here was the true Latin fighter, or at least what an uninformed American public thought was a true Latin fighter, since we know nothing about Hispanic culture and Hispanic civilization, but we do know the word "macho," a cliché that describes nothing but signifies everything. Durán is the true Latin, macho almost to the point of irritation, the man who said to Howard Cosell that he would make Leonard "fight like a man." Here was the racial contrast that made the almost unendurable publicity for the first fight possible. Durán became the prototypical Latin fighter, many people forgetting, first, the fact that not all Latins are aggressive punchers, and that the fighters who gave Durán the hardest times in the ring—the Viruet brothers, Saoul Mamby, Zeferino Gonzalez, and Vilomar Fernandez—were all Latins who understood that discretion is the better part of the manly art of self-defense, and chose to box with Durán rather than slug it out; and, second, the fact that Durán, over the years, has learned to become a better than passable boxer and actually beat Jimmy Heair in a lackluster bout by outjabbing him.

Very little more needs to be said about either Durán or Leonard; they became the blond and the brunette of the romance of American sports. Durán, we know, was the little tough guy from Panama who knocked out horses as a teenager, quit school at the age of thirteen after having reached the third grade, won the lightweight title in 1972 from Ken Buchanan on a low blow, then refused to honor the return-bout clause of the contract, the man sportswriter Dick Young called "the Animal" (a term he would never dream of using to describe a black fighter) and promoter Don King called "the Little Killer." Durán's bully boy insouciance brings to mind both the late Bruce Lee and jazz trumpeter Miles Davis, both of whom were also little tough guys, who, at the height of their fame, swaggered and swashbuckled in front of their audiences as if they were preening themselves for some secret fertility rite.

Leonard is the young man who has brought, as Howard Cosell tells us, "class" to boxing. He is articulate, handsome, smiles a lot, never discusses politics and, aside from one illegitimate child who was later legitimized through marriage, has very little of the taint of ghetto upon him. He gives talks about good sportsmanship to elementary school kiddies and signs autographs for Jewish ladies vacationing in the Catskills. But in truth Leonard wants so desperately to become a personality, recognizable in the same way that white movie stars and entertainers are, that he seems to be holding himself aloft for the highest bidder. Leonard, in short, wants to end up like such white ex-jocks as Bruce Jenner or Joe Namath. What we are witnessing is not the rise and fall of Sugar Ray Leonard but the selling of "Sugar." Leonard is such a shrewd young man that we can get no real sense of the army of people behind him; he seems to be the only *auteur* of his scenario. He wants to be liked, so he makes himself *likable* in about the only way a black person can in this society, by being inoffensive. (Ali, of course, was terribly offensive to this Herrenvolk democracy's taste and values, and he paid a dear price for that.) Leonard is not interested in airing his excesses or becoming, to use the 1920s phrase, "a race man"; he is not mythopoeic material. He is bland and cute, and gives the overwhelming impression of being harmless; his coolness is without subtlety, his manner as polished and chilled as a depthless lake in winter.

Unlike other fighters, and most especially unlike Durán, Leonard anesthetizes the general public to the corruption and horrors of boxing because he does not look as if he came from a ghetto and gives the impression that boxing is not the only thing he can do. His presence, unlike, say, that of Leon Spinks, is not a *j'accuse* to the sport of boxing and to the society that supports it.

As a cultural event, as an event which produces a pattern of symbols and meanings, professional boxing, like most sports, is a social ritual, a drama in the most Aristotelean sense that elicits the feelings of pity and fear most vividly. Ideally, deep inside we should fear the winner and pity the loser and somehow if the match fails to produce these "cleansing" emotions, then it has failed to complete us. By completion I mean what Clifford Geertz once said, that the involvement in our cultural forms and rituals gives us definition, finishes an "incomplete or unfinished animal." And in sports, particularly boxing, the ritual is very much like the Christian Communion: we partake of the body and soul of the athlete, the last and exquisite god, touchingly vulnerable. We have become so accustomed to racial contrast in boxing matches that they have become nearly meaningless, just so much shoddy and cheerless brutality, without it. The masks of racial identification that our fighters wear are similar to the masks worn by the actors in ancient Greece; they are not masks that hide, not psychological masks, but rather masks that reveal all, masks of the primitive which are, as it were, giant, lurid images of the ego beneath. Probably boxing comes closest, of all sports, to producing the primitive responses of pity and fear because the sport *is* so primitive—so naked, if you will. It is appropriate that boxing should now be the possession of the cool medium of television (boxers, like other athletes, have become "TV heroes") where the drama has been modernized to adopt a tone of muted stridency.

So, in our cultural hearts racial contrast and, what is concomitant with it, racial identification are important for the completion of ourselves. The cultural weight of the first Durán-Leonard fight is that it reinforced the emotional perception, if not the intellectual idea, that men are different physically and psychologically because they belong to different races. Despite the mass of scientific evidence to the contrary, we still secretly wish to believe that the mask we wear, namely our skin color and our racial background, like the ancient Greek mask, makes us what we are. So, Durán becomes the stereotypical fiery, macho Latin and Leonard becomes the stereotypical cool, slick boxing black.

Racial contrast awakens the still uglier need of racial identification, something which the ludicrous boxing film *Rocky* exploited in such an obvious, almost embarrassing way. Even today in boxing a cry can be heard which goes back as far as 1915: the cry for a "Great White Hope" who, supposedly, will save boxing for its white fans. As an example of how racial contrast brings about racial identification, consider Gerry Cooney, a promising young Irish heavyweight. Cooney was propelled to the position of number one contender in the official rankings of the World Boxing Council and the World Boxing Association, largely on the basis of beating a very inept white fighter named Dino Dennis. According to CBS sports broadcaster Dick Stockton, the public "demanded" that Cooney fight for the title (or, since nearly every division has two title-holders, it is more accurate to say "fight for *a* title")—a demand based on his very impressive win over once highly regarded Philadelphia heavyweight Jimmy Young. However, before Young lost to Cooney he was defeated by a young black fighter named Michael Dokes and beaten twice by a black Puerto Rican, Osvaldo Ocasio. The public did not "demand" that either of these fighters should immediately fight for the title. Nor did anyone think that the significance of Cooney's victory was more than slightly diluted by the fact that Young had not won an important fight since his loss to Ken Norton a few years ago. Apparently the catharsis of pity and fear produced by boxing is effected more profoundly when the viewer is of the same race as one, and only one, of the boxers.

World champions from the British Isles such as middleweight Alan Minter and lightweight Jim Watt disguise this urge of racial identification under the cloak of nationalism. Those of us with only a passing acquaintance with the history of Britain are well aware that the British nation is, in truth, the British race and that the British wish to stay as alabaster white as the heroine of an Ann Radcliffe or Jane Austen novel. Besides, when black British junior middleweight champion Maurice Hope has fought, no band of brass-playing beefeaters file in the ring before the fight to play national airs and the British fight fans at ringside do not sing "God Save the Queen" with tears in their eyes—which is what actually happened before Minter's defense against Marvin Hagler and Watt's defense against Sean O'Grady of Oklahoma.

And now we must await the article in some leading sports publication such as *Inside Sports* or *Sports Illustrated* or, perhaps, in *Esquire* or *The Ring*, that will ask the asinine question: Are black fighters better than Latin fighters? The article will then offer as possible evidence for an affirmative answer the recent successes blacks have had with Hispanic adversaries: Hilmer Kenty's knockout win over Ernesto Espana for the lightweight title; Aaron Pryor's knockout win over Antonio Cervantes for the junior welterweight title; Tommy Hearns's devastation of Pipino Cuevas for the WBA's version of the welterweight title; Marvin Johnson's victory over Victor Galindez for the light-heavyweight title; Jessie Burnet's victory over Victor Galindez to become the number one contender for the newly created cruiseweight crown; Leo Randolph's upset over Ricardo Cardona for the junior featherweight title. But this current trend means nothing. American fighters are coming out of amateur programs better trained than many Latin fighters who fight out of foreign countries. As many of the South American countries improve their amateur athletics, their fighters will generally gain parity with black U.S. fighters. Furthermore, such brilliant Latin fighters as Roberto Durán, Wilfredo Gomez, Alexis Arguello, Wilfred Benitez, and Salvador Sanchez have had great success against black fighters in the past and probably will continue to be successful in the future. Finally, outside of Muhammad Ali, the two most eminent fighters of the decade 1970–1980 were Durán and now-retired middleweight champion Carlos Monzon. No black fighter, aside from Ali, dominated his division the way these two Latin fighters did and neither man had, through the decade of the seventies, ever lost a title fight. Let us hope that such an article dies before it is written, since the current *slight* superiority of black fighters has absolutely nothing to do with race and we need no sportswriter to make implications to the contrary in a national publication.

Note 2

I remember very well that I could not sleep the night that Benny Kid Paret was knocked into a coma by Emile Griffith in a welterweight championship bout in March of 1962. I had watched that fight on television and when Paret was carried from the ring, unconscious, and, for all intents and purposes, lifeless, I felt myself quivering on the inside. That night I prayed to God to save Paret's life. Indeed, I remember being on my knees and praying very hard, having learned in church that God answers those who truly believe. I thought I truly believed but Benny Kid Paret died anyway. Not only did I learn something about the inscrutable whimsicalness of God but also about the precariousness of the life of a fighter. It was then that I felt that professional prizefighting should be banned, not because it was brutal (a kid who grew up in my neighborhood could not be that morbidly thin-skinned and survive), and not even because it was absurd (whether life itself is absurd is debatable but certainly all sports are), but because it was so uncaring. Boxing as an official bureaucracy hates boxers. Some boxing bureaucrats somewhere allowed a woefully out-of-condition middleweight named Willie Classen to fight and die in the ring, allowed a flashy Philadelphian named Gypsy Joe Harris to fight although he was legally blind in one eye; these same officials and bureaucrats now tolerate a parade of bums and stiffs who, fighting under various aliases, endanger their health and degrade the sport by being allowed to fight opponents who are infinitely superior to them. Seven fighters died in one year as a result of beatings which they sustained in the ring, one being a young Welsh bantamweight named Johnny Owen, who was knocked out by champion Lupe Pintor in the twelfth round of their title fight. Owen never regained consciousness and died in a Los Angeles hospital a few weeks later.

So far, the average death rate has been one fighter every two months. And yet nothing has been done to safeguard the fighters; various state boxing commissions have not coordinated their records to prevent, say, a fighter who was knocked out forty days ago in Maryland from fighting in Pennsylvania or Nevada; if a ringside doctor is present at a fight it is almost always a general

practitioner, possibly an internist, doctors who are expert at examining cuts, but almost never a neurologist, a doctor who would
recognize the signs of incipient brain damage; nothing has been
done to change the rules of professional boxing, either reducing
the number of rounds or changing the style of the gloves or
introducing a standing eight count in professional fights; the only
things the WBC and the WBA are concerned about are squabbling
over who is the true champion of a division or compiling a ranking
system often with the money of promoters and television networks in mind; so, suddenly, a very uncreditable bum becomes
a contending fighter—this, of course, means that many a fighter's
record is more fiction than fact.

These are old complaints. Indeed, every few years some hard-
boiled, reform-minded sports reporter like the one portrayed by
Humphrey Bogart in the 1956 cinéma vérité classic, *The Harder
They Fall*, recites this list as a kind of litany to stir the soul of
the great mass of the unconcerned. The fact that these complaints
are not new should tend to bother us rather than bore us. After
all, these cries of reform reveal that the only major innovations
that have taken place in the last 120 years of professional fighting
have been placing gloves on a fighter's fists and reducing championship fights from interminable lengths to twenty rounds and,
finally, to fifteen. But it should be obvious to all that professional
prizefighting cannot be reformed, not with so many bogus and
even criminal entities, outlaws to their very bootstraps, struggling
for corporate hegemony while the boxers are seen as so much
meat hanging on tenterhooks (the most moving scene in the film
Rocky is when Sylvester Stallone is punching a carcass in a
slaughterhouse. Heavy-handed but still striking symbolism). The
solution for this sport is quite simple: Professional fighting must
go the way of cock fighting and dog fighting and be banished
from our realm. Then, the amateur program, which is more sanely
supervised, can be offered in colleges, and poor boys from our
mean streets can be given an education and the possibility of
actually qualifying for work from which they may get a pension
in their old age. We have seen how, as a cultural phenomenon,
boxing brings out deplorable urges to see ourselves racially, and
we have only to walk into any local gym, get to know any two-

bit fighter, to learn that as a nonsymbolic part of our social system fighting is an ugly sport. The one word that comes to mind more than any other watching the fighters work in the gym is "proletariat." These men are honestly, and in a most ghastly way, *toiling*, and what is most striking is how much more grotesque this work is than, say, the nightmare of an assembly line. And proletariat is such an appropriate word for fighters whom we also call stiffs and bums, words that grew out of the working class vocabulary—a stiff being someone who is managing to survive in the working world, a bum being a stiff who has temporarily been cast out of the working world, and hence is just "bumming around."

As an ardent, I might say, passionate lover of professional boxing, a follower of my boxing heroes since I was a young boy, and as one who appreciates the working-class folklore that surrounds boxing, it is particularly difficult to call for its demise. I remember listening with intense fascination while patrons in the local barbershop spoke of the exploits of Sonny Liston; I can recall the agonizing disappointment when my uncle failed to take me to see the Joey Giardello–Dick Tiger middleweight championship bout; there comes to mind the anguish when I read that the once magnificent heavyweight Cleveland "Big Cat" Williams, who was nearly shot to death a few years before, was going to fight Muhammad Ali for the title, a hopeless mismatch, and I can remember aggrieved amazement when I heard that the promising young junior lightweight Tyrone Everett had been shot to death by his girlfriend. Perhaps, in the end, only a true lover of the sport can understand why proles deserve a better fate.

Note 3

Eugene "Cyclone" Hart was once a prospect for the middleweight title. He had a left hook that was the best that that division had seen since the days of Ray Robinson; he would whip it around with his whole body, producing a crushing blow. Unfortunately, Hart was not a good defensive fighter and tended to get discouraged and disoriented if his left hook failed to produce results within the first few rounds. He had recently lost a fight by knockout to Vito Antuofermo who was to become, briefly, the undisputed middleweight champ, when I met him in circumstances which were probably not very flattering to Hart. He had been arrested for disorderly conduct and, at that particular time, I was working with the Release-on-Own-Recognizance Program (ROR), which was funded by the Law Enforcement Assistance Agency. My job was to interview prisoners before their arraignments to discover if they were eligible for release on their own recognizance—or as they called it, free bail. I cannot speak about other projects that LEAA gives money to, but I certainly can say that my job was a monumental waste of my time and the taxpayers' money. But that topic of discussion must wait for another time. Of course, once I discovered that Cyclone Hart was "in the tank," I made sure to finagle his paperwork so I could interview him. Quite naturally, once I got him to my desk I promptly forgot his bail interview—he did not need one anyway since he had never been arrested before and the charge was so minor that "free bail" was a foregone conclusion—and we sat and talked boxing.

"Are you still going to fight?" I asked. "Lots of people say you're washed up."

"Well, I'm sure gonna try," he said. I remember how hard and strong his body was. He had the hips of a dancer, the shoulders of a halfback. "I think I can still make it. I got a few good fights in me and I might still get a title shot. That's what I'm hangin' around for: a title shot."

"I thought you were going to knock Antuofermo out of the box early," I said.

"Yeah, so did I, but he's a pretty tough cat."

We talked for a while about some other of the local fighters like Jerome Artis, Bad Bad Bennie Briscoe and Sammy Goss. When he rose to return to his cell he said: "Yeah, I'm still hangin' in. I mean, what else can I do? My luck might change."

I had expected him to make a sort of sign with his fists when he said that, but he merely held his hands relaxed at his sides. His lack of gesture was as surprising to me as walking down a flight of stairs and anticipating a final step when none is there. Cyclone Hart was a washed-up fighter at the age of twenty-seven.

"I still might get a title shot," he said as a policeman led him away.

"Yes," I called after him from my desk, "that's nice work if you can get it."

Postscript: Leonard-Durán II

The hardest thing to teach a young boy bent upon becoming a professional prizefighter, according to any cigar-chomping, gibbous old fight trainer, is to get up and continue fighting after the youngster has been knocked down and hurt. In most cases, a fighter is knocked down by a punch he did not see and it is only human nature to want to avoid the unknown and not to wish to continue. It takes hours and hours of the most severe sort of training to make a fighter overcome that natural instinct. Robert Jarrett, a black man who is neither a cigar-chomper nor gibbous, explained this to me one winter afternoon. He is a former professional prizefighter who now trains black youngsters in the Richard Allen projects in Philadelphia in the "sweet science." "Once a kid learns this," he pontificated, "he becomes a man." I did not disagree. But when I see a decked fighter get up and continue to fight, or, in most instances, continue to get beaten to a pulp, I know it is not "heart" or courage which makes him stand up, but a sort of Skinnerian conditioning which has effectively dulled his brain so that he has no real idea when he is hurt or how badly.

Professional boxing, in recent months, has come to resemble professional wrestling in the absurd perversity of its demeanor—lacking, however, wrestling's vulgar hilarity. Wrestling, like Roller Derby, realizes its own sense of burlesque and continually teases and insults its lower-class audience with a sort of mock drama as if it were masterminded by some Grub Street exile; boxing has now mistaken its hysteria for the most profound theater. It has, in a word, become not just a joke spoken in poor taste, but a joke gone in the teeth.

The abrupt ending of the Durán-Leonard rematch, with Durán, for whatever reason, walking away from Leonard in the eighth round, was a pathetic ending to a rivalry which had so engaged the imagination and symbolism of our culture. Perhaps Durán walked away because he was "taking a dive," although one would be hard put to imagine what corporate interest could induce him to embarrass himself so in front of his family, friends, fans, and countrymen, or what corporate interest would want him to; or perhaps he walked away because he experienced an epiphany which revealed at once and at last to his eyes the absurdity of his profession; or perhaps, and this is more likely, he felt very sick: The once poor, lean street urchin, who when he first began as a professional was easily able to make the 135-pound limit for lightweights, may have, in acquiring fame and riches, eaten his way not only out of the lightweights but perhaps out of the welterweights as well. Crash dieting and the use of diuretics are poor methods of training. Alas, this is what happens to those who live life in the fast lane. At any rate, this poetic battle which was to pit the war machine's frenzy against the body electric's gallantry became just another tainted, bizarre contest. This fight which was to justify the existence of boxing wound up justifying its swift execution.

This bout kept the spirit of several other championship fights: Muhammad Ali's painful return, in which, donning another disguise of Melville's Confidence Man, he paid the price of passing blood for a week in exchange for ten million dollars and the opportunity to show the world what early male menopause is like. After acting and Third World diplomacy failed, only boxing remained for this most self-conscious man to engage his puerile exhibitionism. More recently, there was the fight for the junior welterweight championship of the world between Aaron Pryor, the black champion, and Gaetan Hart, the white Canadian challenger. Not only did this fight exploit, as usual, racial contrast and racial identification, but the network that televised the fight reminded the viewers at every opportunity that Hart had seriously injured one fighter in the ring and killed another. Implied in this grotesque reporting, and in the whole raison d'être for Hart, an extremely mediocre fighter to be fighting for the championship, was the obscene question: Would Pryor be Hart's next victim? Hart had eighteen losses on his record; normally no fighter with such a propensity for losing would have been even remotely considered for a championship fight, and the two men he severely battered in the ring were even more inept as fighters than he was and probably should not have been allowed to fight. Pryor knocked out Hart in the sixth round of a mismatch.

In early November I went to an elementary school gymnasium in Ithaca, New York, to watch a local amateur fight card. The first bout of the evening was between two ten-year-old kids, one black, the other white, representing two different boxing clubs. The white youngster was game and tried very hard but the black boy had real talent, the look and hunger of a possible future professional prizefighter, and he thoroughly thrashed his opponent and easily won the fight. As I watched the black boy being congratulated by his friends and as my eyes circled the gym and viewed Ithaca's lower class out in mass to support its relatives and friends I asked myself, why? Why does this youngster want to be a fighter? Why would his family be proud if he became one? His chances of having a career like Ali, Durán, or Leonard are so remote that no bookie would give any sort of betting line on the possibility. And the cost of this misplaced ambition is so much deeper and heavier than if a middle-class kid who plays tennis, another "solitary ego" sport, wished to become John McEnroe.

Tennis is a bourgeois, respected recreation, second only to jogging; no stigma is attached to its pursuit by the white middle and upper classes, and the failure to succeed as a tennis professional does not affect the middle-class youngster's mobility or the possibility that he can cultivate other humane or profitable interests. In other words, a tennis career and, say, an MBA degree, are not incompatible. They are phenomena of the same world and they represent the same bourgeois values.

Boxing is part of another culture, available to a boy who cannot be a singer, a preacher, or a thief (which are really the only other job training programs readily available to the lower class). His success is measured by his movement up the fight card until, finally, he becomes the featured attraction, the main event, and the high rollers of the upper class, caught between ennui and debauchery, come to watch him fight and to bet on the outcome. For the poor, any ambition is ultimately to make money, to change their lives, to make them better. But, as James Brown sang in the mid-sixties, "Money won't change you . . ." A poor person with money is simply, to the eyes of the middle and upper classes, the beast displaced, the tolerated savage, the simpleton with poor taste. And the poor boy himself discovers that the rage which he nurtured to become champion, the rage which pushed him from his birth, the rage against that stultifying bourgeois monolith which made his life miserable, either still gnaws at him like a burning ulcer or has left him completely burned out by the absence of desire. Thus, he finds himself naked and vulnerable, in a nest of vipers. And further, he discovers that it was the rage, and the rage alone, that not only kept him alive but made him human. Money won't change you, indeed. But as James Brown sang in the same song, "Time will take you out."

As I watched the youngster in the ring I thought for a moment about Benny Briscoe, the Philadelphia middleweight, an aging 38, who had several times fought for the title and each time came up empty. Losses to Carlos Monzon and Roderigo Valdes for the title and losses to such up-and-coming middleweights as Marvin Hagler and Vito Antuofermo climaxed a career of frustration and bitterness. Bennie will never be champion and, although he continues to fight, he must hold down another job in order to live.

On any given weekday, in any gym in America, there are ten-year-old boys banging away at heavy bags and sweating in desperation as they pursue that Belle Dame sans Merci—a professional boxing title.

On any given weekday, Bennie Briscoe hauls trash in the ghetto of North Philadelphia. The long journey from the gym to the professional prize ring ended as it began: on the streets. As the corner boys say, Briscoe still "lives on the block."

Gerald Early

"I ONLY LIKE IT BETTER WHEN THE PAIN COMES"*

More Notes Toward a Cultural Definition of Prizefighting

To all the black boys of Philadelphia
who are the small princes of our wounded order

I. *The Exiles*

On a summer day many years ago Jeff Chandler beat my cousin, Gino Fernandez, in a fight on the grounds of the Nebinger school- yard. I think both Jeff and Gino were nine or ten, which means that I was about fourteen or fifteen. I doubt if now it is remotely possible to recall the reason for the fight. I lived in South Phil- adelphia and my cousin, who lived in West Philadelphia, would from time to time come to visit me and spend a few days. I remember well how we enjoyed each other as boys, finding much to do with our days together. This was to change as Gino grew older; toward the end of his life I rarely saw him and when I did we had little enough to say. In recent years, I have come to feel

---

*The title comes from an article which appeared in the March 1983 issue of *The Ring* which was entitled "1982: The Year of the Notables and Quotables" (pp. 18–29). The full quotation of Frank (the Animal) Fletcher is on page 22 and it reads as follows: "I hate to say it, but it's true that I only like it better when pain comes."

quite badly about this estrangement even though it was not my fault that it occurred. On this particular day of the fight, I suppose that my cousin's being from West Philadelphia and therefore a stranger in the neighborhood may have had something to do with the antagonism between the boys. Jeff probably instigated the fight because he was always, as I remember him, a very tough small boy who took a great deal of pride in his ability to fight.

The battle was not a very long one. It started out evenly enough but the crowd of boys who nearly smothered the combatants were quite partisan in favor of Jeff, giving him the sort of "home court advantage" that revealed to me instantly that my cousin was doomed. Gino did, though, fight quite well for several minutes. Suddenly, Jeff hit him with an uppercut to the solar plexus so perfectly executed that any prizefighter would have been proud to have thrown it; its technique was not simply flawless, it was rich in artistic refulgence. My cousin crumpled to the ground in agony. He was crying, a sure sign of capitulation. Jeff walked away, surrounded by his cloud of admiring and cheering witnesses. He felt no sympathy for the loser and, in truth, it was proper that he did not. After all, each boy knew the risks of the encounter before it began, and to commit oneself to any action is to commit oneself to the etiquette of promptly paying certain immediate psychic costs for failure. So, after a minute or two of taunts and jeers directed at me about my "punk cousin," I was left alone to tend to Gino, who was now sobbing heavily and deeply ashamed. I picked him up, extricated a balled-up, snotty handkerchief from my pocket, and wiped his face. We walked together almost in the pose of big brother and little brother: I held my arm around his shoulder and he walked with his head down. I told him not to cry, that everything would be all right, that he would surely have better days. I was quite wrong in this prediction, for if anyone was to have better days it was to be Jeff Chandler. My cousin, at the age of sixteen, was to have his head blown off by a sawed-off shotgun fired at close range by a sniper during a street gang war. Jeff Chandler would later become the World Boxing Association bantamweight champion. The fates of these boys, poor black boys of the streets, far from being unique, take on a sort of dreary, deadening, clichéd familiarity. Both fought for street gangs as adolescents and either could have drawn the other's fortune or misfortune. Chandler could very easily have ended up on a slab in the morgue, and my cousin might well have become a professional fighter. This is perhaps not only how the Bigger Thomases of black America are born, but also how they are made.

Although my cousin lived and died in West Philadelphia, his funeral took place in a South Philadelphia funeral home. The deep oddity of that fact is that the funeral came very close to not taking place at all in that location. The South Philadelphia street gang nearest to the funeral home was the Fifth and South Streets gang, the very gang that Jeff Chandler was then fighting for. And these boys were not going to have their turf invaded by the comrades-in-arms of a fallen West Philadelphia gang member. I remember that at the funeral there were nearly as many cops as bereaved relatives and friends, and such a guarded atmosphere that one might have thought some cruel political dictator was being buried. If there had not been so many police officers present, my cousin's funeral might very well have sparked more bloodshed.

I do not think any group of people could have felt more diminished and deranged by all this than my family did. Here, after all, was a young, wayward Jehovah's Witness boy who was murdered according to the arcane but deadly rules of the ghetto rites of passage. My family, both its South Philadelphia and West Philadelphia branches, had never thought it even lived in a ghetto, much less that it would be brutalized by its hard reality. My mother was stunned to learn that Gino was a member of a street gang. I was an undergraduate at the University of Pennsylvania at the time and this whole horrible incident made me feel degraded.

Jeff Chandler is a very good professional fighter, amazingly good when one considers that he has had no amateur career to speak of. He had a few amateur fights, then decided that it would be better to fight for money and glory than for trophies and glory, especially since the amount of effort would be about the same. He has beaten everyone in his weight division worth beating, and would love to fight his Latin counterpart—Lupe Pintor, the

World Boxing Council bantamweight champion—in a title uni-
fication bout. But the young Mexican wants nothing to do with
Chandler, so the hard Philadelphian will probably move on to the
featherweight division and hope that he can make more money
fighting bigger fellows. Because of the death of Tyrone Everett,
the retirement of Joe Frazier, the deterioration of Matthew Saad
Muhammad and Jimmy Young, and the unfulfillment of Curtis
Parker and Frank Fletcher, Chandler has become the top Philadelphia fighter. That is quite an accomplishment because that
town produces many good fighters, and the training sessions,
both in the gym and on the streets, are wars of the bloodiest and
most demanding kind. Chandler, simply put, is a survivor in a
place and in an occupation where most are swallowed whole in
midcareer.

II. The Kings in the Tower

Alexis Arguello, great champion of the featherweight, junior
lightweight, and lightweight divisions, is known to be a friendly,
easygoing fellow outside of the ring. He numbers among his
friends many fighters who are potential rivals. He seems particularly proud of his friendship with Sugar Ray Leonard who despite his retirement is still a potential rival because everyone
knows that retirement announcements in boxing do not mean
much. The story goes that once in a social context Arguello met
Roberto Durán, great champion of the lightweight and welterweight divisions, and came up to shake hands and chat with him.
At this time Durán was still considered to be, by those who are
supposed to know, pound-for-pound the best fighter in all of
boxing, and there was more than a little talk of a possible big
money bout between him and Arguello. Durán, known for his
haughty disdain for and intense dislike of opponents, looked
aghast at the approaching Arguello and, while backing away from
him, screamed, "Get away from me! I'm not your friend! Get
away from me!"

As crazy as it seems, Durán merely took one of boxing's learned
inclinations to both its neurotic and its rational limits. It would
seem only to complicate matters a great deal to be friendly with

the men one is required to fight. A boxer must inflict a lot of punishment in the normal course of a fight in order to expect to win, and it would seem that he might feel less compromised or uneasy in his actions if the opponent was not a friend. On the other hand, it is quite natural for people who share a particular profession also to share friendships; who can know better than a prizefighter the rewards of achievement or the frustrations of defeat in the prizefighting profession?

Durán does not wish to be friendly with boxers who may be potential opponents because it makes the psychological part of training that much harder. This is often referred to as "psyching yourself up," which means creating an artificial hatred for your opponent, so that you may more efficiently and brutally beat him up. There is more at work here than the incredibly fierce sense of Darwinian competition that characterizes the spirit of play in other professional sports. Boxing, after all, is the only sport whose object is to hurt your opponent—to place him in such pain, to inflict such severe injury upon him, that he cannot or will not continue to fight. The emotional incentive for this must be deeper than the mere quest for championship belts and big money, although, to be sure, those latter items do spur fighters on. Boxers must be driven by other needs as well when they enter the ring: They must have "something to prove," or they must "hold a grudge" against their opponent for some imaginary or petty slight, or they must feel like particularly evil bastards who can, to use John L. Sullivan's phrase, "lick any son of a bitch in the house." In short, the bouts become quests for manhood.

Leonard Gardner's fine novel about second-rate boxers in California, *Fat City*, contains a scene in which the reader sees the pathetic desperation of this psyching up of the boxer, this dredging up of courage from the spirit to stem the tide of the deep fear of it all:

> "Hoping never done nothing," [said Buford Wills.] "It *wanting* that do it. You got to want to win so bad you can taste it. If you want to win bad enough you win. They no way in hell this dude going beat me. He too old. I going be all over him. I going kick him so bad, everytime he take a bite of food tomorrow he going

think of me. He be one sore son-of-a-bitch. He going *know* he been in a fight. I get him before he get me. I going hit him with everything. I won't just *beat* that motherfucker, I going *kill* him." Buford was small and thin. His hair, divided at one side with a razor-blade part, was cropped close. His nose turned up, his nostrils flared, his lips were soft and full and his hooded eyes were narrowed in a constant frown. The year before, only fourteen, he had lied about his age and won the Golden Gloves novice flyweight title in San Francisco. Tonight he was fighting the champion of Fort Ord. "You want to know what make a good fighter?"

"What's that?" [asked Ernie Munger.]

"It believing in yourself. That the will to win. The rest condition. You want to kick ass, you kick ass."

"I hope you're right."

"You don't want to kick ass, you get your own ass whipped."

"I want to kick ass. Don't worry about that."

"You just shit out of luck."

"I said I wanted to kick ass."

"You got to want to kick ass *bad*. They no manager or trainer or pill can do it for you."

"I want to kick ass as bad as you do."

"Then you go out and kick ass."

One of the two interrelated cultural needs that boxing serves suggests that the antagonism of the opponents is very much like that of a morality play, a morality play about the very nature of capitalistic society. Despite the fact that boxing is an international sport, practiced everywhere on the globe, America has become and has been for some time the center of professional fighting. Most of the best fighters are Americans; most of the big money originates here, and most of the publicity as well. In short, boxing is an American pastime. Moreover, one must not lose sight of the fact that modern professional boxing in its traceable history was a product of Britain; boxing in its course to its present identity is not just Western, not simply American, but particularly Anglo-Saxon. It should come as a surprise to no one, knowing modern prizefighting's national and racial origins, that the sport extols most simply and directly the values that the Anglo-Saxon male has historically cherished most: the indomitable will of the individual, aggressive conquest, and contempt for humiliation and submission. It is, perhaps, intended to be the height of irony that Wills, the black boy, the historical victim of the Anglo-Saxon's will to power, should teach Ernie Munger, the white boy, the Western values of male conquest. Wills's little speech sounds as much like the street-corner version of the philosophy of Robinson Crusoe as it does like the advice of a senior boardroom executive to a junior upstart. It is one of the striking ironies of the novel that boxing, a sport which so ruthlessly symbolizes the success ethic of American society, produces men who are so ill-equipped to be anything but failures. Thus, one of the true oddities of the symbolism of boxing is that the minority male, in becoming like the paradigmatic, mythological Anglo-Saxon male, wears a kind of white face.

Durán's little episode with Alexis Arguello might remind one of the incredible invisible burden of the champion boxer, the great "asskicker." Gardner's novel is exclusively concerned with pugs, or as Camus called them, "lowbrow gods." But the intensity of emotional commitment is greater when the fights mean more: more money, more prestige for the winner, more humiliation for the loser. Durán's insecurity has its source in the very deep doubt he must have about his self-image in his chosen profession. Durán is afraid, not so much of being beaten, but of being reduced, lessened, by showing any signs that would make him less committed to his line of work. One must remember that it was Durán who once said after beating an opponent that if he had been in shape he would have sent him to the morgue, not the hospital; it was Durán who once saluted Sugar Ray Leonard's wife by pointing his middle finger and calling her *puta* (whore); and it was Durán who spat in Leonard's face at the end of their first bout. This need for the commitment, the overwhelming identification not with boxing but with what it means to be an asskicker, is probably the main reason that Durán is still fighting even though he should have retired a few years ago. Durán is more the mythical Anglo-Saxon male than the Anglo-Saxon himself, and if that identification proves meaningless, then Durán is forced to ask himself what his blustering quest for manhood means. This is why he is still fighting and embarrassing himself. He does not want to think about what it would mean to stop: Then, he would be like a soldier without a war.

A film that clearly presents, in a huge metaphorical gesture, the secret fear of the male is the 1950s science fiction classic, *The Incredible Shrinking Man*. Slowly, as the hero's body becomes smaller and smaller, the audience finds him overwhelmed not by life generally, not by his job, his government, his culture, or by his general intercourse with other people—but by his home and his wife. The woman becomes an overprotective giant and the home a wild hive of booby traps which threaten him at every turn. One is, of course, reminded of Leslie Fiedler and his talk about those many nineteenth-century American Adams who were trying to escape the very things that Herman Melville's Tommo was returning to at the end of *Typee*: home and mother. In *The Incredible Shrinking Man* there is a parodic inversion by which the man finds himself being swallowed by his home and his wife (whose relative largeness and maternal concern make her a mother figure); he must do battle against objects of his own home: a cat and a spider. The hero thus discovers that living in his home has become the ultimate pioneering adventure as he hunts for food and water and, in the final symbol of pathetic power, uses a straight pin for a sword. Grant Williams, who portrays the hero, ultimately loses his battle as his body simply vanishes by the end of the film.

This neurotic vision, or rather this dream or parable of the neurotic, trapped male, poses a very essential question about the sport of boxing: what is its secret, primeval appeal to its viewers? Part of the answer, no doubt, lies in the boxer's puritanical regimen: the hard training, the abstinence from sex before a fight, the Spartan diet. The boxer's leanness and physical conditioning become a sign of his virtue, a virtue worth a great deal in a land where the fatness of sin is the sin of fatness. But more deeply, the answer rests somewhere in the fact that the male is not needed as a cultural image for his courage, stamina, and heart, all of those manly virtues about which he has woven myths; he is needed as a psychological emblem to illustrate the capacity of dumb suffering. It is the torment and disfigurement of the male body that helps the male to achieve the godhead. Norman Mailer would find in a film like *The Incredible Shrinking Man* the most endearing symbolism.

The first section of Mailer's *The Fight* opens and closes with images of the male body; the opening chapter describes "the Prince of Heaven," Muhammad Ali, in a training session, the beautiful body hiding both power and grace within its limbs:

> To the degree that boxing is carnality, meat against meat, Ali was master when it was time to receive, he got the juice out of it, the aesthetic juice of the punches he blocked or clipped, plus all the libidinal juice of Bossman Jones banging away on his gut. . . .
>
> Now it was as if Ali carried the idea to some advanced place where he could assimilate punches faster than other fighters, could literally transmit the shock through more parts of his body, or direct it to the best path, as if ideally he was working toward the ability to receive that five-punch combination (or six or seven!) yet be so ready to ship the impact out to each arm, each organ and each leg, that the punishment might be digested, and the mind remain clear. It was a study to watch Ali take punches.

The descriptions seem complementary. In the first, the body as mythic image lies between art and sex; and in the second, the body is the mechanism that must be controlled and manipulated by the mind. Both denote so precisely the precarious precision of the boxer's psychological tightrope walk between seizing and creating the moment or squandering it. Mailer is indeed concerned with the wider symbol of the black male's tightrope walking. But Mailer's representation is not so much a psychology of the male body as it is an anthropology of the male body. Somehow, through the imagery at the beginning of Ali's body as self-fulfilling sex, as art, and as machine, and the imagery at the end of the first section of the spindly, ugly body of Ali's talkative trainer, Drew Brown, the reader is presented with the history of male culture, from prince to clown, from the improvisations of the body to the improvisations of language (when the body, as in the case of Brown, fails as adequate symbolism). The polar realities of Brown and Ali as male figures symbolize the morality of masculinity: Ali puts his body on the line and is, thus, a hero-warrior. Drew Brown weaves with his mouth and is like a jester, a gnome, or as Mailer calls him, "The King of the Flunkies." It is Brown who creates Ali's chants and poetry and it is with Brown that Mailer "plays the dozens." So, although Ali was known as "the Mouth," Mailer's fascination and that of the entire Western culture with Ali has, in truth, always been with his heroic body. Boxing becomes, for Mailer, the most primitive yet the highest moment for the male psyche. The one-on-one encounter, the rewards of its brinksmanship, the egotistic excesses of its one-upmanship, is what boxing and the male body mean.

The major problem with Mailer's fight book is that he spends a good number of his pages, far too many really, writing about race. This comes about because this book, like most of Mailer's fight pieces, is about Muhammad Ali, and with Ali as a subject I suppose one is, perforce, confronted with the issue of race. Yet I think white writers like Mailer use Ali as an excuse to write about race, or more precisely, about blacks: What a wonderful opportunity to clear the chest and spleen of numerous phobias and neuroses! When Mailer writes about race or about blacks he invariably is going to sound like the writer who penned that inglorious essay, "The White Negro"—which means that he is liable to sound foolish. He will not sound utterly foolish, just foolish enough to make any knowing reader accept his good portions with a great deal of suspicion. Consider these passages:

> But [Norman Mailer's] love affair with the Black soul, a senti-mental orgy at its worst, had been given a drubbing through the seasons of Black Power. He no longer knew whether he loved Blacks or secretly disliked them, which had to be the dirtiest secret in his American life. Part of the woe of the first trip to Africa, part of that irrationally intense detestation of Mobutu . . . must be a cover for the rage he was feeling toward Blacks, any Blacks. . . .

> . . . [H]is animosity switched a continent over to Black Ameri-cans with their arrogance, jive, ethnic put-down costumes, cater-wauling soul, their thump-your-testicle organ sound and black new vomitous egos like the slag of all of alienated sewage-com-pacted heap U.S.A.; then he knew that he had not only come to

report on a fight but to look a little more into his own outsized feelings of love and—could it be?—sheer hate for the existence of Blacks on earth.

Mailer was in Zaire to report on the heavyweight championship fight between Ali and George Foreman which took place in a hastily constructed stadium in the fall of 1974. Thus, the reader is confronted with Mailer's image of the land of bogeys and boots, the land without rational order, and the image becomes a quest on Mailer's part for the legitimation of his own rational white mind and his confessed inability to understand that mind which symbolizes for him the nonwhite other. It is Mailer's being in Africa and covering a fight between two black fighters that ultimately leads to the sort of psychic flatulence that the two quotations reveal. For Mailer, the black is always the id-dominated beast, the heart of the white man's darkness; and always, in Mailer's tone, there is that juvenile penis envy that might as well be hate because it amounts to such an insulting kind of love. He writes elsewhere in the book:

> So much resentment had developed for black style, black snob-
> bery, black rhetoric, black pimps, superfly, and all the virtuoso
> handling of the ho. The pride Blacks took in their skill as pimps!

It is no wonder that Mailer loves boxing, or rather loves the symbolism of boxing. His engagement with the black experience has always been limited to the male side of all matters—when Mailer says "Blacks" he means male (an observation also made by Michelle Wallace in her book *Black Macho and the Myth of the Superwoman*). And his engagement with boxing has come about largely because its symbolism can be worked out in such an exclusively male arena and in exclusively male terms. What is amazing, in this regard, is Mailer's lack of growth in the years between the publication of "The White Negro" (1957) and *The Fight* (1975). Jazz and the black subterranean urban life served the same purpose in the pages of the essay as boxing and traveling in Africa do in the book. Consider the similarity to the book in tone and content of these quotations from the essay:

Knowing in the cells of his existence that life was war, nothing but war, the Negro (all exceptions admitted) could rarely afford the sophisticated inhibitions of civilization, and so he kept for his survival the art of the primitive, he lived in the enormous present, he subsisted for his Saturday night kicks, relinquishing the pleasures of the mind for the more obligatory pleasures of the body. . . .

It is therefore no accident that psychopathy is most prevalent with the Negro. Hated from outside and therefore hating himself, the Negro was forced into the position of exploring all those moral wildernesses of civilized life which the Square automatically condemns as delinquent or evil or immature or morbid or self-destructive or corrupt. . . . But the Negro, not being privileged to gratify his self-esteem with the heady satisfactions of categorical condemnation, chose to move instead in that other direction where all situations are equally valid, and in the worst of perversion, promiscuity, pimpery, drug addiction, rape, razor-slash, bottle-break, what-have-you, the Negro discovered and elaborated a morality of the bottom.

Mailer expresses a very simple and very old idea here, namely, that the black male is metaphorically the white male's unconsciousness personified. What is of deeper interest in that formulation is Mailer's homogenization of the black male personality; in effect any black male, from jazz musician to boxer to pimp to bank robber, any black male who is estranged from the bourgeois culture for whatever reason (and the reasons and the choices are far from being the same) is, for Mailer, the same outcast, the same uninhibited, uncivilized self, the same untraumatized noble savage. Ironically, if the black or Latin prizefighter within the code of his own world has absorbed the masculine rites and morality of the Anglo-Saxon West, then as symbol in the larger world he is simply a new type of minstrel, a black face hidden behind an even deeper blackface: the secret shadow-self of the white man's mind. In Mailer's vision, the boxers become clockwork psychopaths; each round in a fight is nothing more than a three-minute drill in regulated aggression, orchestrated and articulated by the writers outside the ring who have come to see boxing not as a sport but as imagistic psychotherapeutic ethics.

For Mailer, the good id (Ali) whips the bad id (Foreman). One wishes that Mailer had taken to heart D. H. Lawrence's warning about "cherishing illusions about the race soul, the eternal Negroid soul. . . ."

There is nothing easier than to rake Mailer over the coals for his sexism. I do not intend to do that—first of all because he has been a frequent and quite easy target for feminists in recent years. Secondly, any male who really enjoys boxing is drawn to it at least partly because it is an all-male province, no matter how silly its bravado or how pointlessly dangerous its risks.

The reason why Mailer's book would be open to attack by feminists is related to his conjuring up of Ernest Hemingway whenever he gets the opportunity. Hemingway haunts Mailer and, in this particular instance, one is apt to think that *Death in the Afternoon* looms like a large shadow over Mailer's text. And it is the image of Hemingway that makes one think that Mailer's love of the all-male world of boxing is not the simple recitation of a particular preference but an actual statement of repudiation of any sexually mixed world. To chant the name of Hemingway is merely to give the imprint of genius to any meditation on a world without women.

But in the end, Mailer did not take Hemingway's advice. He tried to write an epic about boxing. The actual fight between Muhammad Ali and George Foreman had to be one of the most boring on record. The only reason it was of any interest is that everyone in the world was convinced that Ali would lose badly. After all, Foreman had bounced Joe Frazier and Ken Norton around like rubber balls, and those two last fighters gave Ali fits in the ring. But as Angelo Dundee has said, "Styles make a fight," and for this fight with Foreman, Ali had the right style. It was exciting *that* he won, but not *how* he won. The fight took on the same pattern round after round: Ali leaning against the ropes covering up while Foreman flailed away like a windmill. Finally, Foreman was too tired to hold his arms up anymore and Ali knocked him out in the eighth round; a flyweight could have knocked Foreman out by then. Ali's strategy worked only because Foreman was such an abysmally stupid fighter. And the long-term bodily effects of the rope-a-dope strategy, which a very lazy

Ali adopted as a main feature in his subsequent fights, have yet
to be fully realized. Suffice it to say that in the long run Ali may
be the big loser. Mailer devotes nearly forty pages in his book
to describing the actual combat, a rather dangerous thing to do.
A third-rate writer for *The Ring* could have described it in a
thousand-word column. Mailer wants to write an epic; he wants
to invest his writing with the images of larger-than-life heroes
and villains and larger-than-life tragedy and drama. But as Hemingway wrote, ". . . nor is overwritten journalism made literature
by the injection of a false epic quality. Remember this too: All
bad writers are in love with the epic."

If Ernest Hemingway's presence overshadows Norman Mailer's
fight pieces, then A. J. Liebling is haunted by the old Victorian
fight journalist, Pierce Egan. Liebling's book on boxing, *The Sweet
Science* (the title is derived from a phrase coined by Egan), is
doubtless the best nonfiction book on boxing since Egan penned
pieces on the bare-knuckle brawlers of England in a publication
called *Boxiana*. Liebling's essays, which originally appeared in
The New Yorker, are a purist's journey through the major bouts
of the fifties: Sugar Ray Robinson's fights with Joey Maxin and
Randy Turpin, Marciano's two bouts with Jersey Joe Wolcott, his
two bouts with Ezzard Charles, and his fight with Archie Moore.
Liebling also covers an early Floyd Patterson fight, Moore's battle
with his archnemesis Harold Johnson, and a minor Sandy Saddler
fight.

Liebling writes as a journalist; he is not obsessed with the epic,
so his pieces are not pretentious like Mailer's. At his best, he
reminds one of the best of Red Smith. Indeed, Liebling positively
revels in the seedy hotel, the wrinkled topcoat, the greasy collar
persona of the boxing writer. And because he writes here in the
guise of the boxing writer, he is also a purist who loves to listen
to the old boys and keep a sharp eye out for the oddballs. The
book is filled with presences like Freddie Brown, old time, raspy-
voiced trainer whose last famous pupil was the foul-tempered but
brilliant Roberto Durán; Al Weill, manager of Rocky Marciano
and seeker of "young broken fighters"; Charlie Goldman, trainer
of Marciano, who says, "One of the troubles with fighters now is

they don't start before they're interested in dames"; and Run-
yonesque-type characters like Prince Monolulu, an Ethiopian prince
who plays the ponies in England, preaches Zionism on Sundays,
and has moderate success betting on fights.

Yet in reading this book one gets the impression that Liebling
is well aware that he has approached the end of an epoch. The
boxers and the bouts, the managers and trainers, the auditoriums
where the fights are held, and the audiences that witness them
are all part of the past. Liebling sees televised fights as heralding
the downfall of the sport:

> The immediate crisis in the United States, forestalling the one
> high living standards might bring on, has been caused by the
> popularization of a ridiculous gadget called television. This is uti-
> lized in the sale of beer and razor blades. The clients of the tele-
> vision companies, by putting on a free boxing show almost every
> night of the week, have knocked out of business the hundreds of
> small-city and neighborhood boxing clubs where youngsters had
> a chance to learn their trade and journeymen to mature their
> skills. Consequently the number of good new prospects dimin-
> ishes with every year, and the peddlers' public is already being
> asked to believe that a boy with perhaps ten or fifteen fights
> behind him is a topnotch performer. Neither advertising agencies
> nor brewers, and least of all the networks, give a hoot if they
> push the Sweet Science back into a period of genre painting.
> When it is in a coma they will find some other way to peddle their
> peanuts.

The purist's obsession with standards is not simply a crotchety
moralism but a quest for integrity in a world where such a quality
is fast vanishing. As it happened, Liebling was right; television
absolutely distorted and detached the viewer's ability to see or
understand prizefighting and often interfered with the boxer's
ability to perform. The viewer is distanced from the struggle and
the pain of the ordeal; the vibrating edge of fear and brutality is
blunted, is in fact reduced and packaged. Indeed, far from being
able "to experience" a fight on television, one is simply manipulated by the camera angles and the commentators. One reacts
to the grossness of the occasion without sensing its subtleties.

The fighters, in many cases little more than honorable schoolboys who have been advanced too many grades without benefit of instruction, are often in more danger of being seriously injured than would be the case if they were more seasoned performers. Finally, to have taken from the province of the enthusiast and put up for public sale not only the big money and big name fights, but the little ordinary ones as well, is to have reduced the sport to its one most prominent and marketable characteristic—the charismatic flowing of blood. As one of the characters in Budd Schulberg's novel, *The Harder They Fall*, puts it: boxing is "show business with blood."

In the end, it is Liebling's very self-consciousness about his quest for integrity that makes *The Sweet Science* reek of a high-brow quaint conservatism. To Liebling, the televised boxing match might have been the beginning of a high-tech, grossly inartistic seizure of the manly art of self-defense. But it must be admitted that before television the world of boxing was one of gangsterism, fixed fights, racial baiting and discrimination, severe punch-drunkenness, down-and-out fighters without two nickels to rub together, petty whores, fleece artists, dishonest officials, and a general miasma of corruption and filth. Television was not ruining an art form; it was buying into a money-making den of iniquity. Nearly any sense of this side of boxing is absent from Liebling's essays. Boxing is not, after all, merely a series of cunningly contrived pieces about its characters written in order to make a low-class endeavor palatable to the highbrow readers of *The New Yorker*. This is where Liebling's purist bent leads him astray: the age of the 1940s and early 1950s in pre-television boxing was not the golden age of bare-knuckle fighters that Pierce Egan described during the Victorian era. Perhaps the 1830s, 1840s, and 1850s were as innocent as Egan wanted his readers to believe, but the 1940s and 1950s demanded more than the picturesque. Liebling's aim, I think, is clear; *The Sweet Science* was meant to be the romance of modern prizefighting; sports-writing as *belles lettres*. The book was not even meant to be historical romanticism like Egan's pieces but rather sheer requiem for the last artists of integrity. This is why the book is framed with the images of two great black fighters who are in the twilight of their careers: Joe Louis and Archie Moore, two supreme artists making their last stands. When Liebling writes, "[a] boxer, like a writer, must stand alone," the reader knows that the book is making an early claim to its easy moral victory. *The Sweet Science* is nothing more than an effective long good-bye.*

III. *Young Man Streetfighter: An American Sketch*

Let me begin by warning the reader that this will not be an unhappy story.

In the neighborhood where I grew up there was a block called Fairhill Street. Every black American ghetto must have one of these streets, where the houses are so dilapidated, so absolutely ruined that the bricks bulge out in a manner that suggests a kind of sterile pregnancy. Even the inanimate objects seem swollen with grief. Many of the houses, as I remember, were boarded up with wood or sheets of metal, and yellow paper signs would be posted on the front doors which read: THIS PROPERTY IS DECLARED UNFIT FOR HUMAN HABITATION. Of course, people continued to live in these buildings and no one thought anything at all about it. If you were to ask these people why they did not move to more suitable quarters, they would simply tell you that they could afford nothing else; they had no place else to live. They were, I think, wretchedly poor, the poorest black people in the neighborhood. The young children would run around barefoot in the summer, with dirty, cut-up feet, mostly because the parents could not afford the fancy PF Flyers and Converses that I and other children wore. The girls on this block were always pregnant before the age of fifteen and the boys in jail before sixteen. In those days, people on welfare did not receive food stamps; they were given government-issued food popularly referred to as "surplus." At

---

*It is deeply ironic that the greatest fighter of all time, Muhammad Ali, should be a creature of television. The world's greatest ring artist shamelessly sold himself like any sponsor's product. Liebling died in 1963, before Ali won the heavyweight title for the first time. Wherever he is now, he must be terribly chagrined by it all.

school, it was easy to spot the kids whose families received surplus; they always brought lunches that consisted of the whitest white bread in the world and thick, pink, rubbery pieces of Spam or potted meat. Those of us who thought we were better off than our Fairhill Street friends—if only, as in the case of most of us, by the fewest of dollars—would revel in our lunches of greasy steak sandwiches and submarines or glazed doughnuts and soda pop bought from the corner store.

On this street was an empty lot, covered with broken glass, garbage, and the occasional dead body of an animal, where one could usually find members of the Fifth and South Streets gang. And it was on this lot that I saw the greatest fistfight of my life, better than any professional fight I have seen before or since. On a certain day in my youth, Frank White, the warlord of the Seventh Street gang, and Tabu, the warlord of the Fifth and South Streets gang, fought in that strange ring for the championship of the streets.

It was an extremely hot August day in my twelfth or thirteenth summer. I was loafing in the playground with the boys of the Fifth and South Streets gang. Some of them were playing basketball; most were simply lounging in the shade, listening to R & B on a transistor radio, drinking wine or soda pop, and trying to beat the heat. Tabu was sitting on a bench playing checkers. He loved playing checkers more than anyone else I knew except the old men who played on the front steps of a house on Fairhill Street. Tabu and his opponents always played by the "touch a man, move a man" rule, just as the old men did, which meant that these games were the fastest ever witnessed on a board. Tabu liked me a great deal and this was certainly a curious thing because I had little merit or influence among these boys; I was simply one of the fellows who hung around the fringes. He had a great deal of respect for my intelligence (even in those days I was known for being a bookish boy) which I thought surprising since virtually no one else did. It was an even exchange since I had a great deal of respect for the way he used his dukes. It was a nice friendship; he always called me Slim because he did not like the name Gerald, and I always called him Tabu because I never knew any other name to call him.

Seeing Tabu in my mind's eye, it is hard to imagine that he was the warlord, the best fighter in the gang. He surely had the physique—he was lean and muscular and as hard as steel. But he did not seem to have the temperament. He loved to play basketball and checkers and talk to girls and laugh. He never seemed angry enough with anyone about anything to want to fight. Yet he did fight quite well and quite often and with a bewildering sense of humor. Whenever he had an opponent—whether in a street fight, basketball game, or checkers match—at an insurmountable disadvantage, he would shout gleefully, "It's game time and your ass is mine!"

On this hot afternoon, word began to spread through the playground that the Seventh Street gang was "coming down strong" looking to kick the asses of the "punk motherfuckers of Fifth and South." The air was suddenly electric with excitement. The boys, once assured that this was no idle rumor, gathered their weapons and massed themselves and began moving out of the playground to meet the enemy. I tagged along mostly to watch. Midway up Fairhill Street we could see the crush of black youthful humanity coming to greet us. We had about fifty members and Seventh Street easily had sixty or seventy. I thought we were outmanned—so much so that, discretion being the better part of valor, it was time to consider beating a hasty retreat. No one else felt that way. When the two gangs did meet face-to-face, there was no violence. The leaders from both groups began to talk, and it was decided, surprisingly, to declare a truce, so that both gangs could unite against the Thirteenth and Fitzgerald Streets gang, the massively manned nemesis of both the Fifth and South and the Seventh Streets gangs. There was some disagreement as to who was to have leadership over this combination and it was decided to have the warlord from each group fight to settle the matter.

The rules of the fight were simple: no kicking, no head-butting, no hitting below the belt, no wrestling, and no rounds. Both boys were to fight until one of them quit. Whoever quit would be the loser.

I did not know Frank White personally but I knew his reputation. He, too, was lean and muscular but much taller than Tabu.

And he had a face that indicated that behind his fire-red eyes was one of the most evil dispositions in all of South Philadelphia. He had a lemon-yellow complexion with freckles and a thick ring of scar tissue around his neck from a knife wound. It was rumored that he had once broken a grown man's jaw in a fistfight. Another rumor was that he had killed a boy in a knife fight and had beaten the rap in court. He looked grim and merciless.

We all sojourned to the empty lot and the principals removed their shirts and shadowboxed a bit to warm up. It was such a hot day that both boys were sweating heavily even before they faced each other. White had very quick hands and a fluid motion; he looked very, very good to me—much better than Tabu, whose facial expression did not even seem to absorb the gravity of the situation. He was smiling and jocular about all of this. I was afraid for him.

The fight started with both boys exchanging evenly, but White soon pulled out in front, using the advantage of his height and reach. He threw rapid-fire left jabs, then followed up with straight rights and left hooks. He was like a smooth-running machine and he never varied his pattern. First, Tabu's nose started to bleed, then his mouth, then little welt marks started to form around his eyes. Tabu was scoring with punches, too. But his hands were not as fast, so he did not land as often. After twenty minutes, both boys were so drenched in sweat that their trousers were soaked and they were nearly exhausted. It was surely surprising that neither passed out from sunstroke. At this point, Tabu was losing badly. Suddenly, he crouched very low as if he were going to spring or lunge a punch. That seemed a sure sign of utter desperation. He stayed in this positon for a minute and allowed White to hit with a jab, then another and another. After throwing the left a half-dozen times without missing, White predictably threw a tremendous straight right; it did not miss, although White afterwards probably wished that it had. It was the punch that Tabu was waiting for; he timed it so that as the punch was thrown, he jerked out of his crouch and thrust his head forward like a bull charging. The blow landed on the top of Tabu's skull and White immediately gave a howl of pain. He had either jammed his knuckles on Tabu's hard head or broken his hand.

In either case, his right hand was useless. Tabu screamed out, "It's game time and your ass is mine!" Tabu swarmed all over White but the fight went on for another twenty minutes before White, after having been struck so vicious a blow on his chest that a surface blood vessel ruptured, finally sat down on the filthy ground and looked up at Tabu and shook his head. The warlord of Seventh Street had quit. It was Tabu's finest hour; he was the undisputed king of the hill insofar as we poor black boys of South Philadelphia were concerned.

As I grew older and no longer hung around with the neighborhood boys, I wondered what had happened to Tabu. About four years ago, when I visited Philadelphia, I learned the news. I was in a record store called Third Street Jazz looking through the stacks when suddenly I heard someone call out, "Hey, Slim. Where you been?" I knew the voice right away. I turned and saw Tabu—but what a change from the street days! He was wearing a three-piece suit, carrying a very expensive-looking attaché case, sporting a neatly trimmed goatee and mustache, and looked for all the world like the landed gentry of black folk. Was this the same person who had once been my hero back on Fairhill Street? He told me what he had been doing: He had a degree from Temple University and worked as an administrator for a municipal agency. He was going to law school at night and contemplated finishing that degree in two more years. He was married, with, as he put it, "four beautiful daughters," all of whom had African names that sounded like pure poetry but which I could not recall the moment after he had spoken them. I was never good at remembering poetry. He still had a good physique but he was beginning to develop a paunchy middle. He told me he played raquetball at a health spa he belonged to. He seemed almost sleek with success.

"I had to quit the gang in order to get serious," he said. "I had to stop fighting. You know, some of those cats are still out there. Into the dope thing. Been to prison. And still into the gang thing. Man, they never grew up. Just want to keep street fighting all their lives. You can't go around fistfighting forever. You got to become a man and put that stuff behind you. I just decided to grow up."

We talked about jazz quite a bit. He had become a big fan of "the music." We were discussing Miles Davis's *Sketches of Spain* album. Tabu shook his head in admiration: "It's the baddest album out there. Man, it's like Miles telling the other trumpet players, 'It's game time and your ass is mine.'" I smiled. Some things never really change.

As I said in the beginning, this was not intended to be an unhappy story about a ghetto boy. It is, in fact, an American success story of the most familiar sort. The lesson of the story is this: Tabu is the only fighter I have ever heard of who was smart enough to quit before he got old.

Ted Hoagland

VIOLENCE, VIOLENCE

It is curious that with such a crushing, befuddling climate of general violence as there is in New York we should still be paying money to go to the prizefights. The fight fan, as one used to picture him, was a kind of overweight frustrated homebody whose life was practically devoid of danger and drama. Middle-aged rather than young, a small businessman or a warehouse foreman, a nostalgic war veteran, he looked about and found the world torpid, so he came to St. Nicholas Arena to holler and twist on his folding chair, throw starts of punches, or did the same thing in front of the television set in a bar. But now this fellow has all the firepower of Vietnam on television, the racial-college riots, the hippies to hate, the burglaries in his building, the fear of being mugged when he is on the street. Going home from the prizefight, he runs a chance of being beaten up worse than the loser was. And boxing, which began as an all-out sport, has not been able to cinch its procedures tighter, the way pro football has, to make for a more modish, highstrung commotion and wilder deeds. It's the simplest pageant of all: Two men fight, rest a minute, and fight some more. Like the mile run, it's tradition-alist and finite, humble in its claims.

Baseball, which seemed the natural man's sport above all, has turned out to be overly ceremonious and time-consuming for the 1960s, and even burlesque and the belly dancers of Eighth Av-

61

enue, forthright as we once supposed they were, have been eclipsed by still more elementary displays of the human physique. The entrepreneurs of boxing didn't at first suspect that their sport had any kick left except as a TV filler for the hinterlands, where the old modes prevail. The custom of weekly fights at St. Nick's or the old Garden had lapsed (since which, both buildings have gone *poof*). But then they tried a few cards at the National Maritime Union hiring hall, counting on the roughhouse seamen to provide a box-office backlog. When the shows sold out, they shifted them to the Felt Forum in the new Madison Square Garden and discovered that the sport pays there as well. As a result, live boxing has become a feature of New York life again. The problem of the promoters is not to streamline the *Geist* to fit the sixties but to find fighters who fight, because unlike many other athletes, prizefighters do not really enjoy their sport very much, as a rule; they fight for the purse. All our Irish and Italian citizens have elevated themselves until they don't have to choose between simonizing cars for a living or the prize ring, and the Negroes and Spanish speakers too are scrambling upward toward better livelihoods, if only in campier sports with lots of legwork, or the various ornate sports where if the team loses the coach loses his job. Boxing isn't like that, and we are bringing in hungry souls from Nigeria, the Philippines, and the Bahamas to do the dirt. People sometimes make the mistake of feeling sorry for boxers, however, and want to abolish the sport, when they should look instead at the man in the neighborhood car wash who *isn't* a fighter—doesn't fly to Seattle for a big card—but runs the steam hose and polishes fenders.

And is it dirt? I'm not one of those professional eyewitnesses who is willing to watch anything just on the grounds that it is happening. I live on Ambulance Alley and don't need to go to the Garden in order to see men in desperate straits. I go to admire a trial of skills, a contest of limited violence between unintimidated adversaries which, even when it does spill out of the ring after a bad decision and the crowd in its anger sways shoulder to shoulder, is very nineteenth century, from the era of cart horses in the street. Every sport is a combat between its participants, but boxing is combat distilled, purer even than combat with weapons. When a referee steps in and stops a fight in which one man is receiving punishment without any hope of recouping, the crowd is not disappointed at seeing the punishment stopped; they are glad enough about that. If they are disappointed, it's because the drama is over, which was true as soon as the fight became one-sided. Boxing's appeal is its drama and grace, a blizzarding grace that amounts to an impromptu, exigent ballet, especially in the lighter and nimbler weights. Hands, arms, feet, legs, head, torso—more is done per moment than in fast ice hockey; and since there is more motion, the athletes in other sports cannot surpass a consummate boxer for grace.

Still, why this extra violence in such a violent time? Is it choreographed like a bullfight; is it like a fine tragedy which one goes to although one's own life is tangled enough? Of course it isn't these things at all. There is no program, no unity, no meaning as such unless a parable fortuitously develops, and the spectators are there for the combat. Writers of the Hemingway-Mailer axis have been fascinated by the combat, locating relevancies and identities in the pre-fight rituals, but they have not made claims for the sport as an art. Ten years ago, when we did not live alongside such an ocean of violence, some of us went to the fights perhaps as one keeps an aquarium. We realized most of the world was under water, but we were high and dry with Eisenhower, and knowing that life is salt and life is action, life is tears and life is water, we kept a fish tank to represent the four-fifths of the world that breathed with gills.

But nowadays we're flooded and swimming for dear life, no matter where we happen to live. That we nevertheless prefer our sports violent—the irreducible conciseness of boxing—is evidence of a relation to violence, a need and a curiosity, so basic that it cannot be sated. Though we do tire of the delirium in the streets, we are only tiring of the disorder. Make it concise, put ropes or white lines around it, and we will go, we will go, just as people on vacation go down to the roaring sea.

Elliott J. Gorn

THE MANASSA MAULER AND THE FIGHTING MARINE

An Interpretation of the Dempsey-Tunney Fights

I often have heard boxing fans remark that the prize ring reveals life the way it really is. The elemental combat between two individuals, the primal physical struggle, the quest for glory and fear of humiliation, all contribute to the belief that men in the ring are in touch with life's underlying realities. Significantly, depicting "life the way it really is" is precisely the role anthropologist Clifford Geertz ascribes to religious worldviews. Religions, Geertz tells us, do not just buttress social systems or justify conditions as men and women find them. They also explain the way the world works, cut behind surface appearances, and offer visions of underlying order which give meaning to daily life. Through drama and ritual, religion depicts the "really real" with idealized clarity. Religious symbols unmask the way the universe is in sheer actuality and demonstrate the moving forces behind mundane affairs. The truism that America's popular religion is sports takes on new significance in light of Geertz's observation. And in the pantheon of the 1920s, no gods shone more brightly than the heroes of the ring.

While one might carry this analogy too far, sports often become freighted with meanings which render them akin to art, drama, and religion. The Dempsey-Tunney fights of the 1920s provide striking examples of how, in subtle ways, cultural phenomena

Jack Dempsey v. Gene Tunney, Chicago, 1927—the most famous knock-down in history.

like sports may reveal larger social tensions. My focus therefore is on the complex symbols, metaphors, and allusions that gave meaning to these battles. They were interesting fights, and would have attracted widespread attention in any era. But a close reading of the press coverage shows that people interpreted them in a manner particularly germane to their times. The Dempsey-Tunney matches generated middle- and even upper-class interest far beyond boxing's traditional lower-class base. The mainstream press—"middlebrow" journals like *Time* magazine and newspapers carrying syndicated stories from the major wire services—invoked broad patterns of symbolism to depict the two boxers. Amidst descriptions of uppercuts, left hooks, and counterpunches, a subliminal battle raged among old Victorian norms, new corporate imperatives, and the values of a consumer society. However, before discussing the cultural shadowboxing that lay beneath the championship bouts, we need to consider some of the pertinent background.*

The sheer magnitude of these spectacles was both striking and unprecedented. In Philadelphia in 1926, 120,000 people saw Dempsey battle Tunney as part of the nation's sesquicentennial celebration. A year later roughly the same number paid over two and one half million dollars to witness the rematch in Chicago's Soldier's Field. At the first fight, movie stars like Charlie Chaplin, William S. Hart, Tom Mix, and Norma Talmadge, as well as sports heroes such as Babe Ruth, John McGraw, and Jacob Ruppert, were in attendance. The wealthy and powerful also sat at the ringside. According to Randy Roberts, Jack Dempsey's biographer, Andrew Mellon, Charles Schwab, Vincent Astor, Percy Rockefeller, W. Averill Harriman, Harry Payne Whitney, William Randolph Hearst, and Joseph Pulitzer, along with assorted governors, mayors, cabinet secretaries, and diplomats, all huddled in the Philadelphia rain. Of course, boxing had been a popular sport with working-class males since the middle of the nineteenth century. But the open presence of socially prominent persons—including a number of women—would have scandalized middle-class Victorians a generation or two before.

For those unable to be corrupted in Philadelphia and Chicago, the miracle of radio carried the fights home. During the second battle, a special network of over seventy independent stations brought the voice of ringside announcer Graham McNamee to

*This essay is necessarily a speculative venture. What reporters write is not invariably what masses of people think. Nonetheless, I have attempted to isolate broad themes which emerged repeatedly in the middle-class press. Because many newspaper stories were syndicated or came from wire services like the Associated Press, the fights were covered with substantial uniformity around the country. By focusing on the most often-repeated symbolism, I hope to capture an essential core of perceptions held by fans and reporters alike.

an estimated fifty million Americans, nearly half the nation's population. Clusters of excited listeners gathered in hotels, saloons, exclusive clubs, drugstores, barbershops, and newspaper offices across the country. It was reported that eleven people died of heart failure listening to the second bout. Moreover, following days of intensive buildup in sports sections, American newspapers screamed the results of both fights with block-letter headlines. Even the staid *New York Times* announced the first fight's outcome with a three-tier banner across page one, followed by seven solid pages—in the main section, not the sports section—of coverage.

Promotion, hype, and commercialism swirled around the Dempsey-Tunney bouts. Advertising helped make the identification of fans with fighters clear. For example, just before the first fight, the *Saturday Evening Post* ran an advertisement for "cantilever shoes," the sort of footwear any business or professional man might purchase. Below a picture of two men boxing, the copy read, "Footwork: Every man is in the ring from morning till night. An athlete in the ring, on the baseball diamond, or on the gridiron, is no better than his feet. For if his feet fail he cannot play the game. The same is true of the man who just fights the daily battle." By the twenties, there was nothing unusual about associating athletes with products, nor about modern media techniques being used to sell sports heroes. What was new was the scale of the sports coverage and the ease with which business organizations, the press, local booster associations, and the respectable middle class, found common ground. In a corporate, increasingly bureaucratic society, sports were perceived as good business, good press, good for morals, and good for morale.

The private sector relied on sports to promote not just products, but a whole new business ideology. "I don't know anything about selling automobiles," Notre Dame football coach Knute Rockne told a gathering of Studebaker salesmen. "I never sold one in my life; but perhaps a few remarks here on the psychology that is necessary for success in a football organization might not be out of place because it seems to me that the same psychology that makes for success in a football organization will make for success in any organization." Whether playing sports, selling goods, or managing a company, there was a special psychological power, an ability to assert one's will over others, that brought victory. The supersalesman—a hallmark of the twenties business culture—exuded personal magnetism, charisma, and youthful vitality, much like the successful athlete. Rockne stressed the need for ambition, hard work, and aggressiveness, but always within the bounds of corporate teamwork. The will to win was now a bureaucratic, not an individualistic imperative: "You men are facing keen competition this year, perhaps facing more opposition than you ever faced in your lives, but I say that is the sort of thing you should thrill to—any kind of challenge. . . . I think the Studebaker organization has demonstrated that you can go better when the going is tough, so I say to you that this year you should thrill to this challenge."

If it is naive to view the sporting mania of the twenties apart from commercial promotion and corporate ideologies, it is equally naive to interpret the apotheosis of sport as something purely contrived for the sake of profit and foisted on the American public like so much snake oil. Even the most cynical observers like Ring Lardner questioned the intelligence, but never the sincerity, of the fans. It was the depth of public interest, its almost devotional quality, which so impressed commentators. Hoopla and ballyhoo notwithstanding, athletic events could stir men deeply.

Commentators accounted for their era's explosion of sporting interest in a variety of ways. Disillusionment with the War, failure of the bright promises of the Progressive Era, the growing complexity and interdependence of business life, and the modern pressures against meaningful rural and urban communities, all caused Americans to seek release from social problems. In a fragmented nation, sports as well as movies, radio and other aspects of the burgeoning mass culture helped bridge the divisions of ethnicity, social class, and region with a shared sense of national identity. Higher pay and the shortened working hours of the prosperous twenties sent many Americans looking for entertainment, while rapid urbanization placed a premium on mass spectacles. Moreover, journalists were well aware that sedentary white-collar and bored blue-collar workers responded to images of youthful heroism. More than mere escapism, sports preserved such values as courage, autonomy, and physical skill which the modern world threatened to erode. The Dempsey-Tunney fights resonated on these and other levels. Each boxer came to represent key values in American life, and the two men together in the ring symbolized central tensions and contradictions of the 1920s.

The public persona of James Joseph "Gene" Tunney was a veritable catalogue of middle-class, Victorian values. Handsome, tall, blond, his face unscarred despite sixty professional fights, he seemed entirely unlike other pugilists. Tunney was born in Greenwich Village, New York, the son of respectable Irish-American working-class parents. The press described him as a sterling example of the fruits of clean living, a man who shunned profanity, tobacco, and alcohol, and who avoided the gamblers and racketeers so closely associated with prizefighting. Tunney devoted himself totally to his career, at all times training hard, staying in excellent physical condition and pursuing his professional goals with dogged determination. From his countenance beamed an ever-present smile of poise and confidence, and always a gentleman, he treated others with courtesy and consideration.

Tunney spoke articulately, surprising members of the press by his lack of grunts and monosyllables. Reporters commented on his intellectual tastes, his knowledge of literature and philosophy, and his habit of relaxing with Shakespeare's plays or novels by W. Somerset Maugham. His great personal appeal allegedly extended interest in professional boxing to new groups of people, including women and members of the learned professions. Finally, Tunney's image was enhanced by his service during the Great War. As soon as America joined the conflict, he offered himself to the nation, enlisting in the Marine Corps. By the war's end, he had become light heavyweight champion of the American Expeditionary Force, and thereby earned his ring name, the "Fighting Marine."

Few really believed Tunney could beat the champion Dempsey. Still, those at ringside were deeply moved as the stalwart young challenger strode confidently into the arena on the night of September 23, 1926, for the first fight. At ringside, several of his armed forces comrades rose to attention and sang the Marine Corps Hymn. As the Fighting Marine stood at ring center, bathed in light, the wild cheers of a packed stadium rained down on him. The betting odds stood as high as three to one against Tunney. But many Americans favored the challenger because his career embodied central cultural values about which they believed passionately. His self-reliance, impeccable personal life, and desire to rise in the world evoked the old Victorian ethos in contrast to the hedonism and moral corruption of the twenties. Tunney embodied hard work, the cultivation of finely honed skills, clean living, and patriotism. His triumph would be that of an individual who lived by social rules and succeeded through self-control.

Simply put, Tunney virtually leaped from the pages of Horatio Alger's novels because he represented success through virtuous individual effort. His victory would help validate crucial cultural myths on which the middle class had been raised. Even upwardly mobile members of the working class took vicarious pleasure in Tunney's triumphs. For example, psychologist Frank Winer, the son of poor Jewish immigrants who settled in a tough factory town, recalled Tunney as his great boyhood hero. Militant union supporters and political radicals, his parents encouraged their children to develop courage and the ability to defend themselves. For young Winer, the Fighting Marine was a perfect blend of self-improvement, social idealism, and physical toughness.*

But the Tunney symbolism contained additonal layers of meaning. The challenger's popularity was based on his fusion of the older ethic of virtuous individualism with important values of the industrial era. Tunney's connection with machine culture often became explicit: GENE SHOWS HE HAS NO CARBON IN RING MACHINERY, a *Chicago Tribune* headline declared. On the day of the first Dempsey-Tunney bout, the Fighting Marine arrived in Philadelphia by airplane, still perceived as a courageous way to

---

*My interest in these fights has a personal basis. My father, too, found Tunney a perfect symbol for Jewish working-class aspirations, and he raised his children with stories of "Gentleman" Gene, the intellectual boxer.

travel in the twenties. Newspapers carried pictures of him in front of a two-seater, his hair swept back, his lips set in a confident Tunney smile. Moreover, Tunney knew the science of boxing, discussed musculature and bone structure with reporters, and emphasized the importance of psychology and a positive mental attitude. Finally, the continual references to his armed services background reminded fans that the Fighting Marine was a team player, a man who accomplished goals through corporate structures.

Tunney's ring style reinforced his public persona. The Fighting Marine was a fine athlete, but he did not have singular size, strength, or speed. Although he knocked out half of his opponents, it was often said that he lacked the "killer instinct," had no taste for blood, simply was not a violent fighter. Tunney was a defensive boxer, a counterpuncher who waited for openings, and gradually wore down his opponents. The press emphasized that he was not a born pugilist but a "synthetic" one, a practitioner of "ring science," a "ring-general"—in short, a "boxer," not a bruiser. Indeed, Tunney's greatest asset was his total subordination of body to mind. Through sheer willpower, discipline, and self-control, it was asserted, he made himself into a title contender. He practiced "studied scientific boxing," approached his profession as a "mechanical business undertaking," applied a "mathematical method of fighting." Tunney's success was interpreted as the rational subordination of impulse to rules, restraint, and self-discipline. Like the thousands of Americans who chanted Emile Coué's mantra of therapeutic self-help, day by day in every way, he got better and better.

To be accurate, however, Tunney's public image was not invariably favorable. In some of the working-class press, and even in middle-class reporting, his self-confidence shaded into arrogance, and it sometimes seemed as though he considered himself too good for boxing and its fans. Especially as he piled up victories, there were grumblings that the Fighting Marine was aloof, stuffy, and pretentious. Worst of all, Tunney could be just plain boring. Both his tightly controlled personality and his defensive boxing style were becoming predictable, especially by the time of the second championship bout with Dempsey. However, these liabilities should not be overemphasized, because they emerged late in the Fighting Marine's career, and were generally eclipsed by his positive image.

In a *New York Times* interview four days before the first Dempsey-Tunney fight, Henry Ford characterized mass production as managerial intelligence, skillfully combining speed, power, and accuracy with economy, system, and continuity—precisely the metaphors used that day to characterize Gene Tunney's boxing style. Efficiency, scientific planning, a positive mental attitude, skillful application of resources, all described Tunney in the ring. Like his mythic contemporary, Charles Lindbergh, Gene Tunney reconciled the contradictory impulses of heroic individualism with the interdependence of an increasingly technological and bureaucratic society. Tunney the man and Tunney the fighter retained great appeal, especially among middle-class Americans, because he symbolically merged venerable bourgeois values and new corporate ones. As a symbol, the Fighting Marine affirmed that America's past and future were of a piece, that virtue and self-reliance could still thrive in a technocratic environment.

If Tunney's image was complex, his opponent's persona was encrusted with contradictions. Always controversial, William Harrison Dempsey seems to have been at once the best-loved and most-hated champion of all time. Dempsey, too, was a poor boy who had made good, a self-reliant individualist; yet he stood in sharp contrast to the Fighting Marine, and his personal history was very well-known to the public. Dempsey's ancestors were mountain people from West Virginia, descendants of the Scotch Irish, but his parents moved west to the mining country of the Rockies late in the nineteenth century. Young Dempsey was born and raised in Manassa, Colorado, and his western heritage was kept constantly in the public mind by his ring name, the "Manassa Mauler." The ninth of thirteen children born to a luckless father and a hardworking mother, Dempsey left home in his teens, hopping boxcars and drifting among the copper mines of Colorado and Utah. His early life evoked the discord of poverty, labor violence, and economic exploitation, for the western mining country still conjured up images of radical workers, rapacious owners, and bloody conflicts like the Ludlow Massacre of 1914.

Half mine laborer and half hobo, Dempsey lived on the fringes of conventional society. The violent, all-male life of the camps had taught him how to defend himself, and he soon recognized his great talents as a fighter. For over half a century mining had been one of the occupations closely associated with pugilism, so Dempsey followed a long tradition in dividing his time between the pits, shafts, and the ring. His older brother helped train him, teaching young Dempsey the traditional way to toughen his skin by pickling it in brine, and the age-old method of strengthening one's jaw by chewing pine tar. As time passed, Dempsey continued riding railroad breakbeams, no longer as a drifter and migrant laborer, but as a seeker of fights with bullies and roughnecks in saloons and mining camps throughout the West. Dempsey earned his living by betting on himself and collecting a small percentage of the winnings from spectators who wagered on him. He confirmed his decision to concentrate purely on the prize ring by taking the name "Jack" Dempsey, after the great nineteenth-century lightweight.

His professional career was good though not spectacular. But gradually, with the help of a cagey and ruthless manager, Jack "Doc" Kearns, the Manassa Mauler worked his way toward the heavyweight title. Thus, in Toledo, Ohio, on a sweltering July Fourth afternoon in 1919, Jack Dempsey stood in the ring prepared to fight for the championship. His opponent was Jess Willard, a six-foot six-inch, 250-pound "man-mountain," the conqueror of Jack Johnson. Shorter by five inches and lighter by sixty pounds, Dempsey was given very little chance of winning. Yet there was something wild and untamed in his appearance. He entered the ring with his face covered by a thick, dark stubble of black beard, and his lean, muscular torso tanned deep bronze. Most important, he wore what would become the subject of so much press coverage and so many photographs, the famous Dempsey scowl. Waiting for the fight to begin, he glared at his opponent with a fierce, smoldering expression of pure rage.

The Manassa Mauler's performance in the ring that day matched his wild appearance. In the first round, Dempsey knocked Willard to the canvas seven times. After three rounds, the "Massacre at

Toledo" was over. Willard, his jaw broken, his cheekbone shattered, his ribs cracked, his face covered with blood, failed to come out for the fourth round. Rumors circulated for the rest of Dempsey's career that his gloves were loaded on the day he won the title.

Over the next eight years, the Manassa Mauler became the greatest single drawing card in the history of American sports. Fan interest certainly reached unprecedented heights when Dempsey fought Tunney. However, in each of three other fights, one of them not even a title bout, nearly 100,000 people paid over a million dollars to watch the champion in action. Total gate receipts for Dempsey's five biggest fights totaled almost nine million dollars, an unheard-of figure until the era of Muhammad Ali and inflated dollars. In contrast, Tunney never drew large crowds before his fights with Dempsey. Indeed, the Fighting Marine's only bout after the Dempsey matches turned into a financial disaster, becoming the sole fight on which promoter Tex Rickard lost money. Tunney's immense popularity in 1926 and 1927, then, came largely as a consequence of his being matched against Dempsey.

Paradoxically, while the fans flocked to see Dempsey fight, they did not always come to cheer him. Even though he fought them on American soil, the ringside crowd on two occasions favored foreign opponents over the Manassa Mauler. In Ring Lardner's "The Battle of the Century"—a thinly veiled fictitious account of Dempsey's 1921 fight against Georges Carpentier—the champion, about to defend his title against a handsome French war hero, lamented, "Here I am, an American that's supposed to be fighting to keep the title in this country, and I doubt if they's a dozen Americans that ain't pulling for me to get knocked for a corpse." Dempsey confirmed Lardner's assessment in his autobiography: "The crowd was pulling hysterically for Georges. They wanted me to lose, even to a foreigner. As the preliminaries drew to an end—maybe I imagined it—I could sense the screaming crowd turning hostile." Five years later, reporters noted that many fans at the first Tunney fight greeted the announcement of Dempsey's name with a loud chorus of boos. One newspaper estimated hyperbolically that out of 115 million Americans, only

100,000 favored Dempsey. As *Time* succinctly put it, "He has never been a popular champion."

Surely these observers exaggerated, for one can also find references to Dempsey's unparalleled popularity. Differences in social background account for at least some of the contradictory attitudes toward the champion. The working-class *Police Gazette*, for example, embraced Dempsey with fewer qualms than middle-class journals. Moreover, crowd reactions may be misleading because, as a general rule, only individuals with substantial incomes could afford to attend the fights. Dempsey's persona also improved with time, as the prosperity of million-dollar gates tempered the image of the hungry young hobo, and the media covered some of the champion's rough edges with a veneer of wholesomeness. Still, today's boxing fans tend to remember the twenties' fascination with Dempsey, but forget that until defeat tamed the Manassa Mauler, much of the public viewed him with a jaundiced eye. As often as not, he was the villain who kept fans spellbound anticipating his downfall.

Contemporary observers accounted for the champion's unfavorable image in a variety of ways. The most important single factor was his avoidance of service during the Great War. Many fans were offended that weaker men fought and died while this exalted ring warrior fled from real battle. The difficulty was compounded by a publicity photograph showing him supporting the war effort by "working" in a shipyard. Clearly visible beneath his overalls were pinstriped slacks and patent leather boots. Despite the claims that he was the sole supporter of his mother, father, and wife during the war, despite his raising hundreds of thousands of dollars in Red Cross campaigns, and despite his vindication in a federal court, Dempsey never lived down the "slacker" charge.

The Manassa Mauler had other image problems, too. He divorced his first wife early in his boxing career, compounding the stigma several years later by marrying a movie star, Estelle Taylor. Moreover, he seemed intent on keeping his title without actively defending it; for three years before agreeing to fight Tunney he avoided challengers. Finally, the Manassa Mauler made no effort to hide his connections with a loose-moraled, thrill-hungry, big-spending crowd. The characters hanging around Dempsey's training camps—gamblers, hucksters, pugs, minor hoods—all failed to help his public image. Dempsey did pay some deference to middle-class values. He gave talks on the fruits of clean living, made movies that upheld traditional notions of morality, saved and invested his money with reasonable prudence, and was the subject of pulp literature that tried to recast him in the Tunney mold of the hardworking, self-made man. While important, these efforts never wholly changed the public's view of Dempsey, and the outlaw image lingered.

Dempsey the boxer confirmed the image of Dempsey the social outlaw. He called himself a "jungle fighter," referring to the old times in the hobo camps and mining towns. Reporters agreed:

> Only when he is in the ring do those days come back. Then his brows blacken . . . his body muscled like a panther cat's, seems to ignite with malice, to burn and flash; then his fists reach out, savagely, lethally, to destroy the weaving shape in front of him and get revenge for something he has just remembered, a wrong done, a score that must be evened, something that happened to him long ago.*

This sense of vengeance, of redressing past grievances, was common in descriptions of the Manassa Mauler. Some reporters even predicted that once in the ring, Dempsey would pile on Tunney all responsibility for recent problems in his business dealings and his marriage. Blind with anger, he would strike out in mad fury against the man who symbolized his persecution.

There are at least hints that Dempsey's rage expressed social antagonisms and that the Manassa Mauler was thus favored by many tough, unreconstructed working-class men like himself. Occasional newspaper references alluded to this, and the *Chicago Tribune* claimed that small bettors across the country placed their wagers on Dempsey while the big money went for Tunney. Although it was not published until the Great Depression, Horace Gregory's "Dempsey, Dempsey" drew upon this identification of hard-hit laborers with the Manassa Mauler:

*Time, 30 August 1926.

> The million men and a million boys,
> come out of hell and crawling back,
> maybe they don't know what they're saying,
> maybe they don't care
> but they know what they mean . . .
> Knock down the big boss,
> O, my little Dempsey,
> my beautiful Dempsey
> with that God in heaven smile
> and quick, god's body leaping
> not afraid, leaping, rising—
> hit him again, he cut my paycheck, Dempsey. . . .

It is speculative but plausible to suggest that because he was not the golden boy, but rather a man who still smelled of the mines, still was a jungle fighter, Dempsey's outlaw image appealed to those most victimized by the gnawing hatreds and injustices of American society.

The champion's boxing style gave credence to claims that he fought out of pure primitive rage. His ring technique seemed brutal, with little apparent science or finesse. Like Dempsey the ex-hobo, Dempsey the fighter lived beyond rules and restraints. Newspapers said he knew no defense, only attack. He violated all accepted principles of boxing, charging out of his corner at full speed from the first round, never taking a step backwards. Columnist Westbrook Pegler declared that Dempsey seemed "as hard and violent as any man living." William O. McGeehan wrote of the champion's "concentrated cruelty" and his "will to kill." Others said that Dempsey lost his head in the ring, went out of control, simply did not know what he was doing. As one reporter put it, he came "slashing and slugging, rushing and tearing in, taking everything offered to crash through with a few of his own." He loved violence, and his greatest asset was his "killer instinct," his ability to follow up an advantage with bloodthirsty, relentless fury.

Newspapers referred constantly to Dempsey's defense of his title against Luis Angel Firpo—the Wild Bull of the Pampas—as part of their buildup to the first Tunney bout. *The Ring* magazine editor Nat Fleischer considered this fight the most exciting he had witnessed in fifty years of reporting. Immediately after the opening bell, Firpo knocked Dempsey to his knees with a right uppercut. Almost before the stunned crowd could catch its breath, the champion rose, charged the Wild Bull, and punched him down with a left to the jaw. Dempsey stood over his fallen opponent, glowering. When Firpo rose, Dempsey punched him back to the canvas. Again and again and again this happened. Somehow Firpo managed to avoid a seventh knockdown. He rushed Dempsey to the ropes, and with a clublike right, sent the champion sailing out of the ring into the arms of reporters. The newspapermen pushed the Manassa Mauler back to the fray, and the bell finally sounded with Dempsey resuming the attack. As the second round opened, the champion charged from his corner and immediately dropped Firpo with rights to the stomach and jaw. The Wild Bull staggered to his feet, but a quick combination by Dempsey ended the bout. In four breathless minutes, the fans had witnessed eleven knockdowns.

Despite the seeming anarchy, Dempsey's ring style was carefully cultivated; he worked hard to develop his distinctive bobbing-and-weaving technique. Still, the champion was usually depicted as a natural product, a born fighter, a purely physical man. He was wild and untamed, a "mauler," a "brawler," a "killer." He fought solely on instinct. Reporters seized upon natural metaphors to describe him. He burned with a flaming ring spirit. A "jungle fighter," he sprang at his prey with pantherlike quickness, cuffed, mauled, and maimed with tigerish ferocity, finished his victims with a lion's relentless savagery. Like a tornado, a whirlwind, a hurricane, he swept up his opponents and carried them along in a fury of devastation. He gave the fans what they wanted—intense, violent action.

Rituals, the anthropologist Victor Turner argues, condense symbols into coherent systems of meaning. While symbols may be multivocal—that is to say they may simultaneously signify many things—rituals bring symbolic meaning into comprehensible patterns. Usually, these patterns are organized around two poles: physiological phenomena like birth, death, sex, and blood, on the one hand, and normative values, moral imperatives, or social goals on the other. "The drama of ritual action," Turner writes, "causes an exchange between these poles in which the biological referents are ennobled and the normative referents are charged with emotional significance." The result is "communitas," a temporary state in which conflicts centering on material interest or social hierarchy are momentarily set aside. Ritually invoking communitas does not eliminate social schisms, but it does temporarily overshadow them, binding individuals together with shared cultural imperatives.

. The extraordinarily powerful images of the Dempsey-Tunney fights evoked precisely such a response. A sense of unity bordering on communion, of powerfully shared experience, comes through in descriptions of the crowds. A correspondent for *Time* groped for a metaphor to capture the fans' absorption in the first fight:

> To conceive of the cup of the stadium as the cup that holds a man's brain; to conceive of the ranked heads as the cells of the brain, each alone yet united in a common consciousness, each fiercely kinetic yet keeping its place in a segment . . . and every cell, every segment, every area of the vast filled hollow burning inward and downward upon the mysterious core of its life—a little white ring with four posts. To conceive of this is not to exaggerate.*

The sense of concentrated group consciousness—of communitas—grew out of the fights' ability to merge the controlled but intense violence of boxing with central cultural themes. Bringing Dempsey and Tunney together in a single ring transformed abstract norms into emotionally satisfying drama, converted a conflict of values into a palpable physical struggle, fused symbols, metaphors, and blood into messages mere words could not convey. The fights, then, were texts—stories we told ourselves about ourselves, to paraphrase Clifford Geertz—inviting exegesis.

By antithesis each man helped define what his opponent stood for, and it was the juxtaposition of the two images that gave the fights their deepest emotional impact. The symbolic Tunney af-

*Time, 4 October 1926.

firmed that hard work and self-help were alive and well. Person-
ifying both liberal individualism and faith in industrial progress,
the Fighting Marine represented the early twentieth century's
rickety ideological merger of heroic action and managerial norms,
personal accomplishment and corporate structures, the virtuous
self-made man in a thoroughly rationalized society. Taming wild
places and wild men—first the wilderness and red Indians, then
the workplace and red radicals—was a hallmark of American
mythology. In their rich symbolism, the Dempsey-Tunney fights
updated and renewed this old national theme of quest for control.
Embodying key norms undergirding a corporate-liberal society,
the Fighting Marine stepped forth to tame the Manassa Mauler,
just as scientific managers and industrial engineers brought non-
rational labor patterns under control, the American Expeditionary
Force subdued the "barbaric" Germans, modern psychology il-
lumined the darkness of the human unconscious, the Justice
Department hounded radicals, and educators conquered the immigrants' ignorance of American ways.

But the symbolism worked in reverse. There was a liberating
quality to the Manassa Mauler's violence, and as Dempsey himself acknowledged, the fans had a love/hate relationship with
him.* Against the Fighting Marine, the champion's nihilistic
aggression found specific focus. In opposition to Tunney's discipline, rational pursuit of goals, and subordination of passions
to self-control, Dempsey vented his wrath against the growing
constraints of a complex society. Where Tunney symbolized the
glorious fulfillment of industrial culture, Dempsey represented
the secret impulse to smash through the restrictions imposed on
men by bourgeois, bureaucratic society. Dempsey embodied
spontaneity, personal expressiveness, the acting out of human
passions, all in opposition to the social subordination that chan-
neled individuals into narrow roles and tasks.

Boxing, like other sports of the 1920s, remained primarily a
male passion, and the tensions I have been describing addressed

---

*When his ring career ended—after age and defeat humbled him—Dempsey
was rarely reviled, but became one of the most popular and sought-after figures
in American sports history. Tunney, in contrast, seemed increasingly priggish,
aloof, even arrogant in victory.

conflicts over what it meant to be a man in modern America. Responsibility, hard work, and conscientiousness fulfilled one version of masculinity, but denied another. If the bourgeois values that Tunney stood for remained genuinely compelling, Dempsey the outlaw figure who overthrew the same confining norms tapped a deep subterranean well of discontent with the direction of American society in the 1920s. Here was an aggressive assertion of self in a world increasingly cut off from the physical basis of life. As if in response to the triumph of the middle-class male ideal— provider of goods, trustworthy head of household, companion to wife and children—Dempsey and his cronies projected a fantasy image of unreconstructed virility and independence. And in an environment where assembly lines and bureaucratic business organizations reduced work to meaningless routine and co-opted control over the conditions of one's labor, images of the champion violating social rules, wild with rage, out of control, held deep if often unconscious appeal.

But while the fights expressed genuine ambivalence over the direction of American society, one could argue that their ultimate impact was quite conservative. Both Dempsey and Tunney, after all, were professional entertainers, products of image-making in-dustries—communications, public relations, advertising, and show business—which were hallmarks of the rising mass society, handmaidens of the consumer age. In a sense, Dempsey was as much in the mainstream of twenties culture as Tunney, because his spontaneity and impulsiveness, his love of fast cars, fancy clothes, and Hollywood highlife, exemplified an emergent new ethos. Advertising men now manipulated images of animality and wildness—of letting oneself go—as effective marketing devices. Indeed, the consumer values of self-gratification and self-indul-gence were as essential to an advanced capitalist society seeking new markets for mass-produced goods as the old ethic of hard work and steady habits. Movie screens, magazine pages, and radio airwaves were filled with images of youthful rebellion against traditional canons of upright behavior. However, what mass-media images offered was less a call to action than an invitation to more passive consumption, for cultural "liberation" readily degenerated into escapism from social, political, or economic problems. The twenties' "revolution" in manners and morals proved a rather tame uprising, leading men and women on shopping sprees rather than to the barricades. Taken on this level, spectacles like the Dempsey-Tunney fights were part of a larger fantasy world of popular idols, status symbols, and leisure-time pleasures that offered Americans vicarious release from an oppressively rationalized society.

Yet even if we accept the now-familiar argument that the mass media tend to trivialize social or cultural conflicts, this does not mean that those conflicts cease to exist. One cannot read the accounts of the Dempsey-Tunney fights without sensing that despite the hype and media exploitation, Americans found the images of the two boxers profoundly moving. The tension between repressive social demands and the ideal of individual liberation is as old as civilization itself, but the symbolism that clung to Dempsey and Tunney reified this age-old theme for the 1920s. More than merely two splendid athletes, the fighters dramatized conflicting values that grew out of tensions in the new mass society. The fans' quixotic, almost schizophrenic, reactions to the boxers bore testimony to a larger ambivalence over the contradictions in the culture of the 1920s. Momentarily, the ring afforded the nation a kaleidoscopic vision of itself. Dempsey and Tunney embodied the most fundamental cultural oppositions: bourgeois propriety, faith in progress, the spirit of improvement and productivity, all in the context of a corporate-bureaucratic social order, arrayed against an urge to break through the new social dependencies that limited human freedom, cravings for spontaneity and impulsiveness, and the desire for titillating goods and images as compensation for suffocating workaday life. Americans reacted so passionately to the fights, loved and hated both boxers, because the bouts presented the "really real" through the dramatic symbolism of violent human combat.

Of course, boxing matches could not resolve normative conflicts. If they could, victory would have belonged to the forces of rationality and self-control, for, in the event, it was Gene Tunney who won two clear-cut ten-round decisions from Jack Dempsey, keeping the old Manassa Mauler at bay with his fine defensive skills. The most dramatic—indeed poetic—moment came in the seventh round of the second fight. Dempsey caught Tunney with a left hook to the jaw, followed by a flurry of punches, sending the Fighting Marine to the canvas. The Manassa Mauler stood over Tunney, ready to knock him down again, but the referee enforced the rules, refusing to begin the count until Dempsey retired to a neutral corner. Tunney thus acquired precious extra seconds, rose on the count of nine, and managed to keep Dempsey out of range for the rest of the round. "Enough running. Come on and fight," Dempsey blurted in frustration, but the "long count" was his last moment of glory in the ring. In boxing as in American life, spontaneity and impulsiveness found expression, only to be confined within the bounds of rational, rule-bound institutions. For a moment, anyway, cultural dilemmas found catharsis, but certainly not resolution. After all, it was just prize-fighting.

A. J. Liebling

AHAB AND NEMESIS

Back in 1922, the late Heywood Broun, who is not remembered primarily as a boxing writer, wrote a durable account of a combat between the late Benny Leonard and the late Rocky Kansas for the lightweight championship of the world. Leonard was the greatest practitioner of the era, Kansas just a rough, optimistic fellow. In the early rounds Kansas messed Leonard about, and Broun was profoundly disturbed. A radical in politics, he was a conservative in the arts, and Kansas made him think of Gertrude Stein, *les Six*, and nonrepresentational painting, all novelties that irritated him.

"With the opening gong, Rocky Kansas tore into Leonard," he wrote. "He was gauche and inaccurate, but terribly persistent." The classic verities prevailed, however. After a few rounds, during which Broun continued to yearn for a return to a culture with fixed values, he was enabled to record: "The young child of nature who was challenging for the championship dropped his guard, and Leonard hooked a powerful and entirely orthodox blow to the conventional point of the jaw. Down went Rocky Kansas. His past life flashed before him during the nine seconds in which he remained on the floor, and he wished that he had been more faithful as a child in heeding the advice of his boxing teacher. After all, the old masters did know something. There is still a

84

kick in style, and tradition carries a nasty wallop."

I have often thought of Broun's words in the years since Rocky Marciano, the reigning heavyweight champion, scaled the fistic summits, as they say in *Journal-Americanese*, by beating Jersey Joe Walcott. The current Rocky is gauche and inaccurate, but besides being persistent he is a dreadfully severe hitter with either hand. The predominative nature of this asset has been well stated by Pierce Egan, the Edward Gibbon and Sir Thomas Malory of the old London prize ring, who was less preoccupied than Broun with ultimate implications. Writing in 1821 of a milling cove named Bill Neat, the Bristol Butcher, Egan said, "He possesses a requisite above all the art that *teaching* can achieve for any boxer; namely, *one hit* from his right hand, given in proper distance, can gain a victory; but three of them are positively enough to dispose of a giant." This is true not only of Marciano's right hand but of his left hand, too—provided he doesn't miss the giant entirely. Egan doubted the advisability of changing Neat's style, and he would have approved of Marciano's. (The champion has an apparently unlimited absorptive capacity for percussion—Egan would have called him an "insatiable glutton"—and inexhaustible energy, "a prime bottom fighter"). "Shifting," or moving to the side, and "milling in retreat," or moving back, are innovations of the late eighteenth century that Rocky's advisers have carefully kept from his knowledge, lest they spoil his natural prehistoric style. Egan excused these tactics only in boxers of feeble constitution.

Archie Moore, the light-heavyweight champion of the world, who hibernates in San Diego, California, and estivates in Toledo, Ohio, is a Brounian rather than an Eganite in his thinking about style, but he naturally has to do more than think about it. Since the rise of Marciano, Moore, a cerebral and hyperexperienced light-colored pugilist who has been active since 1936, has suffered the pangs of a supreme exponent of *bel canto* who sees himself crowded out of the opera house by a guy who can only shout. As a sequel to a favorable review I wrote of one of his infrequent New York appearances, when his fee was restricted to a measly five figures, I received a sad little note signed "The most unappreciated fighter in the world, Archie Moore." A fellow who has as much style as Moore tends to overestimate the intellect—he develops the kind of Faustian mind that will throw itself against the problem of perpetual motion, or of how to pick horses first, second, third, *and* fourth in every race. Archie's note made it plain to me that he was honing his harpoon for the White Whale.

When I read newspaper items about Moore's decisioning a large, playful porpoise of a Cuban heavyweight named Nino Valdes and scoop-netting a minnow like Bobo Olson, the middleweight champion, for practice, I thought of him as a lonely Ahab, rehearsing to buck Herman Melville, Pierce Egan, and the betting odds. I did not think that he could bring it off, but I wanted to be there when he tried. What would *Moby Dick* be if Ahab had succeeded? Just another fish story. The thing that is eternally diverting is the struggle of man against history—or what Albert Camus, who used to be an amateur middleweight, has called the Myth of Sisyphus. (Camus would have been a great man to cover the fight, but none of the syndicates thought of it.) When I heard that the boys had been made for September 20, 1955, at the Yankee Stadium, I shortened my stay abroad in order not to miss the Encounter of the Two Heroes, as Egan would have styled the rendezvous.

In London on the night of September thirteenth, a week before the date set for the Encounter, I tried to get my eye in for fight-watching by attending a bout at the White City greyhound track between Valdes, who had been imported for the occasion, and the British Empire heavyweight champion, Don Cockell, a fat man whose gift for public suffering has enlisted the sympathy of a sentimental people. Since Valdes had gone fifteen rounds with Moore in Las Vegas the previous May, and Cockell had excruciated for nine rounds before being knocked out by Marciano in San Francisco in the same month, the bout offered a dim opportunity for establishing what racing people call a "line" between Moore and Marciano. I didn't get much of an optical workout, because Valdes disposed of Cockell in three rounds. It was evident that Moore and Marciano had not been fighting the same class of people this season.

This was the only fight I ever attended in a steady rainstorm. It had begun in the middle of the afternoon, and, while there was a canopy over the ring, the spectators were as wet as speckled trout. "The weather, it is well known, has no terrors to the admirers of Pugilism of Life," Egan once wrote, and on his old stamping ground this still holds true. As I took my seat in a rock pool that had collected in the hollow of my chair, a South African giant named Ewart Potgieter, whose weight had been announced as twenty-two stone ten, was ignoring the doctrine of apartheid by leaning on a Jamaican colored man who weighed a mere sixteen stone, and by the time I had transposed these statistics to three hundred and eighteen pounds and two hundred and twenty-four pounds, respectively, the exhausted Jamaican had acquiesced in resegregation and retired. The giant had not struck a blow, properly speaking, but had shoved downward a number of times, like a man trying to close an overfilled trunk.

The main bout proved an even less grueling contest. Valdes, eager to get out of the chill, struck Cockell more vindictively than is his wont, and after a few gestures invocative of commiseration the fat man settled in one corner of the ring as heavily as suet pudding upon the unaccustomed gastric system. He had received what Egan would have called a "ribber" and a "nobber," and when he arose it was seen that the latter had raised a cut on his forehead. At the end of the third round, his manager withdrew him from competition. It was not an inspiring occasion, but after the armistice eight or nine shivering Cubans appeared in the runway behind the press section and jumped up and down to register emotion and restore circulation. *"Ahora Marciano!"* they yelled. "Now for Marciano!" Instead of being grateful for the distraction, the other spectators took a poor view of it. "Sit down, you chaps!" one of them cried. "We want to see the next do!" They were still parked out there in the rain when I tottered into the Shepherd's Bush underground station and collapsed, sneezing, on a train that eventually disgorged me at Oxford Circus, with just enough time left to buy a revivifying draught before eleven o'clock, when the pubs closed. How the mugs I left behind cured themselves I never knew. They had to do it on Bovril.

Because I had engagements that kept me in England until a few days before the Encounter, I had no opportunity to visit the training camps of the rival American Heroes. I knew all the members of both factions, however, and I could imagine what they were thinking. In the plane on the way home, I tried to envision the rival patterns of ratiocination. I could be sure that Marciano, a kind, quiet, imperturbable fellow, would plan to go after Moore and make him fight continuously until he tired enough to become an accessible target. After that he would expect concussion to accentuate exhaustion and exhaustion to facilitate concussion, until Moore came away from his consciousness, like everybody else Rocky had ever fought. He would try to remember to minimize damage to himself in the beginning, while there was still snap in Moore's arms, because Moore is a sharp puncher. (Like Bill Neat of old, Marciano hits at his opponent's arms when he cannot hit past them. "In one instance, the arm of Oliver [a Neat adversary] received so paralyzing a shock in stopping the blow that it appeared almost useless," Egan once wrote.) Charlie Goldman would have instructed Marciano in some rudimentary maneuver to throw Moore's first shots off, I felt sure, but after a few minutes Rocky woud forget it, or Archie would figure it out. But there would always be Freddie Brown, the "cut man," in the champion's corner to repair superficial damage. One reason Goldman is a great teacher is that he doesn't try to teach a boxer more than he can learn. What he had taught Rocky in the four years since I had first seen him fight was to shorten the arc of most of his blows without losing power thereby, and always to follow one hard blow with another—"for insurance"—delivered with the other hand, instead of recoiling to watch the victim fall. The champion had also gained confidence and presence of mind; he has a good fighting head, which is not the same thing as being a good mechanical practitioner: "A *boxer* requires a *nob* as well as a *statesman* does a HEAD, coolness and calculation being essential to *second* his efforts," Egan wrote, and the old historiographer was never more correct. Rocky was thirty-one, not in the first flush of youth for a boxer, but Moore was only a few days short of thirty-nine, so age promised to be in the champion's favor if he kept pressing.

Moore's strategic problem, I reflected on the plane, offered more choices and, as a corollary, infinitely more chances for error. It was possible, but not probable, that jabbing and defensive skill would carry him through fifteen rounds, even on those old legs,

but I knew that the mere notion of such a *gambade* would revolt
Moore. He is not what Egan would have called a shy fighter.
Besides, would Ahab have been content merely to go the distance
with the White Whale? I felt sure that Archie planned to knock
the champion out, so that he could sign his next batch of letters
"The most appreciated and deeply opulent fighter in the world."
I surmised that this project would prove a mistake, like Mr.
Churchill's attempt to take Gallipoli in 1915, but it would be the
kind of mistake that would look good in his memoirs. The basis
of what I rightly anticipated would prove a miscalculation went
back to Archie's academic background. As a young fighter of
conventional tutelage, he must have heard his preceptors say
hundreds of times, "They will all go if you hit them right." If a
fighter did not believe that, he would be in the position of a
Euclidian without faith in the hundred-and-eighty-degree tri-
angle. Moore's strategy, therefore, would be based on working
Marciano into a position where he could hit him right. He would
not go in and slug with him, because that would be wasteful,
distasteful, and injudicious, but he might try to cut him up, in
an effort to slow him down so he could hit him right, or else try
to hit him right and then cut him up. The puzzle he reserved for
me—and Marciano—was the tactic by which he would attempt
to attain his strategic objective. In the formation of his views, I
believed, Moore would be handicapped, rather than aided, by his
active, skeptical mind. One of the odd things about Marciano is
that he isn't terribly big. It is hard for a man like Moore, just
under six feet tall and weighing about a hundred and eighty
pounds, to imagine that a man approximately the same size can
be immeasurably stronger than he is. This is particularly true
when, like the light-heavyweight champion, he has spent his
whole professional life contending with boxers—some of them
considerably bigger—whose strength has proved so near his own
that he could move their arms and bodies by cunning pressures.
The old classicist would consequently refuse to believe what he
was up against.

The light-heavyweight limit is a hundred and seventy-five pounds,
and Moore can get down to that when he must, in order to defend
his title, but in a heavyweight match each Hero is allowed to

weigh whatever he pleases. I was back in time to attend the weighing-in ceremonies, held in the lobby of Madison Square Garden at noon on the day set for the Encounter, and learned that Moore weighed 188 and Marciano $188\frac{1}{4}$—a lack of disparity that figured to encourage the rationalist's illusions. I also learned that, in contrast to Jack Solomons, the London promoter who held the Valdes-Cockell match in the rain, the I.B.C., which was promoting the Encounter, had decided to postpone it for twenty-four hours, although the weather was clear. The decision was based on apprehension of Hurricane Ione, which, although apparently veering away from New York, might come around again like a lazy left hook and drop in on the point of the stadium's jaw late in the evening. Nothing like that happened, but the postponement brought the town's theaters and bars another evening of good business from the out-of-town fight trade, such as they always get on the eve of a memorable Encounter. ("Not a bed could be had at any of the villages at an early hour on the preceding evening; and Uxbridge was crowded beyond all former precedent," Egan wrote of the night before Neat beat Oliver.) There was no doubt that the fight had caught the public imagination, ever sensitive to a meeting between Hubris and Nemesis, as the boys on the quarterlies would say, and the bookies were laying 18-5 on Nemesis, according to the boys on the dailies, who always seem to hear. (A friend of mine up from Maryland with a whim and a five-dollar bill couldn't get ten against it in ordinary barroom money anywhere, although he wanted Ahab.)

The enormous—by recent precedent—advance sale of tickets had so elated the I.B.C. that it had decided to replace the usual card of bad preliminary fights with some not worth watching at all, so there was less distraction than usual as we awaited the appearance of the Heroes on the fateful evening. The press seats had been so closely juxtaposed that I could fit in only sidewise between two colleagues—the extra compression having been caused by the injection of a prewar number of movie stars and politicos. The tight quarters were an advantage, in a way, since they facilitated my conversation with Peter Wilson, an English prize-ring correspondent, who happened to be in the row behind me. I had last seen Mr. Wilson at White City the week before, at a time when the water level had already reached his shredded-Latakia mustache. I had feared that he had drowned at ringside, but when I saw him at the Stadium, he assured me that by buttoning the collar of his mackintosh tightly over his nostrils he had been able to make the garment serve as a diving lung, and so survive. Like all British fight writers when they are relieved of the duty of watching British fighters, he was in a holiday mood, and we chatted happily. There is something about the approach of a good fight that renders the spirit insensitive to annoyance; it is only when the amateur of the Sweet Science has some doubts as to how good the main bout will turn out to be that he is avid for the satisfaction to be had from the preliminaries. This is because after the evening is over, he may have only a good supporting fight to remember. There were no such doubts—even in the minds of the mugs who had paid for their seats—on the evening of September twenty-first.

At about ten-thirty the champion and his faction entered the ring. It is not customary for the champion to come in first, but Marciano has never been a stickler for protocol. He is a humble, kindly fellow, who even now will approach an acquaintance on the street and say bashfully, "Remember me? I'm Rocky Marciano." The champion doesn't mind waiting five or ten minutes to give anybody a punch in the nose. In any case, once launched from his dressing room under the grandstand, he could not have arrested his progress to the ring, because he had about forty policemen pushing behind him, and three more clearing a path in front of him. Marciano, tucked in behind the third cop like a football ball-carrier behind his interference, had to run or be trampled to death. Wrapped in a heavy blue bathrobe and with a blue monk's cowl pulled over his head, he climbed the steps to the ring with the cumbrous agility of a medieval executioner ascending the scaffold. Under the hood he seemed to be trying to look serious. He has an intellectual appreciation of the anxieties of a champion, but he has a hard time forgetting how strong he is; while he remembers that, he can't worry as much as he knows a champion should. His attendants—quick, battered little Goldman; Al Weill, the stout, excitable manager, always stricken just before the bell with the suspicion that he may have made a bad match; Al Columbo—are all as familiar to the crowd as he is.

Ahab's party arrived in the ring a minute or so later, and Charlie Johnston, his manager—a calm sparrow hawk of a man, as old and wise in the game as Weill—went over to watch Goldman put on the champion's gloves. Freddie Brown went to Moore's corner to watch *his* gloves being put on. Moore wore a splendid black silk robe with a gold lamé collar and belt. He sports a full mustache above an imperial, and his hair, sleeked down under pomade when he opens operations, invariably rises during the contest, as it gets water sloshed on it between rounds and the lacquer washes off, until it is standing up like the top of a shaving brush. Seated in his corner in the shadow of his personal trainer, a brown man called Cheerful Norman, who weighs two hundred and thirty-five pounds, Moore looked like an old Japanese print I have of a "Shogun Engaged in Strategic Contemplation in the Midst of War." The third member of his group was Bertie Briscoe, a rough, chipper little trainer, whose more usual charge is Sandy Saddler, the featherweight champion—also a Johnston fighter. Mr. Moore's features in repose rather resemble those of Orson Welles, and he was reposing with intensity.

The procession of other fighters and former fighters to be introduced was longer than usual. The full galaxy was on hand, including Jack Dempsey, Gene Tunney, and Joe Louis, the *têtes de cuvée* of former-champion society; ordinary former heavyweight champions, like Max Baer and Jim Braddock, slipped through the ropes practically unnoticed. After all the celebrities had been in and out of the ring, an odd dwarf, advertising something or other—possibly himself—was lifted into the ring by an accomplice and ran across it before he could be shooed out. The referee, a large, craggy, oldish man named Harry Kessler, who, unlike some of his better-known colleagues, is not an ex-fighter, called the men to the center of the ring. This was his moment; he had the microphone. "Now Archie and Rocky, I want a nice, clean fight," he said, and I heard a peal of silvery laughter behind me from Mr. Wilson, who had seen both of them fight before. "Protect yourself at all times," Mr. Kessler cautioned them unnecessarily. When the principals shook hands, I could see Mr.

Moore's eyebrows rising like storm clouds over the Sea of Azov. His whiskers bristled and his eyes glowed like dark coals as he scrunched his eyebrows down again and enveloped the Whale with the Look, which was intended to dominate his willpower. Mr. Wilson and I were sitting behind Marciano's corner, and as the champion came back to it I observed his expression, to determine what effect the Look had had upon him. More than ever, he resembled a Great Dane who has heard the word "bone."

A moment later the bell rang and the Heroes came out for the first round. Marciano, training in the sun for weeks, had tanned to a slightly deeper tint than Moore's old ivory, and Moore, at 188, looked, if anything, bigger and more muscular than Marciano; much of the champion's weight is in his legs, and his shoulders slope. Marciano advanced, but Moore didn't go far away. As usual, he stood up nicely, his arms close to his body and his feet not too far apart, ready to go anywhere but not without a reason—the picture of a powerful, decisive intellect unfettered by preconceptions. Marciano, pulling his left arm back from the shoulder, flung a left hook. He missed, but not by enough to discourage him, and then walked in and hooked again. All through the round he threw those hooks, and some of them grazed Moore's whiskers; one even hit him on the side of the head. Moore didn't try much offensively; he held a couple of times when Marciano worked in close.

Marciano came back to his corner as he always does, unimpassioned. He hadn't expected to catch Moore with those left hooks anyway, I imagine; all he had wanted was to move him around. Moore went to his corner inscrutable. They came out for the second, and Marciano went after him in brisker fashion. In the first round he had been throwing the left hook, missing with it, and then throwing a right and missing with that, too. In the second he tried a variation—throwing a right and then pulling a shoulder back to throw the left. It appeared for a moment to have Moore confused, as a matador might be confused by a bull who walked in on his hind legs. Marciano landed a couple of those awkward hooks, but not squarely. He backed Moore over toward the side of the ring farthest from me, and then Moore knocked him down.

Some of the reporters, describing the blow in the morning papers, called it a "sneak punch," which is journalese for one the reporter didn't see but technically means a lead thrown before the other man has warmed up or while he is musing about the gate receipts. This had been no lead, and although I certainly hadn't seen Moore throw the punch, I knew that it had landed inside the arc of Marciano's left hook. ("Marciano missed with the right, trun the left, and Moore stepped inside it," my private eye, Whitey Bimstein, said next day, confirming my diagnosis, and the film of the fight bore both of us out.) So Ahab had his harpoon in the Whale. He had hit him right if ever I saw a boxer hit right, with a classic brevity and conciseness. Marciano stayed down for two seconds. I do not know what took place in Mr. Moore's breast when he saw him get up. He may have felt, for the moment, like Don Giovanni when the Commendatore's statue grabbed at him—startled because he thought he had killed the guy already—or like Ahab when he saw the Whale take down Fedallah, harpoons and all. Anyway, he hesitated a couple of seconds, and that was reasonable. A man who took nine to come up after a punch like that would be doing well, and the correct tactic would be to go straight in and finish him. But a fellow who came up on two was so strong he would bear investigation.

After that, Moore did go in, but not in a crazy way. He hit Marciano some good, hard, classic shots, and inevitably Marciano, a trader, hit him a few devastating swipes, which slowed him. When the round ended, the edge of Moore's speed was gone, and he knew that he would have to set a new and completely different trap, with diminished resources. After being knocked down, Marciano had stopped throwing that patterned right-and-left combination; he has a good nob. "He never trun it again in the fight," Whitey said next day, but I differ. He threw it in the fifth, and again Moore hit him a peach of a right inside it, but the steam was gone; this time Ahab couldn't even stagger him. Anyway, there was Moore at the end of the second, dragging his shattered faith in the unities and humanities back to his corner. He had hit a guy right, and the guy hadn't gone. But there is no geezer in Moore, any more than there was in the master of the Pequod.

Both came out for the third very gay, as Egan would have said. Marciano had been hit and cut, so he felt acclimated, and Moore was so mad at himself for not having knocked Marciano out that he almost displayed animosity toward him. He may have thought that perhaps he had not hit Marciano *just* right; the true artist is always prone to self-reproach. He would try again. A minute's attention from his squires had raised his spirits and slicked down his hair. At this point, Marciano set about him. He waddled in, hurling his fists with a sublime disregard of probabilities, content to hit an elbow, a biceps, a shoulder, the top of a head—the last supposed to be the least profitable target in the business, since, as every beginner learns, "the head is the hardest part of the human body," and a boxer will only break his hands on it. Many boxers make the systematic presentation of the cranium part of their defensive scheme. The crowd, basically anti-intellectual, screamed encouragement. There was Moore, riding punches, picking them off, slipping them, rolling with them, ducking them, coming gracefully out of his defensive efforts with sharp, patterned blows—and just about holding this parody even on points. His face, emerging at instants from under the storm of arms— his own and Rocky's—looked like that of a swimming walrus. When the round ended, I could see that he was thinking deeply. Marciano came back to his corner at a kind of suppressed dogtrot. He didn't have a worry in the world.

It was in the fourth, though, that I think Sisyphus began to get the idea he couldn't roll back the Rock. Marciano pushed him against the ropes and swung at him for what seemed a full minute without ever landing a punch that a boxer with Moore's background would consider a credit to his workmanship. He kept them coming so fast, though, that Moore tired just getting out of their way. One newspaper account I saw said that at this point Moore "swayed uncertainly," but his motions were about as uncertain as Margot Fonteyn's, or Arthur Rubinstein's. He is the most premeditated and best-synchronized swayer in his profession. After the bell rang for the end of the round, the champion hit him a right for good measure—he usually manages to have something on the way all the time—and then pulled back to disclaim any uncouth intention. Moore, no man to be conned, hit him a corker of a punch in return, when he wasn't expecting it. It was a gesture of moral reprobation and also a punch that would give any normal man something to think about between rounds. It was a good thing Moore couldn't see Marciano's face as he came back to his corner, though, because the champion was laughing.

The fifth was a successful round for Moore, and I had him ahead on points that far in the fight. But it took no expert to know where the strength lay. There was even a moment in the round when Moore set himself against the ropes and encouraged Marciano to swing at him, in the hope the champion would swing himself tired. It was a confession that he himself was too tired to do much hitting.

In the sixth Marciano knocked Moore down twice—once, early in the round, for four seconds, and once, late in the round, for eight seconds, with Moore getting up just before the bell rang. In the seventh, after that near approach to obliteration, the embattled intellect put up its finest stand. Marciano piled out of his corner to finish Moore, and the stylist made him miss so often that it looked, for a fleeting moment, as if the champion were indeed punching himself arm-weary. In fact, Moore began to beat him to the punch. It was Moore's round, certainly, but an old-timer I talked to later averred that one of the body blows Marciano landed in that round was the hardest of the fight.

It was the eighth that ended the competitive phase of the fight. They fought all the way, and in the last third of the round the champion simply overflowed Archie. He knocked him down with a right six seconds before the bell, and I don't think Moore could have got up by ten if the round had lasted that long. The fight by then reminded me of something that Sam Langford, one of the most profound thinkers—and, according to all accounts, one of the greatest doers—of the prize ring, once said to me: "Whatever that other man wants to do, don't let him do it." Merely by moving in all the time and punching continually, Marciano achieves the same strategic effect that Langford gained by finesse. It is impossible to think, or to impose your thought, if you have to keep on avoiding punches.

Moore's "game," as old Egan would have called his courage, was beyond reproach. He came out proudly for the ninth, and stood and fought back with all he had, but Marciano slugged him down, and he was counted out with his left arm hooked over the middle rope as he tried to rise. It was a crushing defeat for the higher faculties and a lesson in intellectual humility, but he had made a hell of a fight.

The fight was no sooner over than hundreds of unsavory young yokels with New England accents began a kind of mountain-goat immigration from the bleachers to ringside. They leaped from chair to chair and, after they reached the press section, from typewriter shelf to typewriter shelf and, I hope, from movie star to movie star. "Rocky!" they yelled. "Brockton!" Two of them, as dismal a pair of civic ambassadors as I have seen since I worked on the Providence *Journal & Evening Bulletin*, stood on Wilson's typewriter and yelled "Providence!" After the fighters and the hick delinquents had gone away, I made my way out to Jerome Avenue, where the crowd milled, impenetrable, under the "El" structure.

If you are not in a great hurry to get home (and why should you be at eleven-thirty or twelve on a fight night?), the best plan is to walk up to the station north of the stadium and have a beer in a saloon, or a cup of tea in the 167th Street Cafeteria, and wait until the whole mess clears away. By that time you may even get a taxi. After this particular fight I chose the cafeteria, being in a contemplative rather than a convivial mood. The place is of a genre you would expect to find nearer Carnegie Hall, with blond woodwork and modern functional furniture imported from Italy— an appropriate background for the evaluation of an aesthetic experience. I got my tea and a smoked-salmon sandwich on a soft onion roll at the counter and made my way to a table, where I found myself between two young policemen who were talking about why Walt Disney has never attempted a screen version of Kafka's "Metamorphosis." As I did not feel qualified to join in that one, I got out my copy of the official program of the fights and began to read the high-class feature articles as I munched my sandwich.

One reminded me that I had seen the first boxing show ever held in Yankee Stadium—on May 12, 1923. I had forgotten that it *was* the first show, and even that 1923 was the year the stadium opened. In my true youth the Yankees used to share the Polo Grounds with the Giants, and I had forgotten that, too, because I never cared much about baseball, although, come to think of it, I used to see the Yankees play occasionally in the nineteen teens, and should have remembered. I remembered the boxing show itself very well, though. It happened during the spring of my second suspension from college, and I paid five dollars for a high-grandstand seat. The program merely said that it had been "an all-star heavyweight bill promoted by Tex Rickard for the Hearst Milk Fund," but I found that I could still remember every man and every bout on the card. One of the main events was between old Jess Willard, the former heavyweight champion of the world, who had lost the title to Jack Dempsey in 1919, and a young heavyweight named Floyd Johnson. Willard had been coaxed from retirement to make a comeback because there was such a dearth of heavyweight material that Rickard thought he could still get by, but as I remember the old fellow, he couldn't fight a lick. He had a fair left jab and a right uppercut that a fellow had to walk into to get hurt by, and he was big and soft. Johnson was a mauler worse than Rex Layne, and the old man knocked him out. The other main event, *ex aequo,* had Luis Angel Firpo opposing a fellow named Jack McAuliffe II, from Detroit, who had had only fifteen fights and had never beaten anybody, and had a glass jaw. The two winners, of whose identity there was infinitesimal preliminary doubt, were to fight each other for the right to meet the great Jack Dempsey. Firpo was so crude that Marciano would be a Fancy Dan in comparison. He could hit with only one hand—his right—he hadn't the faintest idea of what to do in close, and he never cared much for the business anyway. He knocked McAuliffe out, of course, and then, in a later "elimination" bout, stopped poor old Willard. He subsequently became a legend by going one and a half sensational rounds with Dempsey, in a time that is now represented to us as the golden age of American pugilism.

I reflected with satisfaction that old Ahab Moore could have whipped all four principals on that card within fifteen rounds, and that while Dempsey may have been a great champion, he had less to beat than Marciano. I felt the satisfaction because it proved that the world isn't going backward, if you can just stay young enough to remember what it was really like when you were really young.

Gay Talese

THE LOSER

At the foot of a mountain in upstate New York, about sixty miles from Manhattan, there is an abandoned country clubhouse with a dusty dance floor, upturned barstools, and an untuned piano; and the only sounds heard around the place at night come from the big white house behind it—the clanging sounds of garbage cans being toppled by raccoons, skunks, and stray cats making their nocturnal raids down from the mountain.

The white house seems deserted, too; but occasionally, when the animals become too clamorous, a light will flash on, a window will open, and a Coke bottle will come flying through the darkness and smash against the cans. But mostly the animals are undisturbed until daybreak, when the rear door of the white house swings open and a broad-shouldered Negro appears in gray sweat clothes with a white towel around his neck.

He runs down the steps, quickly passes the garbage cans and proceeds at a trot down the dirt road beyond the country club toward the highway. Sometimes he stops along the road and throws a flurry of punches at imaginary foes, each jab punctuated by hard gasps of his breathing—"*hegh-hegh-hegh*"—and then, reaching the highway, he turns and soon disappears up the mountain.

At this time of morning, farm trucks are on the road, and the other drivers wave at the runner. And later in the morning other motorists see him, and a few stop suddenly at the curb and ask:

"Say, aren't you Floyd Patterson?"

"No," says Floyd Patterson. "I'm his brother, Raymond."

The motorists move on, but recently a man on foot, a disheveled man who seemed to have spent the night outdoors, staggered behind the runner along the road and yelled, "Hey, Floyd Patterson!"

"No, I'm his brother Raymond."

"Don't tell *me* you're not Floyd Patterson. I know what Floyd Patterson looks like."

"Okay," Patterson said, shrugging, "if you want me to be Floyd Patterson, I'll be Floyd Patterson."

"So let me have your autograph," said the man, handing him a rumpled piece of paper and a pencil.

He signed it—"Raymond Patterson."

One hour later Floyd Patterson was jogging his way back down the dirt path toward the white house, the towel over his head absorbing the sweat from his brow. He lives alone in a two-room apartment in the rear of the house, and has remained in almost complete seclusion since getting knocked out a second time by Sonny Liston.

In the smaller room is a large bed he makes up himself, several record albums he rarely plays, a telephone that seldom rings. The larger room has a kitchen on one side and, on the other, adjacent to a sofa, is a fireplace from which are hung boxing trunks and T-shirts to dry, and a photograph of him when he was the champion, and also a television set. The set is usually on except when Patterson is sleeping, or when he is sparring across the road inside the clubhouse (the ring is rigged over what was once the dance floor), or when, in a rare moment of painful honesty, he reveals to a visitor what it is like to be the loser.

"Oh, I would give up anything to just be able to work with Liston, to box with him somewhere where nobody would see us, and to see if I could get past three minutes with him," Patterson was saying, wiping his face with the towel, pacing slowly around the room near the sofa. "I *know* I can do better. . . . Oh, I'm not talking about a rematch. Who would pay a nickel for another

Patterson-Liston fight? I know *I* wouldn't. . . . But all I want to do is get past the first round."

Then he said, "You have no idea how it is in the first round. You're out there with all those people around you, and those cameras, and the whole world looking in, and all that movement, that excitement, and 'The Star-Spangled Banner,' and the whole nation hoping you'll win, including the President. And do you know what all this does? It blinds you, just blinds you. And then the bell rings, and you go at Liston and he's coming at you, and you're not even aware that there's a referee in the ring with you.

"Then you can't remember much of the rest, because you don't want to. . . . All you recall is, all of a sudden you're getting up, and the referee is saying, 'You all right?' and you say, 'Of *course* I'm all right,' and he says, 'What's your name?' and you say, 'Patterson.'

"And then, suddenly, with all this screaming around you, you're down again, and you know you have to get up, but you're extremely groggy, and the referee is pushing you back, and your trainer is in there with a towel, and people are all standing up, and your eyes focus directly at no one person—you're sort of floating.

"It is not a *bad* feeling when you're knocked out," he said. "It's a *good* feeling, actually. It's not painful, just a sharp grogginess. You don't see angels or stars; you're on a pleasant cloud. After Liston hit me in Nevada, I felt, for about four or five seconds, that everybody in the arena was actually in the ring with me, circled around me like a family, and you feel warmth toward all the people in the arena after you're knocked out. You feel lovable to all the people. And you want to reach out and kiss everybody—men and women—and after the Liston fight somebody told me I actually blew a kiss to the crowd from the ring. I don't remember that. But I guess it's true because that's the way you feel during the four or five seconds after a knockout. . . .

"But then," Patterson went on, still pacing, "this good feeling leaves you. You realize where you are, and what you're doing there, and what has just happened to you. And what follows is a hurt, a confused hurt—not a physical hurt—it's a hurt combined with anger; it's a what-will-people-think hurt; it's an ashamed-of-my-own-ability hurt . . . and all you want then is a hatch door in the middle of the ring—a hatch door that will open and let you fall through and land in your dressing room instead of having to get out of the ring and face those people. The worst thing about losing is having to walk out of the ring and face those people. . . ."

Then Patterson walked over to the stove and put on the kettle for tea. He remained silent for a few moments. Through the walls could be heard the footsteps and voices of the sparring partners and the trainer who live in the front of the house. Soon they would be in the clubhouse getting things ready should Patterson wish to spar. In two days he was scheduled to fly to Stockholm and fight an Italian named Amonti, Patterson's first appearance in the ring since the last Liston fight.

Next he hoped to get a fight in London against Henry Cooper. Then, if his confidence was restored, his reflexes reacting, Patterson hoped to start back up the ladder in this country, fighting all the leading contenders, fighting often, and not waiting so long between each fight as he had done when he was a champion in the 90-percent tax bracket.

His wife, whom he finds little time to see, and most of his friends think he should quit. They point out that he does not need the money. Even he admits that, from investments alone on his $8,000,000 gross earnings, he should have an annual income of about $35,000 for the next twenty-five years. But Patterson, who is only twenty-nine years old and barely scratched, cannot believe that he is finished. He cannot help but think that it was something more than Liston that destroyed him—a strange, psychological force was also involved, and unless he can fully understand what it was, and learn to deal with it in the boxing ring, he may never be able to live peacefully anywhere but under this mountain. Nor will he ever be able to discard the false whiskers and moustache that, ever since Johansson beat him in 1959, he has carried with him in a small attaché case into each fight so he can slip out of the stadium unrecognized should he lose.

"I often wonder what other fighters feel, and what goes through their minds when they lose," Patterson said, placing the cups of tea on the table. "I've wanted so much to talk to another fighter about all this, to compare thoughts, to see if he feels some of the same things I've felt. But who can you talk to? Most fighters don't talk much anyway. And I can't even look another fighter in the eye at a weigh-in, for some reason.

"At the Liston weigh-in, the sportswriters noticed this, and said it showed I was afraid. But that's not it. I can never look *any* fighter in the eye because . . . well, because we're going to fight, which isn't a nice thing, and because . . . well, once I actually did look a fighter in the eye. It was a long, long time ago. I must have been in the amateurs then. And when I looked at this fighter, I saw he had such a nice face . . . and then he looked at *me* . . . and *smiled* at me . . . and *I* smiled back! It was strange, very strange. When a guy can look at another guy and smile like that, I don't think they have any business fighting.

"I don't remember what happened in that fight, and I don't remember what the guy's name was. I only remember that, ever since, I have never looked another fighter in the eye."

The telephone rang in the bedroom. Patterson got up to answer it. It was his wife, Sandra. So he excused himself, shutting the bedroom door behind him.

Sandra Patterson and their four children live in a $100,000 home in an upper-middle-class white neighborhood in Scarsdale, New York. Floyd Patterson feels uncomfortable in this home surrounded by a manicured lawn and stuffed with furniture, and, since losing his title to Liston, he has preferred living full-time at his camp, which his children have come to know as "Daddy's house." The children, the eldest of whom is a daughter named Jeannie now seven years old, do not know exactly what their father does for a living. But Jeannie, who watched the last Liston-Patterson fight on closed-circuit television, accepted the explanation that her father performs in a kind of game where the men take turns pushing one another down; he had his turn pushing them down, and now it is their turn.

The bedroom door opened again, and Floyd Patterson, shaking his head, was very angry and nervous.

"I'm not going to work out today," he said. "I'm going to fly down to Scarsdale. Those boys are picking on Jeannie again. She's the only Negro in this school, and the older kids give her a rough time, and some of the older boys tease her and lift up her dress all the time. Yesterday she went home crying, and so today I'm going down there and plan to wait outside the school for those boys to come out, and . . ."

"How old are they?" he was asked.

"Teen-agers," he said. "Old enough for a left hook."

Patterson telephoned his pilot friend, Ted Hanson, who stays at the camp and does public relations work for him, and has helped teach Patterson to fly. Five minutes later Hanson, a lean white man with a crew cut and glasses, was knocking on the door; and ten minutes later both were in the car that Patterson was driving almost recklessly over the narrow, winding country roads toward the airport, about six miles from the camp.

"Sandra is afraid I'll cause trouble; she's worried about what I'll do to those boys; she doesn't want trouble!" Patterson snapped, swerving around a hill and giving his car more gas. "She's just not firm enough! She's afraid . . . she was afraid to tell me about that groceryman who's been making passes at her. It took her a long time before she told me about that dishwasher repairman who comes over and calls her 'baby.' They all know I'm away so much. And that dishwasher repairman's been to my home about four, five times this month already. That machine breaks down every week. I guess he fixes it so it breaks down every week. Last time, I laid a trap. I waited forty-five minutes for him to come, but then he didn't show up. I was going to grab him and say, 'How would you like it if I called *your* wife *baby*? You'd feel like punching me in the nose, wouldn't you? Well, that's what I'm going to do—if you *ever* call her *baby* again. You call her Mrs. Patterson, or Sandra, if you know her. But you don't know her, so call her Mrs. Patterson.' And then I told Sandra that these men, this type of white man, he just wants to have some fun with colored women. He'll never marry a colored woman, just wants to have some fun. . . ."

Now he was driving into the airport's parking lot. Directly ahead, roped to the grass airstrip, was the single-engine green Cessna that Patterson bought and learned to fly before the second Liston fight. Flying was a thing Patterson had always feared—a fear shared by, maybe inherited from, his manager, Cus D'Amato, who still will not fly.

D'Amato, who took over training Patterson when the fighter

was seventeen or eighteen years old and exerted a tremendous influence over his psyche, is a strange but fascinating man of fifty-six who is addicted to Spartanism and self-denial and is possessed by suspicion and fear: He avoids subways because he fears someone might push him onto the tracks; never has married; never reveals his home address.

"I must keep my enemies confused," D'Amato once explained. "When they are confused, then I can do a job for my fighters. What I do not want in life, however, is a sense of security; the moment a person knows security, his senses are dulled—and he begins to die. I also do not want many pleasures in life; I believe the more pleasures you get out of living, the more fear you have of dying."

Until a few years ago, D'Amato did most of Patterson's talking, and ran things like an Italian *padrone*. But later Patterson, the maturing son, rebelled against the Father Image. After losing to Sonny Liston the first time—a fight D'Amato had urged Patterson to resist—Patterson took flying lessons. And before the second Liston fight, Patterson had conquered his fear of height, was master at the controls, was filled with renewed confidence—and knew, too, that even if he lost, he at least possessed a vehicle that could get him out of town, fast.

But it didn't. After the fight, the little Cessna, weighed down by too much luggage, became overheated ninety miles outside of Las Vegas. Patterson and his pilot companion, having no choice but to turn back, radioed the airfield and arranged for the rental of a larger plane. When they landed, the Vegas air terminal was filled with people leaving town after the fight. Patterson hid in the shadows behind a hangar. His beard was packed in the trunk. But nobody saw him.

Later the pilot flew Patterson's Cessna back to New York alone. And Patterson flew in the larger, rented plane. He was accompanied on this flight by Hanson, a friendly, forty-two-year-old, thrice-divorced Nevadan who once was a crop duster, a bartender, and a cabaret hoofer; later he became a pilot instructor in Las Vegas, and it was there that he met Patterson. The two became good friends. And when Patterson asked Hanson to help fly the rented plane back to New York, Hanson did not hesitate, even though he had a slight hangover that night—partly due to being depressed by Liston's victory, partly due to being slugged in a bar by a drunk after objecting to some unflattering things the drunk had said about the fight.

Once in the airplane, however, Ted Hanson became very alert. He had to, because, after the plane had cruised a while at 10,000 feet, Floyd Patterson's mind seemed to wander back to the ring, and the plane would drift off course, and Hanson would say, "Floyd, Floyd, how's about getting back on course?", and then Patterson's head would snap up and his eyes would flash toward the dials. And everything would be all right for a while. But then he was back in the arena, reliving the fight, hardly believing that it had really happened.

"... And I kept thinking, as I flew out of Vegas that night, of all those months of training before the fight, all the roadwork, all the sparring, all the months away from Sandra ... thinking of the time in camp when I wanted to stay up until eleven-fifteen P.M. to watch a certain movie on the late show. But I didn't because I had roadwork the next morning.

"... And I was thinking about how good I'd felt before the fight, as I lay on the table in the dressing room. I remember thinking, 'You're in excellent physical condition, you're in good mental condition—but are you vicious?' But you tell yourself, 'Viciousness is not important now, don't think about it now; a championship fight's at stake, and that's important enough and, who knows? maybe you'll get vicious once the bell rings.'

"... And so you lay there trying to get a little sleep ... but you're only in a twilight zone, half asleep, and you're interrupted every once in a while by voices out in the hall, some guy's yelling 'Hey, Jack,' or 'Hey, Al,' or 'Hey, get those four-rounders into the ring.' And when you hear that, you think, 'They're not ready for you yet.' So you lay there ... and wonder, 'Where will I be to-morrow? Where will I be three hours from now?' Oh, you think all kinds of thoughts, some thoughts completely unrelated to the fight ... you wonder whether you ever paid your mother-in-law back for all those stamps she bought a year ago ... and you remember that time at two A.M. when Sandra tripped on the steps while bringing a bottle up to the baby ... and then you get *mad and ask: 'What am I thinking about these things for?' . . . and you try to sleep . . . but then the door opens and somebody says to somebody else, 'Hey, is somebody gonna go to Liston's dressing room to watch 'em bandage up?'*

". . . And so then you know it's about time to get ready. . . . You open your eyes. You get off the table. You glove up, you loosen up. Then Liston's trainer walks in. He looks at you, he smiles. He feels the bandages and later he says, 'Good luck, Floyd,' and you think, 'He didn't have to say that; he must be a nice guy.'

". . . And then you go out, and it's the long walk, always a long walk, and you think, 'What am I gonna be when I come back this way?' Then you climb into the ring. You notice Billy Eckstine at ringside leaning over to talk to somebody, and you see the reporters—some you like, some you don't like—and then it's 'The Star Spangled Banner,' and the cameras are rolling, and the bell rings.

". . . How could the same thing happen twice? How? That's all I kept thinking after the knockout. . . . Was I fooling these people all these years? . . . Was I ever the champion? . . . And then they lead you out of the ring . . . and up the aisle you go, past those people, and all you want is to get to your dressing room, fast . . . but the trouble was in Las Vegas they made a wrong turn along the aisle, and when we got to the end there was no dressing room there . . . and we had to walk all the way back down the aisle, past the same people, and they must have been thinking, 'Patterson's not only knocked out, but he can't even find his dressing room.'

". . . In the dressing room I had a headache. Liston didn't hurt me physically—a few days later I only felt a twitching nerve in my teeth—it was nothing like some fights I've had: like that Dick Wagner fight in '53 when he beat my body so bad I was urinating blood for days. After the Liston fight, I just went into the bathroom, shut the door behind me, and looked at myself in the mirror. I just looked at myself, and asked, 'What happened?' and then they started pounding on the door, and saying, 'Com'on out, Floyd, com'on out; the press is here, Cus is here, com'on out, Floyd.'

". . . And so I went out, and they asked questions, but what

can you say? What you're thinking about is all those months of training, all the conditioning, all the depriving; and you think, 'I didn't have to run that extra mile, didn't have to spar that day, I could have stayed up that night in camp and watched the late show. . . . I could have fought this fight tonight in no condition. . . .'"

"Floyd, Floyd," Hanson had said, "let's get back on course."

Again Patterson would snap out of his reverie, and refocus on the omniscope, and get his flying under control. After landing in New Mexico, and then in Ohio, Floyd Patterson and Ted Hanson brought the little plane into the New York airstrip near the fight camp. The green Cessna that had been flown back by the other pilot was already there, roped to the grass at precisely the same spot it was on this day five months later when Floyd Patterson was planning to fly it toward perhaps another fight—this time a fight with some schoolboys in Scarsdale who had been lifting up his little daughter's dress.

Patterson and Ted Hanson untied the plane, and Patterson got a rag and wiped from the windshield the splotches of insects. Then he walked around behind the plane, inspected the tail, checked under the fuselage, then peered down between the wing and the flaps to make sure all the screws were tight. He seemed suspicious of something. D'Amato would have been pleased.

"If a guy wants to get rid of you," Patterson explained, "all he has to do is remove these little screws here. Then, when you try to come in for a landing, the flaps fall off, and you crash."

Then Patterson got into the cockpit and started the engine. A few moments later, with Hanson beside him, Patterson was racing the little plane over the grassy field, then soaring over the weeds, then flying high above the gentle hills and trees. It was a nice takeoff.

Since it was only a forty-minute flight to the Westchester airport, where Sandra Patterson would be waiting with a car, Floyd Patterson did all the flying. The trip was uneventful until, suddenly behind a cloud, he flew into heavy smoke that hovered above a forest fire. His visibility gone, he was forced to the instruments. And at this precise moment, a fly that had been buzzing in the back of the cockpit flew up front and landed on the instrument panel in front of Patterson. He glared at the fly, watched it crawl slowly up the windshield, then shot a quick smash with his palm against the glass. He missed. The fly buzzed safely past Patterson's ear, bounced off the back of the cockpit, circled around.

"This smoke won't keep up," Hanson assured. "You can level off."

Patterson leveled off.

He flew easily for a few moments. Then the fly buzzed to the front again, zigzagging before Patterson's face, landed on the panel and proceeded to crawl across it. Patterson watched it, squinted. Then he slammed down at it with a quick right hand. Missed.

Ten minutes later, his nerves still on edge, Patterson began the descent. He picked up the radio microphone—"Westchester tower . . . Cessna 2729 uniform . . . three miles northwest . . . land in one-six on final . . ."—and then, after an easy landing, he climbed quickly out of the cockpit and strode toward his wife's station wagon outside the terminal.

But along the way a small man smoking a cigar turned toward Patterson, waved at him, and said, "Say, excuse me, but aren't you . . . aren't you . . . Sonny Liston?"

Patterson stopped. He glared at the man, bewildered. He wasn't sure whether it was a joke or an insult, and he really did not know what to do.

"Aren't you Sonny Liston?" the man repeated, quite serious.

"No," Patterson said, quickly passing by the man, "I'm his brother."

When he reached Mrs. Patterson's car, he asked, "How much time till school lets out?"

"About fifteen minutes," she said, starting up the engine. Then she said, "Oh, Floyd, I just should have told Sister, I shouldn't have . . ."

"*You* tell Sister; *I'll* tell the boys."

Mrs. Patterson drove as quickly as she could into Scarsdale, with Patterson shaking his head and telling Ted Hanson in the back, "Really can't understand these school kids. This is a religious school, and they want $20,000 for a glass window—and yet, some of them carry these racial prejudices, and it's mostly the Jews who are shoulder-to-shoulder with us, and . . ."

"Oh, Floyd," cried his wife, "Floyd, I have to get along here . . . you're not here, you don't live here, I . . ."

She arrived at the school just as the bell began to ring. It was a modern building at the top of a hill, and on the lawn was the statue of a saint, and behind it a large white cross. "There's Jeannie," said Mrs. Patterson.

"Hurry, call her over here," Patterson said.

"Jeannie! Come over here, honey."

The little girl, wearing a blue school uniform and cap, and clasping books in front of her, came running down the path toward the station wagon.

"Jeannie," Floyd Patterson said, rolling down his window, "point out the boys who lifted your dress."

Jeannie turned and watched as several students came down the path; then she pointed to a tall, thin curly-haired boy walking with four other boys, all about twelve to fourteen years of age.

"Hey," Patterson called to him, "can I see you for a minute?"

All five boys came to the side of the car. They looked Patterson directly in the eye. They seemed not at all intimidated by him.

"You the one that's been lifting up my daughter's dress?" Patterson asked the boy who had been singled out.

"Nope," the boy said, casually.

"Nope?" Patterson said, caught off guard by the reply.

"Wasn't him, mister," said another boy. "Probably was his little brother."

Patterson looked at Jeannie. But she was speechless, uncertain. The five boys remained there, waiting for Patterson to do something.

"Well, er, where's your little brother?" Patterson asked.

"Hey, kid!" one of the boys yelled. "Come over here."

A boy walked toward them. He resembled his older brother; he had freckles on his small, upturned nose, had blue eyes, dark curly hair and, as he approached the station wagon, he seemed equally unintimidated by Patterson.

"You been lifting up my daughter's dress?"

"Nope," the boy said.

"*Nope!*" Patterson repeated, frustrated.

"Nope, I wasn't lifting it. I was just touching it a little. . . ."

The other boys stood around the car looking down at Patterson, and other students crowded behind them, and nearby Patterson saw several white parents standing next to their parked cars; he became self-conscious, began to tap nervously with his fingers against the dashboard. He could not raise his voice without creating an unpleasant scene, yet could not retreat gracefully; so his voice went soft, and he said, finally:

"Look, boy, I want you to stop it. I won't tell your mother—that might get you in trouble—but don't do it again, okay?"

"Okay."

The boys calmly turned and walked, in a group, up the street.

Sandra Patterson said nothing. Jeannie opened the door, sat in the front seat next to her father, and took out a small blue piece of paper that a nun had given her and handed it across to Mrs. Patterson. But Floyd Patterson snatched it. He read it. Then he paused, put the paper down, and quietly announced, dragging out the words, *"She didn't do her religion. . . ."*

Patterson now wanted to get out of Scarsdale. He wanted to return to camp. After stopping at the Patterson home in Scarsdale and picking up Floyd Patterson, Jr., who is three, Mrs. Patterson drove them all back to the airport. Jeannie and Floyd, Jr., were seated in the back of the plane, and then Mrs. Patterson drove the station wagon alone up to camp, planning to return to Scarsdale that evening with the children.

It was four P.M. when Floyd Patterson got back to the camp, and the shadows were falling on the clubhouse, and on the tennis court routed by weeds, and on the big white house in front of which not a single automobile was parked. All was deserted and quiet; it was a loser's camp.

The children ran to play inside the clubhouse; Patterson walked slowly toward his apartment to dress for the workout.

"What could I do with those schoolboys?" he asked. "What can you do to kids of that age?"

It still seemed to bother him—the effrontery of the boys, the realization that he had somehow failed, the probability that, had those same boys heckled someone in Liston's family, the schoolyard would have been littered with limbs.

While Patterson and Liston both are products of the slum, and while both began as thieves, Patterson had been tamed in a special school with help from a gentle Negro spinster; later he became a Catholic convert, and learned not to hate. Still later he bought a dictionary, adding to his vocabulary such words as "vicissitude" and "enigma." And when he regained his championship from Johansson, he became the Great Black Hope of the Urban League.

He proved that it is not only possible to rise out of a Negro slum and succeed as a sportsman, but also to develop into an intelligent, sensitive, law-abiding citizen. In proving this, however, and in taking pride in it, Patterson seemed to lose part of himself. He lost part of his hunger, his anger—and as he walked up the steps into his apartment, he was saying, "I became the good guy. . . . After Liston won the title, I kept hoping that he would change into a good guy, too. That would have relieved me of the responsibility, and maybe I could have been more of the bad guy. But he didn't. . . . It's okay to be the good guy when you're winning. But when you're losing, it is no good being the good guy."

Patterson took off his shirt and trousers and, moving some books on the bureau to one side, put down his watch, his cuff links, and a clip of bills.

"Do you do much reading?" he was asked.

"No," he said. "In fact, you know I've never finished reading a book in my whole life? I don't know why. I just feel that no writer today has anything for me; I mean, none of them has felt any more deeply than I have, and I have nothing to learn from them. Although Baldwin to me seems different from the rest. What's Baldwin doing these days?"

"He's writing a play. Anthony Quinn is supposed to have a part in it."

"Quinn?" Patterson asked.

"Yes."

"Quinn doesn't like me."

"Why?"

"I read or heard it somewhere; Quinn had been quoted as saying that my fight was disgraceful against Liston, and Quinn said something to the effect that he could have done better. People often say that—*they* could have done better! Well I think that if *they* had to fight, *they* couldn't even go through the experience of waiting for the fight to begin. They'd be up the whole night before, and would be drinking, or taking drugs. They'd probably get a heart attack. I'm sure that if I was in the ring with Anthony Quinn, I could wear him out without even touching him. I would do nothing but pressure him, I'd stalk him, I'd stand close to him. I wouldn't touch him, but I'd wear him out and he'd collapse. But Anthony Quinn's an old man, isn't he?"

"In his forties."

"Well, anyway," Patterson said, "getting back to Baldwin, he seems like a wonderful guy. I've seen him on television and, before the Liston fight in Chicago, he came by my camp. You meet Baldwin on the street and you say, 'Who's this poor slob?'— he seems just like another guy, and this is the same impression *I* give people when they don't know me. But I think Baldwin and me, we have much in common, and someday I'd just like to sit somewhere for a long time and talk to him. . . ."

Patterson, his trunks and sweat pants on, bent over to tie his shoelaces, and then, from a bureau drawer, took out a T-shirt across which was printed *Deauville*. He has several T-shirts bearing the same name. He takes good care of them. They are souvenirs from the high point of his life. They are from the Deauville Hotel in Miami Beach, which is where he trained for the third Ingemar Johansson match in March of 1961.

Never was Floyd Patterson more popular, more admired than during that winter. He had visited President Kennedy; he had been given a $35,000 jeweled crown by his manager; his greatness was conceded by sportswriters—and nobody had any idea that Patterson, secretly, was in possession of a false moustache and dark glasses that he intended to wear out of Miami Beach should he lose the third fight to Johansson.

It was after being knocked out by Johansson in their first fight that Patterson, deep in depression, hiding in humiliation for months in a remote Connecticut lodge, decided he could not face the public again if he lost. So he bought false whiskers and a moustache, and planned to wear them out of his dressing room after a defeat. He had also planned, in leaving his dressing room, to linger momentarily within the crowd and perhaps complain out loud about the fight. Then he would slip undiscovered through the night and into a waiting automobile.

Although there proved to be no need for bringing disguise into the second or third Johansson fights, or into a subsequent bout in Toronto against an obscure heavyweight named Tom Mc-Neeley, Patterson brought it anyway; and, after the first Liston fight, he not only wore it during his thirty-hour automobile ride from Chicago to New York, but he also wore it while in an airliner bound for Spain.

"As I got onto this plane, you'd never have recognized me," he said. "I had on this beard, moustache, glasses, and hat—and I also limped, to make myself look older. I was alone. I didn't care what plane I boarded; I just looked up and saw this sign at the terminal reading 'Madrid,' and so I got on that flight after buying a ticket.

"When I got to Madrid I registered at a hotel under the name 'Aaron Watson.' I stayed in Madrid about four or five days. In the daytime I wandered around to the poorer sections of the city, limping, looking at the people, and the people stared back at me and must have thought I was crazy because I was moving so slow and looked the way I did. I ate food in my hotel room. Although once I went to a restaurant and ordered soup. I hate soup. But I thought it was what old people would order. So I ate it. And after a week of this, I began to actually think I was somebody else. I began to believe it. And it is nice, every once in a while, being somebody else."

Patterson would not elaborate on how he managed to register under a name that did not correspond to his passport; he merely explained, "With money, you can do anything."

Now, walking slowly around the room, his black silk robe over his sweat clothes, Patterson said, "You must wonder what makes a man do things like this. Well, I wonder too. And the answer is, I don't know . . . but I think that within me, within every human being, there is a certain weakness. It is a weakness that exposes itself more when you're alone. And I have figured out that part of the reason I do the things I do, and cannot seem to conquer that one word—*myself*—is because . . . is because . . . I am a coward."

He stopped. He stood very still in the middle of the room, thinking about what he had just said, probably wondering whether he should have said it.

"I am a coward," he then repeated, softly. "My fighting has little to do with that fact, though. I mean you can be a fighter—and a *winning* fighter—and still be a coward. I was probably a coward on the night I won the championship back from Ingemar. And I remember another night, long ago, back when I was in the amateurs, fighting this big, tremendous man named Julius Griffin. I was only a hundred fifty-three pounds. I was petrified. It was all I could do to cross the ring. And then he came at me, and moved close to me . . . and from then on I don't know anything. I have no idea what happened. Only thing I know is, I saw him on the floor. And later somebody said, 'Man, I never saw anything like it. You just jumped up in the air, and threw thirty different punches. . . .' "

"When did you first think you were a coward?" he was asked.

"It was after the first Ingemar fight."

"How does one see this cowardice you speak of?"

"You see it when a fighter loses. Ingemar, for instance, is not a coward. When he lost the third fight in Miami, he was at a party later at the Fountainebleau. Had I lost, I couldn't have gone to that party. And I don't see how he did. . . ."

"Could Liston be a coward?"

"That remains to be seen," Patterson said. "We'll find out what he's like after somebody beats him, how he takes it. It's easy to do anything in victory. It's in defeat that a man reveals himself. In defeat I can't face people. I haven't the strength to say to people, 'I did my best, I'm sorry, and whatnot.' "

"Have you no hate left?"

"I have hated only one fighter," Patterson said. "And that was Ingemar in the second fight. I had been hating him for a whole year before that—not because he beat me in the first fight, but because of what he did after. It was all that boasting in public, and his showing off his right-hand punch on television, his thundering right, his 'toonder and lightning.' And I'd be home watching him on television, and *hating* him. It is a miserable feeling, hate. When a man hates, he can't have any peace of mind. And for one solid year I hated him because, after he took everything away from me, deprived me of everything I was, he *rubbed it in.* On the night of the second fight, in the dressing room, I couldn't wait until I got into the ring. When he was a little late getting into the ring, I thought, 'He's holding me up; he's trying to un-settle me—well, I'll get him!' "

"Why couldn't you hate Liston in the second match?"

Patterson thought for a moment, then said, "Look, if Sonny Liston walked into this room now and slapped me in the face, then you'd see a fight. You'd see the fight of your life because, then, a principle would be involved. I'd forget he was a human being. I'd forget I was a human being. And I'd fight accordingly."

"Could it be, Floyd, that you made a mistake in becoming a prizefighter?"

"What do you mean?"

"Well, you say you're a coward; you say you have little capacity for hate; and you seemed to lose your nerve against those school-boys in Scarsdale this afternoon. Don't you think you might have been better suited for some other kind of work? Perhaps a social worker, or—"

"Are you asking why I continue to fight?"

"Yes."

"Well," he said, not irritated by the question, "first of all, I love boxing. Boxing has been good to me. And I might just as well ask you the question, 'Why do you write?' Or, 'Do you retire from writing every time you write a bad story?' And as to whether I should have become a fighter in the first place, well, let's see how I can explain it. . . . Look, let's say you're a man who has been in an empty room for days and days without food . . . and then they take you out of that room and put you into another room where there's food hanging all over the place . . . and the first thing you reach for, you eat. When you're hungry, you're not choosy, and so I chose the thing that was closest to me. That was boxing. One day I just wandered into a gymnasium and boxed a boy. And I beat him. Then I boxed another boy. I beat him, too. Then I kept boxing. And winning. And I said, 'Here, finally, is something I can do!'

"Now I wasn't a sadist," he quickly added, "but I liked beating people because it was the only thing I could do. And whether boxing was a sport or not, I wanted to make it a sport because it was a thing I could succeed at. And what were the requirements? Sacrifice. That's all. To anybody who comes from the Bedford-Stuyvesant section of Brooklyn, sacrifice comes easy. And so I kept fighting, and one day I became heavyweight champion, and I got to know people like you. And you wonder how I can sacrifice, how I can deprive myself so much. You just don't realize where I've come from. You don't understand where I was when it began for me.

"In those days, when I was about eight years old, everything I got, I stole. I stole to survive, and I did survive, but I seemed to hate myself. My mother told me I used to point to a photograph of myself hanging in the bedroom and say, 'I don't like that boy!' One day my mother found three large X's scratched with a nail or something over that photograph of me. I don't remember doing it. But I do remember feeling like a parasite at home. I remember how awful I used to feel at night when my father, a longshoreman, would come home so tired that, as my mother fixed food before him, he would fall asleep at the table because he was that tired. I would always take his shoes off and clean his feet. That was my job. And I felt so bad because here I was, not going to school, doing nothing, just watching my father come home; and on Friday nights it was even worse. He would come home with his pay, and he'd put every nickel of it on the table so my mother could buy food for all the children. I never wanted to be around to see that. I'd run and hide. And then I decided to leave home and start stealing—and I did. And I would never come home unless I brought something that I had stolen. Once I remember I broke into a dress store and stole a whole mound of dresses, at two A.M., and here I was, this little kid, carrying all those dresses over the wall, thinking they were all the same size, my mother's size, and thinking the cops would never notice me walking down the street with all those dresses piled over my head. They did, of course. . . . I went to the Youth House. . . ."

Floyd Patterson's children, who had been playing outside all this time around the country club, now became restless and began to call him, and Jeannie started to pound on his door. So Patterson picked up his leather bag, which contained his gloves, his mouth-piece and adhesive tape, and walked with the children across the path toward the clubhouse.

He flicked on the light switches behind the stage near the piano. Beams of amber streaked through the dimly lit room and flashed onto the ring. Then he walked to one side of the room, outside the ring. He took off his robe, shuffled his feet in the rosin, skipped rope, and then began to shadowbox in front of the spit-stained mirror, throwing out quick combinations of lefts, rights, lefts, rights, each jab followed by a *"hegh-hegh-hegh-hegh."* Then, his gloves on, he moved to the punching bag in the far corner, and soon the room reverberated to his rhythmic beat against the bobbing bag—rat-tat-tat-*tetteta*, rat-tat-tat-*tetteta*, rat-tat-tat-*tetteta*, rat-tat-tat-*tetteta*!

The children, sitting on pink leather chairs moved from the bar to the fringe of the ring, watched him in awe, sometimes flinching at the force of his pounding against the leather bag.

And this is how they would probably remember him years from now: a dark, solitary, glistening figure punching in the corner of a forlorn spot at the bottom of a mountain where people once came to have fun—until the clubhouse became unfashionable, the paint began to peel, and Negroes were allowed in.

As Floyd Patterson continued to bang away with lefts and rights, his gloves a brown blur against the bag, his daughter slipped quietly off her chair and wandered past the ring into the other room. There, on the other side of the bar and beyond a dozen round tables, was the stage. She climbed onto the stage and stood behind a microphone, long dead, and cried out, imi-tating a ring announcer, "Ladieees and gentlemen . . . tonight we present . . ."

She looked around, puzzled. Then, seeing that her little brother had followed her, she waved him up to the stage and began again: "Ladieees and gentlemen . . . tonight we present . . . *Floydie Pat-terson* . . ."

Suddenly, the pounding against the bag in the other room stopped. There was silence for a moment. Then Jeannie, still behind the microphone and looking down at her brother, said, "Floydie, come up here!"

"No," he said.

"Oh, come up here!"

"*No,*" he cried.

Then Floyd Patterson's voice, from the other room, called: "Cut it out . . . I'll take you both for a walk in a minute."

He resumed punching—rat-tat-tat-*tetteta*—and they returned to his side. But Jeannie interrupted, asking, "Daddy, how come you sweating?"

"Water fell on me," he said, still pounding.

"Daddy," asked Floyd, Jr., "how come you spit water on the floor before?"

"To get it out of my mouth."

He was about to move over to the heavier punching bag when the sound of Mrs. Patterson's station wagon could be heard moving up the road.

Soon she was in Patterson's apartment cleaning up a bit, patting the pillows, washing the teacups that had been left in the sink. One hour later the family was having dinner together. They were together for two more hours; then, at ten P.M., Mrs. Patterson washed and dried all of the dishes, and put the garbage out in the can—where it would remain until the raccoons and skunks got to it.

And then, after helping the children with their coats and walking out to the station wagon and kissing her husband good-bye, Mrs. Patterson began the drive down the dirt road toward the highway. Patterson waved once, and stood for a moment watching the taillights go, and then he turned and walked slowly back toward the house.

Norman Mailer

KING OF THE HILL

Ego! It is the great word of the twentieth century. If there is a single word our century has added to the potentiality of language, it is ego. Everything we have done in this century, from monumental feats to nightmares of human destruction, has been a function of that extraordinary state of the psyche which gives us authority to declare we are sure of ourselves when we are not.

Muhammad Ali begins with the most unsettling ego of all. Having commanded the stage, he never pretends to step back and relinquish his place to other actors—like a six-foot parrot, he keeps screaming at you that he is the center of the stage. "Come here and get me, fool," he says. "You can't, 'cause you don't know who I am. You don't know *where* I am. I'm human intelligence and you don't even know if I'm good or evil." This has been his essential message to America all these years. It is intolerable to our American mentality that the figure who is probably most prominent to us after the president is simply not comprehensible, for he could be a demon or a saint. Or both! Richard Nixon, at least, appears comprehensible. We can hate him or we can vote for him, but at least we disagree with each other about him. What kills us about Cassius Clay is that the disagreement is inside us. He is *fascinating*—attraction and repulsion must be in the same package. So, he is obsessive. The more we don't want to think about him, the more we are obliged to. There is a reason

Ali-Frazier, New York City, 1971

for it. He is America's Greatest Ego. He is also, as I am going to
try to show, the swiftest embodiment of human intelligence we
have had yet, he is the very spirit of the twentieth century, he is
the prince of mass man and the media. Now, perhaps temporarily,
he is the fallen prince. But there still may be one holocaust of
an urge to understand him, or try to, for obsession is a disease.
Twenty little obsessions are twenty leeches on the mind, and one
big obsession can become one big operation if we refuse to live

with it. If Muhammad Ali defeats Frazier in the return bout, then he'll become the national obsession and we'll elect him president yet—you may indeed have to vote for any man who could defeat a fighter as great as Joe Frazier and still be Muhammad Ali. That's a combination!

Yes, ego—that officious and sometimes efficient exercise of ignorance-as-authority—must be the central phenomenon of the twentieth century, even if patriotic Americans like to pretend it does not exist in their heroes. Which, of course, is part of the holy American horseball. The most monstrous exhibition of ego by a brave man in many a year was Alan Shepard's three whacks at a golf ball while standing on the moon. There, in a space suit, hardly able to stand, he put a club head on an omnipurpose tool shaft, and, restricted to swinging with one arm, dibbled his golf ball on the second try. On the third it went maybe half a mile— a nonphenomenal distance in the low gravitational field of the lunar sphere.

"What's so unpleasant about that?" asked a pleasant young jet-setter.

Aquarius, of the old book, loftily replied, "Would you take a golf ball into St. Patrick's and see how far you can hit it?"

The kid nodded his head. "Now that you put it that way, I guess I wouldn't, but I was excited when it happened. I said to my wife, 'Honey, we're playing golf on the moon.' "

Well, to the average fight fan, Cassius Clay has been golf on the moon. Who can comprehend the immensity of ego involved? Every fighter is in a whirligig with his ego. The fight game, for example, is filled with legends of fighters who found a girl in an elevator purposefully stalled between floors for two minutes on the afternoon of a main-event fight. Later, after he blew the fight, his irate manager blew his ears. "Were you crazy?" the manager asked. "Why did you do it?"

"Because," said the fighter, "I get these terrible headaches every afternoon, and only a chick who knows how, can relieve them."

Ego is driving a point through to a conclusion you are obliged to reach without knowing too much about the ground you cross between. You suffer for a larger point. Every good prizefighter must have a large ego, then, because he is trying to demolish a man he doesn't know too much about, he is unfeeling—which is the ground floor of ego; and he is full of techniques—which are the wings of ego. What separates the noble ego of the prize-fighters from the lesser ego of authors is that the fighter goes through experiences in the ring that are occasionally immense, incommunicable except to fighters who have been as good, or to women who have gone through every minute of an anguish-filled birth, experiences that are finally mysterious. Like men who climb mountains, it is an exercise of ego which becomes something like soul—just as technology may have begun to have transcended itself when we reached to the moon. So, two great fighters in a great fight travel down subterranean rivers of exhaustion and cross mountain peaks of agony, stare at the light of their own death in the eye of the man they are fighting, travel into the crossroads of the most excruciating choice of karma as they get up from the floor against all the appeal of the sweet swooning catacombs of oblivion—it is just that we do not see them this way, because they are not primarily men of words, and this is the century of words, numbers, and symbols. Enough.

We have come to the point. There are languages other than words, languages of symbol and languages of nature. There are languages of the body. And prizefighting is one of them. There is no attempting to comprehend a prizefighter unless we are willing to recognize that he speaks with a command of the body which is as detached, subtle, and comprehensive in its intelligence as any exercise of mind by such social engineers as Herman Kahn or Henry Kissinger. Of course, a man like Herman Kahn is by report gifted with a bulk of three hundred pounds. He does not move around with a light foot. So many a good average prizefighter, just a little punchy, does not speak with any particular éclat. That doesn't mean he is incapable of expressing himself with wit, style, and an aesthetic flair for surprise when he boxes with his body, any more than Kahn's obesity would keep us from recognizing that his mind can work with strength. Boxing is a dialogue between bodies. Ignorant men, usually black, and usually next to illiterate, address one another in a set of *conversational* exchanges which go deep into the heart of each other's matter. It is just that they converse with their physiques. But unless you believe that you cannot receive a mortal wound from an incisive remark, you may be forced to accept the novel idea that men doing friendly boxing have a conversation on which they can often thrive. William Buckley and I, in a discussion in a living room for an evening, will score points on one another, but enjoy it. On television, where the stakes may be more, we may still both enjoy it. But put us in a debating hall with an argument to go on without cease for twenty-four hours, every encouragement present to humiliate each other, and months of preparation for such a debate, hooplas and howlers of publicity, our tongues stuck out at one another on TV, and repercussions in Vietnam depending on which one of us should win, then add the fatigue of harsh lights, and a moderator who keeps inter-rupting us, and we are at the beginning of a conversation in which at least one of us will be hurt, and maybe both. Even hurt seriously. The example is picayune, however, in relation to the demands of a fifteen-round fight—perhaps we should have to debate nonstop for weeks under those conditions before one of us was carried away comatose. Now the example becomes clearer: Boxing is a rapid debate between two sets of intelligence. It takes place rapidly because it is conducted with the body rather than the mind. If this seems extreme, let us look for a connection. Picasso could never do arithmetic when he was young because the number 7 looked to him like a nose upside down. So to learn arithmetic would slow him up. He was a future painter—his intelligence resided somewhere in the coordination of the body and the mind. He was not going to cut off his body from his mind by learning numbers. But most of us do. We have minds which work fairly well and bodies which sometimes don't. But if we are white and want to be comfortable we put our emphasis on learn-ing to talk with the mind. Ghetto cultures, black, Puerto Rican, and Chicano cultures, having less expectation of comfort, tend to stick with the wit their bodies provide. They speak to each other with their bodies, they signal with their clothes. They talk with many a silent telepathic intelligence. And doubtless feel the frustration of being unable to express the subtleties of their states in words, just as the average middle-class white will feel unable to carry out his dreams of glory by the uses of his body. If black people are also beginning to speak our mixture of formal English and jargon-polluted American with real force, so white corporate America is getting more sexual and more athletic. Yet to begin to talk about Ali and Frazier, their psyches, their styles, their honor, their character, their greatness, and their flaws, we have to recognize that there is no way to comprehend them as men like ourselves—we can only guess at their insides by a real jump of our imagination into the science Ali invented—he was the first psychologist of the body.

Okay. There are fighters who are men's men. Rocky Marciano was one of them. Oscar Bonavena and Jerry Quarry and George Chuvalo and Gene Fullmer and Carmen Basilio, to name a few, have faces which would give a Marine sergeant pause in a bar fight. They look like they could take you out with the knob of bone they have left for a nose. They are all, incidentally, white fighters. They have a code—it is to fight until they are licked, and if they have to take a punch for every punch they give, well, they figure they can win. Their ego and their body intelligence are both connected to the same source of juice—it is male pride. They are substances close to rock. They work on clumsy skills to hone them finer, knowing if they can obtain parity, blow for blow with any opponent, they will win. They have more guts. Up to a far-gone point, pain is their pleasure, for their character in combat is their strength to trade pain for pain, loss of faculty for loss of faculty.

One can cite black fighters like them. Henry Hank and Reuben Carter, Emile Griffith and Benny Paret. Joe Frazier would be the best of them. But black fighters tend to be complex. They have veins of unsuspected strength and streaks when they feel as spooked as wild horses. Any fight promoter in the world knew he had a good fight if Fullmer went against Basilio, it was a proposition as certain as the wages for the week. But black fighters were artists, they were relatively moody, they were full of the surprises of Patterson or Liston, the virtuosities of Archie Moore and Sugar Ray, the speed, savagery, and curious lack of substance in Jimmy Ellis, the vertiginous neuroses of giants like Buster

Mathis. Even Joe Louis, recognized by a majority in the years of his own championship as the greatest heavyweight of all time, was surprisingly inconsistent with minor fighters like Buddy Baer. Part of the unpredictability of their performances was due to the fact that all but Moore and Robinson were heavyweights. Indeed, white champions in the top division were equally out of form from fight to fight. It can, in fact, be said that heavyweights are always the most lunatic of prizefighters. The closer a heavyweight comes to the championship, the more natural it is for him to be a little bit insane, secretly insane, for the heavyweight champion of the world is either the toughest man in the world or he is not, but there is a real possibility he is. It is like being the big toe of God. You have nothing to measure yourself by. Lightweights, welterweights, middleweights can all be exceptionally good, fantastically talented—they are still very much in their place. The best lightweight in the world knows that an unranked middleweight can defeat him on most nights, and the best middleweight in the world will kill him every night. He knows that the biggest strongman in a tough bar could handle him by sitting on him, since the power to punch seems to increase quickly with weight. A fighter who weighs two-forty will punch more than twice as hard as a fighter who weighs one-twenty. The figures have no real basis, of course, they are only there to indicate the law of the ring: a good big man beats a good little man. So the notion of prizefighters as hardworking craftsmen is most likely to be true in the light and middle divisions. Since they are fighters who know their limitations, they are likely to strive for excellence in their category. The better they get, the closer they have come to sanity, at least if we are ready to assume that the average fighter is a buried artist, which is to say a *body* artist with an extreme amount of violence in him. Obviously the better and more successful they get, the more they have been able to transmute violence into craft, discipline, even body art. That is human alchemy. We respect them and they deserve to be respected.

But the heavyweights never have such simple sanity. If they become champions they begin to have inner lives like Hemingway or Dostoyevski, Tolstoy or Faulkner, Joyce or Melville or Conrad or Lawrence or Proust. Hemingway is the example above all. Because he wished to be the greatest writer in the history of literature and still be a hero with all the body arts age would yet grant him, he was alone and he knew it. So are heavyweight champions alone. Dempsey was alone and Tunney could never explain himself and Sharkey could never believe himself nor Schmeling nor Braddock, and Carnera was sad and Baer an indecipherable clown; great heavyweights like Louis had the loneliness of the ages in their silence, and men like Marciano were mystified by a power which seemed to have been granted them. With the advent, however, of the great modern black heavyweights, Patterson, Liston, then Clay and Frazier, perhaps the loneliness gave way to what it had been protecting itself against— a surrealistic situation unstable beyond belief. Being a black heavyweight champion in the second half of the twentieth century (with black revolutions opening all over the world) was now not unlike being Jack Johnson, Malcolm X, and Frank Costello all in one. Going down the aisle and into the ring in Chicago was conceivably more frightening for Sonny Liston than facing Patterson that night—he was raw as uncoated wire with his sense of retribution awaiting him for years of prison pleasures and underworld jobs. Pools of paranoia must have reached him like different washes of color from different sides of the arena. He was a man who had barely learned to read and write—he had none of the impacted and mediocre misinformation of all the world of daily dull reading to clot the antenna of his senses—so he was keen to every hatred against him. He knew killers were waiting in that mob, they always were, he had been on speaking terms with just such subjects himself—now he dared to be king— any assassin could strike for his revenge upon acts Liston had long forgot; no wonder Liston was in fear going into the ring, and happier once within it.

And Patterson was exhausted before the fight began. Lonely as a monk for years, his daily gym work the stuff of his meditation, he was the first of the black fighters to be considered, then used, as a political force. He was one of the liberal elite, an Eleanor Roosevelt darling, he was political mileage for the NAACP. Violent, conceivably, to the point of murder if he had not been a fighter, he was a gentleman in public, more, he was a man of the nicest, quietest, most private good manners. But monastic by inclination. Now, all but uneducated, he was appealed to by political blacks to win the Liston fight for the image of the Negro. Responsibility sat upon him like a comic cutback in a silent film where we return now and again to one poor man who has been left to hold a beam across his shoulders. There he stands, hardly able to move. At the end of the film he collapses. That was the weight put on Patterson. The responsibility to beat Liston was too great to bear. Patterson, a fighter of incorruptible honesty, was knocked out by punches hardly anybody saw. He fell in open air as if seized by a stroke. The age of surrealistic battles had begun. In the second fight with Liston, Patterson, obviously more afraid of a repetition of the first nightmare than anything else, simply charged his opponent with his hands low and was knocked down three times and out in the first round. The age of body psychology had begun and Clay was there to conceive it.

A kid as wild and dapper and jaybird as the president of a down-home college fraternity, bow tie, brown-and-white shoes, sweet, happy-go-lucky, *raucous*, he descended on Vegas for the second Patterson-Liston fight. He was like a beautiful boy surrounded by doting aunts. The classiest-looking middle-aged Negro ladies were always flanking him in Vegas as if to set up a female field of repulsion against any evil black magnetic forces in the offing. And from the sanctuary of his ability to move around crap tables like a kitten on the frisk, he taunted black majestic king-size Liston before the fight and after the fight. "You're so ugly," he would jeer, crap table safely between them, "that I don't know how you can get any uglier."

"Why don't you sit on my knee and I'll feed you your orange juice," Liston would rumble back.

"Don't insult me, or you'll be sorry. 'Cause you're just an ugly slow bear."

They would pretend to rush at one another. Smaller men would hold them back without effort. They were building the gate for the next fight. And Liston was secretly fond of Clay. He would chuckle when he talked about him. It was years since Liston had failed to knock out his opponent in the first round. His charisma was majestic with menace. One held one's breath when near him. He looked foward with obvious amusement to the happy seconds when he would take Clay apart and see the expression on that silly face. In Miami he trained for a three-round fight. In the famous fifth round when Clay came out with caustic in his eyes and could not see, he waved his gloves at Liston, a look of abject horror on his face, as if to say, "Your younger brother is now an old blind beggar. Do not strike him." And did it with a peculiar authority. For Clay looked like a ghost with his eyes closed, tears streaming, his extended gloves waving in front of him like a widow's entreaties. Liston drew back in doubt, in bewilderment, conceivably in concern for his new great reputation as an ex-bully; yes, Liston reacted like a gentleman, and Clay was home free. His eyes watered out the caustic, his sight came back. He cut Liston up in the sixth. He left him beaten and exhausted. Liston did not stand up for the bell to the seventh. Maybe Clay had even defeated him earlier that day at the weigh-in when he had harangued and screamed and shouted and whistled and stuck his tongue out at Liston. The Champ had been bewildered. No one had been able ever to stare him in the eyes these last four years. Now a boy was screaming at him, a boy reported to belong to Black Muslims, no, stronger than that, a boy favored by Malcolm X who was braver by reputation than the brave, for he could stop a bullet any day. Liston, afraid only, as he put it, of crazy men, was afraid of the Muslims for he could not contend with their allegiance to one another in prison, their puritanism, their discipline, their martial ranks. The combination was too complex, too unfamiliar. Now, their boy, in a pain of terror or in a mania of courage, was screaming at him at the weigh-in. Liston sat down and shook his head, and looked at the press, the press now become his friend, and wound his fingers in circles around his ear, as if saying, whitey to whitey, "That black boy is nuts." So Clay made Liston Tom it, and when Liston missed the first jab he threw in the fight by a foot and a half, one knew the night would not be ordinary in the offing.

For their return bout in Boston, Liston trained as he had never before. Clay got a hernia. Liston trained again. Hard training as a fighter grows older seems to speak of the dull deaths of the brightest cells in all the favorite organs; old fighters react to training like beautiful women to washing floors. But Liston did it twice, once for Clay's hernia, and again for their actual fight in Maine, and the second time he trained, he aged as a fighter, for he had a sparring partner, Amos Lincoln, who was one of the better heavyweights in the country. They had wars with one another every afternoon in the gym. By the day before the fight, Liston was as relaxed and sleepy and dopey as a man in a steam bath. He had fought his heart out in training, had done it under constant pressure from Clay who kept telling the world that Liston was old and slow and could not possibly win. And their fight created a scandal, for Liston ran into a short punch in the first round and was counted out, unable to hear the count. The referee and timekeeper missed signals with one another while Clay stood over fallen Liston screaming, "Get up and fight!" It was no night for the fight game, and a tragedy for Clay since he had trained for a long and arduous fight. He had developed his technique for a major encounter with Liston and was left with a horde of un-answered questions including the one he could never admit—which was whether there had been the magic of a real knockout in his punch or if Liston had made—for what variety of reasons!—a conscious decision to stay on the floor. It did him no good.

He had taken all the lessons of his curious life and the outra-geously deep comprehension he had of the motivations of his own people—indeed, one could even approach the beginnings of a Psychology of the Blacks by studying his encounters with fight-ers who were black—and had elaborated that into a technique for boxing which was almost without compare. A most cultivated technique. For he was no child of the slums. His mother was a gracious pale-skinned lady, his father a bitter wit pride-oriented on the family name of Clay—they were descendants of Henry Clay, the orator, on the white side of the family, nothing less, and Cassius began boxing at twelve in a police gym, and from the beginning was a phenomenon of style and the absence of pain, for he knew how to use his physical endowment. Tall, relatively light, with an exceptionally long reach even for his size, he developed defensive skills which made the best use of his body. Working apparently on the premise that there was something obscene about being hit, he boxed with his head back and drew it further back when attacked like a kid who is shy of punches in a street fight, but because he had a waist that was more supple than the average fighter's neck, he was able to box with his arms low, surveying the fighter in front of him, avoiding punches by the speed of his feet, the reflexes of his waist, the long spoiling deployment of his arms which were always tipping other fighters off-balance. Added to this was his psychological comprehension of the vanity and confusion of other fighters. A man in the ring is a performer as well as a gladiator. Elaborating his technique from the age of twelve, Clay knew how to work on the vanity of other performers, knew how to make them feel ridiculous and so force them into crucial mistakes, knew how to set such a tone from the first round—later he was to know how to begin it a year before he would even meet the man. Clay knew that a fighter who had been put in psychological knots before he got near the ring had already lost half, three-quarters, no, all of the fight could be lost before the first punch. That was the psychology of the body.

Now, add his curious ability as a puncher. He knew that the heaviest punches, systematically delivered, meant little. There are club fighters who look like armadillos and alligators—you can bounce punches off them forever and they never go down. You can break them down only if they are in a profound state of confusion, and the bombardment of another fighter's fists is never their confusion but their expectation. So Clay punched with a greater variety of mixed intensities than anyone around, he played with punches, was tender with them, laid them on as delicately as you put a postage stamp on an envelope, then cracked them in like a riding crop across your face, stuck a cruel jab like a baseball bat held head on into your mouth, next waltzed you in a clinch with a tender arm around your neck, winged away out of reach on flying legs, dug a hook with the full swing of a baseball bat hard into your ribs, hard pokes of a jab into the face, a mocking soft flurry of pillows and gloves, a mean forearm cutting you off from coming up on him, a cruel wrestling of your neck in a clinch, then elusive again, gloves snake-licking your face like a whip. By the time Clay defeated Liston once and was training for the

second fight, by the time Clay, now champion and renamed Muhammad Ali, and bigger, grown up quickly and not so mysteri-
ously (after the potent ego-soups and marrows of his trip through
Muslim Africa) into a Black Prince, Potentate of his people, new
Poobah of Polemic, yes, by this time, Clay—we will find it more
natural to call him Ali from here on out (for the Prince will behave
much like a young god)—yes, Muhammad Ali, Heavyweight
Champion of the World, having come back with an amazing
commitment to be leader of his people, proceeded to go into
training for the second Liston fight with a commitment and then
a genius of comprehension for the true intricacies of the Science
of Sock. He alternated the best of sparring partners and the most
ordinary, worked rounds of dazzling speed with Jimmy Ellis—
later, of course, to be champion himself before Frazier knocked
him out—rounds that displayed the high aesthetic of boxing at
its best, then lay against the ropes with other sparring partners,
hands at his sides as if it were the eleventh or thirteenth round
of an excruciating and exhausting fight with Liston where Ali
was now so tired he could not hold his hands up, could just
manage to take punches to the stomach, rolling with them,
smothering them with his stomach, absorbing them with backward moves, sliding along the ropes, steering his sparring partner
with passive but offsetting moves of his limp arms. For a minute,
for two minutes, the sparring partner—Shotgun Sheldon was his
name—would bomb away on Ali's stomach much as if Liston
were tearing him apart in later rounds, and Ali weaving languidly,
sliding his neck for the occasional overhead punch to his face,
bouncing from the rope into the punches, bouncing back away
from punches, as if his torso had become one huge boxing glove
to absorb punishment, had penetrated through into some further
conception of pain, as if pain were not pain if you accepted it
with a relaxed heart, yes, Ali let himself be bombarded on the
ropes by the powerful bull-like swings of Shotgun Sheldon, the
expression on his face as remote and as searching for the last
routes into the nerves of each punch going in as a man hanging
on a subway strap will search into the meaning of the market
quotations he has just read on the activities of a curious stock.
So Ali relaxed on the ropes and took punches to the belly with a

faint disdain, as if, curious punches, they did not go deep enough and after a minute of this, or two minutes, having offered his body like the hide of a drum for a mad drummer's solo, he would snap out of his communion with himself and flash a tattoo of light and slashing punches, mocking as the lights on water, he would dazzle his sparring partner, who, arm-weary and punched out, would look at him with eyes of love, complete was his admiration. And if people were ever going to cry watching a boxer in training, those were the moments, for Ali had the far-off concentration and disdain of an artist who simply cannot find anyone near enough or good enough to keep him and his art engaged, and all the while was perfecting the essence of his art which was to make the other fighter fall secretly, helplessly, in love with him. Bundini, a special trainer, an alter ego with the same harsh, demoniac, witty, nonstop powers of oration as Ali himself—he even looked a little like Ali—used to weep openly as he watched the workouts.

Training session over, Ali would lecture the press, instruct them—looking beyond his Liston defense to what he would do to Patterson, mocking Patterson, calling him a rabbit, a white man's rabbit, knowing he was putting a new beam on Patterson's shoulders, an outrageously helpless and heavy beam of rage, fear, hopeless anger, and secret black admiration for the all-out force of Ali's effrontery. And in the next instant Ali would be charming as a movie star on the make speaking tenderly to a child. If he were Narcissus, so he was as well the play of mood in the water which served as mirror to Narcissus. It was as if he knew he had disposed of Patterson already, that the precise attack of calling him a rabbit would work on the weakest link—wherever it was— in Patterson's tense and tortured psyche and Patterson would crack, as indeed, unendurably for himself, he did, when their fight took place. Patterson's back gave way in the early rounds, and he fought twisted and in pain, half crippled like a man with a sacroiliac for eleven brave and most miserable rounds before the referee would call it and Ali, breaking up with his first wife then, was unpleasant in the ring that night, his face ugly and contemptuous, himself well on the way to becoming America's most unpopular major American. That, too, was part of the art—

to get a public to the point of hating him so much the burden
on the other fighter approached the metaphysical—which is where
Ali wanted it. White fighters with faces like rock embedded in
cement would trade punch for punch, Ali liked to get the boxing
where it belonged—he would trade metaphysic for metaphysic
with anyone.

So he went on winning his fights and growing forever more
unpopular. How he inflamed the temper of boxing's white establishment, for they were for the most part a gaggle of avuncular
drunks and hard-bitten hacks who were ready to fight over every
slime-slicked penny, and squared a few of their slippery crimes
by getting fighters to show up semblance-of-sober at any available
parish men's rally and charity church breakfast—"Everything I
am I owe to boxing," the fighter would mumble though his den-
tures while elements of gin, garlic, and goddess-of-a-girlie from
the night before came off in the bright morning fumes.

Ali had them psyched. He cut through moribund coruscated
dirty business corridors, cut through cigar smoke and bushwah,
hypocrisy and well-aimed kicks to the back of the neck, cut through
crooked politicians and patriotic pus, cut like a laser, point of the
point, light and impersonal, cut to the heart of the rottenest meat
in boxing, and boxing was always the buried South Vietnam of
America, buried for fifty years in our hide before we went there,
yes, Ali cut through the flag-dragooned salutes of drunken dawns
and said, "I got no fight with those Vietcongs," and they cut him
down, thrust him into the three and a half years of his martyrdom.
Where he grew. Grew to have a little fat around his middle and
a little of the complacent muscle of the clam to his world-ego.
And grew sharper in the mind as well, and deepened and broad-
ened physically. Looked no longer like a boy, but a sullen man,
almost heavy, with the beginnings of a huge expanse across his
shoulders. And developed the patience to survive, the wisdom to
contemplate future nights in jail, grew to cultivate the suspension
of belief and the avoidance of disbelief—what a rack for a young
man! As the years of hope for reinstatement, or avoidance of
prison, came up and waned in him, Ali walked the tightrope
between bitterness and apathy, and had enough left to beat Quarry
and beat Bonavena, beat Quarry in the flurry of a missed hundred

punches, ho! how his timing was off! beat him with a calculated whip, snake-lick whip, to the corrugated sponge of dead flesh over Quarry's Irish eyes—they stopped it after the third on cuts— then knocked out Bonavena, the indestructible, never stopped before, by working the art of crazy mixing in the punches he threw at the rugged—some of the punches Ali threw that night would not have hurt a little boy—the punch he let go in the fifteenth came in like a wrecking ball from outer space. Bonavena went sprawling across the ring. He was a house coming down.

Yet it may have been the blow that would defeat him later. For Ali had been tired with Bonavena, lackluster, winded, sluggish, far ahead on points but in need of the most serious work if he were to beat Frazier. The punch in the last round was obliged, therefore, to inflame his belief that the forces of magic were his, there to be called upon when most in need, that the silent leagues of black support for his cause—since their cause was as his own—were like some cloak of midnight velvet, there to protect him by black blood, by black sense of tragedy, by the black consciousness that the guilt of the world had become the hinge of a door that they would open. So they would open the way to Frazier's chin, the blacks would open the aisle for his trip to the gods.

Therefore he did not train for Frazier as perhaps he had to. He worked, he ran three miles a day when he could have run five, he boxed some days and let a day and perhaps another day go, he was relaxed, he was confident, he basked in the undemanding winter sun of Miami, and skipped his rope in a gym crowded with fighters, stuffed now with working fighters looking to be seen, Ali comfortable and relaxed like the greatest of movie stars, he played a young fighter working out in a corner on the heavy bag—for of course every eye was on him—and afterward doing sit-ups in the back room and having his stomach rubbed with liniment, he would talk to reporters. He was filled with confidence there was no black fighter he did not comprehend to the root of the valve in the hard-pumping heart, and yes, Frazier, he assured everybody, would be easier than they realized. Like a little boy who had grown up to take on a mountain of responsibility, he spoke in the deep relaxation of the wise, and teased two of the reporters who were present and fat. "You want to drink a lot of water," he said, "good cold water instead of all that liquor rot-your-gut," and gave the smile of a man who had been able to intoxicate himself on water (although he was, by repute, a fiend for soft sweet drinks), "and fruit and good clean vegetables you want to eat and chicken and steak. You lose weight then," he advised out of kind secret smiling thoughts, and went on to talk of the impact of the fight upon the world. "Yes," he said, "you just think of a stadium with a million people, ten million people, you could get them all in to watch, they would all pay to see it live, but then you think of the hundreds of millions and the billions who are going to see this fight, and if you could sit them all down in one place, and fly a jet plane over them, why that plane would have to fly for an hour before it would reach the end of all the people who will see this fight. It's the greatest event in the history of the world, and you take a man like Frazier, a good fighter, but a simple hardworking fellow, he's not built for this kind of pressure, the eyes," Ali said softly, "of that many people upon him. There's an experience to pressure which I have had, fighting a man like Liston in Miami the first time, which he has not. He will cave in under the pressure. No, I do not see any way a man like Frazier can whup me, he can't reach me, my arms are too long, and if he does get in and knock me down I'll never make the mistake of Quarry and Foster or Ellis of rushing back at him, I'll stay away until my head clears, then I begin to pop him again, pop! pop!"—a few jabs—"no there is no way this man can beat me, this fight will be easier than you think."

There was one way in which boxing was still like a street fight and that was in the need to be confident you would win. A man walking out of a bar to fight with another man is seeking to compose his head into the confidence that he will certainly triumph—it is the most mysterious faculty of the ego. For that confidence is a sedative against the pain of punches and yet is the sanction to punch your own best. The logic of the spirit would suggest that you win only if you deserve to win: The logic of the ego lays down the axiom that if you don't think you will win, you don't deserve to. And, in fact, usually don't; it is as if not believing you will win opens you to the guilt that perhaps you have not the right, you are too guilty.

So training camps are small factories for the production of one rare psychological item—an ego able to bear huge pain and administer drastic punishment. The flow of Ali's ego poured over the rock of every distraction, it was an ego like the flow of a river of constant energy fed by a hundred tributaries of black love and the love of the white left. The construction of the ego of Joe Frazier was of another variety. His manager, Yancey "Yank" Durham, a canny foxy light-skinned Negro with a dignified mien, a gray head of hair, gray moustache and a small but conservative worthy's paunch, plus the quick-witted look of eyes that could spot from a half-mile away any man coming toward him with a criminal thought, was indeed the face of a consummate jeweler who had worked for years upon a diamond in the rough until he was now and at last a diamond, hard as the transmutation of black carbon from the black earth into the brilliant sky-blue shadow of the rarest shining rock. What a fighter was Frazier, what a diamond of an ego had he, and what a manager was Durham. Let us look.

Sooner or later, fight metaphors, like fight managers, go sentimental. They go military. But there is no choice here. Frazier was the human equivalent of a war machine. He had tremendous firepower. He had a great left hook, a left hook frightening even to watch when it missed, for it seemed to whistle; he had a powerful right. He could knock a man out with either hand— not all fighters can, not even very good fighters. Usually, however, he clubbed opponents to death, took a punch, gave a punch, took three punches, gave two, took a punch, gave a punch, high speed all the way, always working, pushing his body and arms, short for a heavyweight, up through the middle, bombing through on force, reminiscent of Jimmy Brown knocking down tacklers, Frazier kept on coming, hard and fast, a hang-in, hang-on, go-and-get-him, got-him, got-him, slip and punch, take a punch, wing a punch, whap a punch, never was Frazier happier than with his heart up on the line against some other man's heart, let the bullets fly—his heart was there to stand up at the last. Sooner or later, the others almost all fell down. Undefeated like Ali, winner of twenty-three out of twenty-six fights by knockout, he was a human force, certainly the greatest heavyweight force to come along since Rocky Marciano. (If those two men had ever met, it would have been like two Mack trucks hitting each other head on, then backing up to hit each other again—they would have kept it up until the wheels were off the axles and the engines off the chassis.) But this would be a different kind of fight. Ali would run, Ali would keep hitting Frazier with long jabs, quick hooks and rights while backing up, backing up, staying out of reach unless Frazier could take the punishment and get in. That was where the military problem began. For getting in against the punishment he would take was a question of morale, and there was a unique situation in this fight—Frazier had become the white man's fighter, Mr. Charley was rooting for Frazier, and that meant blacks were boycotting him in their heart. That could be poison to Frazier's morale, for he was twice as black as Clay and half as handsome, he had the rugged decent life-worked face of a man who had labored in the pits all his life, he looked like the deserving modest son of one of those Negro cleaning women of a bygone age who worked from six in the morning to midnight every day, raised a family, endured and occasionally elicited the exasperated admiration of white ladies who would kindly remark, "That woman deserves something better in her life." Frazier had the mien of the son, one of many, of such a woman, and he was the hardest-working fighter in training many a man had ever seen, he was conceivably the hardest-working man alive in the world, and as he went through his regimen, first boxing four rounds with a sparring partner, Kenny Norton, a talented heavy-weight from the coast with an almost unbeaten record, then working on the heavy bag, then the light bag, then skipping rope, ten to twelve rounds of sparring and exercise on a light day, Frazier went on with the doggedness, the concentration, and the pumped-up fury of a man who has had so little in his life that he can endure torments to get everything, he pushed the total of his energy and force into an absolute abstract exercise of will so it did not matter if he fought a sparring partner or the heavy bag, he lunged at each equally as if the exhaustions of his own heart and the clangor of his lungs were his only enemies, and the head of a fighter or the leather of the bag as it rolled against his own head was nothing but some abstract thunk of material, not a thing, not a man, but thunk! thunk! something of an obstacle, thunk! thunk! thunk! to beat into thunk! oblivion. And his breath came in rips and sobs as he smashed into the bag as if it were real, just that heavy big torso-sized bag hanging from its chain—but he attacked it as if it were a bear, as if it were a great fighter and they were in the mortal embrace of a killing set of exchanges of punches in the middle of the eighth round, and rounds of exercise later, skipping rope to an inhumanly fast beat for this late round in the training day, sweat pouring like jets of blood from an artery, he kept swinging his rope, muttering, "Two-million-dollars-and-change, two-million-dollars-and-change," railroad train chugging into the terminals of exhaustion. And it was obvious that Durham, jeweler to his diamond, was working to make the fight as abstract as he could for Frazier, to keep Clay out of it—for they would not call him Ali in their camp—yes, Frazier was fortifying his ego by depersonalizing his opponent, Clay was, thunk! the heavy bag, thunk! and thunk!—Frazier was looking to get no messages from that cavern of velvet when black people sent their good wishes to Ali at midnight, no, Frazier would insulate himself with prodigies of work, hardest-working man in the hell-hole of the world, and on and on he drove himself into the depressions each day of killing daily exhaustion.

That was one half of the strategy to isolate Frazier from Ali, hard work and thinking of thunking on inanimate Clay; the other half was up to Durham who was running front relations with the blacks of North Philly who wandered into the gym, paid their dollar, and were ready to heckle on Frazier. In the four rounds he boxed with Norton, Frazier did not look too good for a while. It was ten days before the fight and he was in a bad mood when he came in, for the word was through the gym that they had discovered one of his favorite sparring partners, just fired that morning, was a Black Muslim and had been calling Ali every night with reports, that was the rumor, and Frazier, sullen and cold at the start, was bopped and tapped, then walloped by Norton moving fast with the big training gloves in imitation of Ali, and Frazier looked very easy to hit until the middle of the third round when Norton, proud of his something like twenty wins and one loss, beginning to get some ideas himself about how to fight champions, came driving in to mix it with Frazier, have it out man to man and caught a right which dropped him, left him looking limp with that half-silly smile sparring partners get when they have been hit too hard to justify any experience or any money they are going to take away. Up till then the crowd had been with Norton. Restricted to one end of the Cloverlay gym, a street-level storefront room which could have been used originally by an automobile dealer, there on that empty, immaculate Lysol-soaked floor, designed when Frazier was there for only Frazier and his partners (as opposed to Miami where Ali would rub elbows with the people) the people, since they were here kept to the end off the street, jeered whenever Norton hit Frazier, they laughed when Norton made him look silly, they called out, "Drop the mother," until Durham held up a gentlemanly but admonishing finger in request for silence. Afterward, however, training completed, Durham approached them to answer questions, rolled with their sallies, jived the people back, subtly enlisted their sympathy for Frazier by saying, "When I fight Clay, I'm going to get him somewhere in the middle rounds," until the blacks quipping back said angrily, "You ain't fighting him, Frazier is."

"Why you call him Clay?" another asked. "He Ali."

"His name is Cassius Clay to me," said Durham.

"What you say against his religion?"

"I don't say nothing about his religion and he doesn't say anything about mine. I'm a Baptist."

"You going to make money on this?"

"Of course," said Durham, "I got to make money. You don't think I work up this sweat for nothing."

They loved him. He was happy with them. A short fat man in a purple suit wearing his revival of the wide-brim bebop hat said to Durham, "Why don't you get Norton to manage? He was beating up on your fighter," and the fat man cackled for he had scored and could elaborate the tale for his ladies later how he had put down Yank who was working the daily rite on the edge of the black street for his fighter, while upstairs, dressed, and sucking an orange, sweat still pouring, gloom of excessive fatigue upon him, Frazier was sitting through his two-hundredth or two-thousandth interview for this fight, reluctant indeed to give it at all. "Some get it, some don't," he had said for refusal, but relented when a white friend who had done roadwork with him interceded, so he sat there now against a leather sofa, dark blue suit, dark T-shirt, mopping his brow with a pink-red towel, and spoke dispiritedly of being ready too early for the fight. He was waking up an hour too early for roadwork each morning now. "I'd go back to sleep but it doesn't feel good when I do run."

"I guess the air is better that hour of the morning."

He nodded sadly. "There's a limit to how good the air in Philly can get."

"Where'd you begin to sing?" was a question asked.

"I sang in church first," he replied, but it was not the day to talk about singing. The loneliness of hitting the bag still seemed upon him as if in his exhaustion now, and in the thoughts of that small insomnia which woke him an hour too early every day was something of the loneliness of all blacks who work very hard and are isolated from fun and must wonder in the just-awakened night how large and pervasive was the curse of a people. "The countdown's begun," said Frazier, "I get impatient about now."

For the fight, Ali was wearing red velvet trunks, Frazier had green. Before they began, even before they were called together by the referee for instructions, Ali went dancing around the ring and glided past Frazier with a sweet little-boy smile, as if to say, "You're my new playmate. We're going to have fun." Ali was laughing. Frazier was having nothing of this and turned his neck to embargo him away. Ali, having alerted the crowd by this big first move, came prancing in again. When Frazier looked ready to block him, Ali went around, evading a contact, gave another sweet smile, shook his head at the lack of high spirit. "Poor Frazier," he seemed to say.

At the weigh-in early that afternoon Ali looked physically resplendent; the night before in Harlem, crowds had cheered him; he was coming to claim his victory on the confluence of two mighty tides—he was the mightiest victim of injustice in America and he was also—the twentieth century was nothing if not a tangle of opposition—he was also the mightiest narcissist in the land. Every beard, dropout, homosexual, junkie, freak, swinger, and plain simple individualist adored him. Every pedantic liberal soul who had once loved Patterson now paid homage to Ali. The mightiest of the black psyches and the most filigreed of the white psyches were ready to roar him home, as well as every family-loving hardworking square American who genuinely hated the war in Vietnam. What a tangle of ribbons he carried on his lance, enough cross-purposes to be the knight-resplendent of television, the fell hero of the medium, and he had a look of unique happiness on television when presenting his program for the course of the fight, and his inevitable victory. He would be as content then as an infant splashing the waters of the bathinette. If he was at once a saint and a monster to any mind that looked for category, any mind unwilling to encounter the thoroughly dread-filled fact that the twentieth-century breed of man now in birth might be no longer half good and half evil—generous and greedy by turns—but a mutation with Cassius Muhammad for the first son—then that mind was not ready to think about Twentieth-Century Man. (And indeed Muhammad Ali had twin poodles he called Angel and Demon.) So now the ambiguity of his presence filled the Garden before the fight was fairly begun; it was as if he had announced to that plural billion-footed crowd assembled under the shadow of the jet which would fly over them that the first enigma of the fight would be the way he would win it, that he would initiate his triumph by getting the crowd to laugh at Frazier, yes, first premise tonight was that the poor black man in Frazier's soul would go berserk if made a figure of roll-off-your-seat amusement.

The referee gave his instructions. The bell rang. The first fifteen seconds of a fight can be the fight. It is equivalent to the first kiss in a love affair. The fighters each missed the other. Ali blocked Frazier's first punches easily, but Ali then missed Frazier's head. That head was bobbing as fast as a third fist. Frazier would come rushing in, head moving like a fist, fists bobbing too, his head working above and below his forearm, he was trying to get through Ali's jab, get through fast and sear Ali early with the terror of a long fight and punches harder than he had ever taken to the stomach, and Ali in turn, backing up, and throwing fast punches, aimed just a trifle, and was therefore a trifle too slow, but it was obvious Ali was trying to shiver Frazier's synapses from the start, set waves of depression stirring which would reach his heart in later rounds and make him slow, deaden nerve, deaden nerve went Ali's jab flicking a snake tongue, whoo-eet! whoo-eet! but Frazier's head was bobbing too fast, he was moving faster than he had ever moved before in that bobbing, nonstop never-a-backward step of his, slogging and bouncing forward, that huge left hook flaunting the air with the confidence it was enough of a club to split a tree, and Ali, having missed his jabs, stepped nimbly inside the hook and wrestled Frazier in the clinch. Ali looked stronger here. So by the first forty-five seconds of the fight, they had each surprised the other profoundly. Frazier was fast enough to slip through Ali's punches, and Ali was strong enough to handle him in the clinches. A pattern had begun. Because Ali was missing often, Frazier was in under his shots like a police dog's muzzle on your arm, Ali could not slide from side to side, he was boxed in, then obliged to go backward, and would end on the ropes again and again with Frazier belaboring him. Yet Frazier could not reach him. Like a prestidigitator Ali would tie the other's punches into odd knots, not even blocking them yet on his elbows or his arms, rather throwing his own punches as defensive moves, for even as they missed, he would brush Frazier to the side with his forearm, or hold him off, or clinch and wrestle a little of the will out of Frazier's neck. Once or twice in the round a long left hook by Frazier just touched the surface of Ali's chin, and Ali waved his head in placid contempt to the billions watching as if to say, "This man has not been able to hurt me at all."

The first round set a pattern for the fight. Ali won it and would win the next. His jab was landing from time to time and rights and lefts of no great consequence. Frazier was hardly reaching him at all. Yet it looked like Frazier had established that he was fast enough to get in on Ali and so drive him to the ropes and to the corners, and that spoke of a fight that would be determined by the man in better condition, in better physical condition rather than in better psychic condition, the kind of fight Ali could hardly want for his strength was in his pauses, his nature passed along the curve of every dialectic, he liked, in short, to fight in flurries, and then move out, move away, assess, take his time, fight again.

Frazier would not let him. Frazier moved in with the snarl of a wolf, his teeth seemed to show through his mouthpiece, he made Ali work. Ali won the first two rounds but it was obvious he could not continue to win if he had to work all the way. And in the third round Frazier began to get to him, caught Ali with a powerful blow to the face at the bell. That was the first moment where it was clear to all that Frazier had won a round. Then he won the next. Ali looked tired and a little depressed. He was moving less and less and calling upon a skill not seen since the fight with Chuvalo when he had showed his old ability, worked on all those years ago with Shotgun Sheldon, to lie on the ropes and take a beating to the stomach. He had exhausted Chuvalo by welcoming attacks on the stomach but Frazier was too incommensurable a force to allow such total attack. So Ali lay on the ropes and wrestled him off, and moved his arms and waist, blocking punches, slipping punches, countering with punches—it began to look as if the fight would be written on the ropes, but Ali was getting very tired. At the beginning of the fifth round, he got up slowly from his stool, very slowly. Frazier was beginning to feel that the fight was his. He moved in on Ali jeering, his hands at his side in mimicry of Ali, a street fighter mocking his opponent, and Ali tapped him with long light jabs to which Frazier stuck out his mouthpiece, a jeer of derision as if to suggest that the mouthpiece was all Ali would reach all night.

There is an extortion of the will beyond any of our measure in the exhaustion which comes upon a fighter in early rounds when he is already too tired to lift his arms or take advantage of openings there before him, yet the fight is not a third over, there are all those rounds to go, contractions of torture, the lungs screaming into the dungeons of the soul, washing the throat with a hot bile that once belonged to the liver, the legs are going dead, the arms move but their motion is limp, one is straining into another will, breathing into the breath of another will as agonized as one's own. As the fight moved through the fifth, the sixth, and the seventh, then into the eighth, it was obvious that Ali was into the longest night of his career, and yet with that skill, that research into the pits of every miserable contingency in boxing, he came up with odd somnambulistic variations, holding Frazier off, riding around Frazier with his arm about his neck, almost entreating Frazier with his arms extended, and Frazier leaning on him, each of them slowed to a pit-a-pat of light punches back and forth until one of them was goaded up from exhaustion to whip and stick, then hook and hammer and into the belly and out, and out of the clinch and both looking exhausted, and then Frazier, mouth bared again like a wolf, going in and Ali waltzing him, tying him, tapping him lightly as if he were a speed bag, just little flicks, until Frazier, like an exhausted horse finally feeling the crop, would push up into a trot and try to run up the hill. It was indeed as if they were both running up a hill. As if Frazier's offensive was so great and so great was Ali's defense that the fight could only be decided by who could take the steepest pitch of the hill. So Frazier, driving, driving, trying to drive the heart out of Ali, put the pitch of that hill up and up until they were ascending an unendurable slope. And moved like somnambulists slowly working and rubbing one another, almost embracing, next to locked in the slow moves of lovers after the act until, reaching into the stores of energy reaching them from cells never before so used, one man or the other would work up a contractive spasm of skills and throw punches at the other in the straining slow-motion hypnosis of a deepening act. And so the first eight rounds went by. The two judges scored six for Frazier, two for Ali. The referee had it even. Some of the press had Ali ahead— it was not easy to score. For if it were an alley fight, Frazier would win. Clay was by now hardly more than the heavy bag to Frazier. Frazier was dealing with a man, not a demon. He was not respectful of that man. But still! It was Ali who was landing the majority of punches. They were light, they were usually weary, but some had snap, some were quick, he was landing two punches to Frazier's one. Yet Frazier's were hardest. And Ali often looked as tender as if he were making love. It was as if he could now feel the whole absence of that real second fight with Liston, that fight for which he had trained so long and so hard, the fight which might have rolled over his laurels from the greatest artist of pugilism to the greatest brawler of them all—maybe he had been prepared on that night to beat Liston at his own, be more

of a slugger, more of a man crude to crude than Liston. Yes, Ali
had never been a street fighter and never a whorehouse knock-
it-down stud, no, it was more as if a man with the exquisite
reflexes of Nureyev had learned to throw a knockout punch with
either hand and so had become champion of the world without
knowing if he were the man of all men or the most delicate of
the delicate with special privilege endowed by God. Now with
Frazier, he was in a sweat bath (a mud pile, a knee, elbow, and
death-thumping chute of a pit) having in this late year the fight
he had sorely needed for his true greatness as a fighter six and
seven years ago, and so whether ahead, behind or even, terror
sat in the rooting instinct of all those who were for Ali for it was
obviously Frazier's fight to win, and what if Ali, weaknesses of
character now flickering to the surface in a hundred little moves,
should enter the vale of prizefighting's deepest humiliation, should
fall out half-conscious on the floor and not want to get up. What
a death to his followers.

The ninth began. Frazier mounted his largest body attack of
the night. It was preparations-for-Liston-with-Shotgun-Sheldon,
it was the virtuosity of the gym all over again, and Ali, like a
catcher handling a fast-ball pitcher, took Frazier's punches, one
steamer, another steamer, wing! went a screamer, a steamer,
warded them, blocked them, slithered them, winced from them,
absorbed them, took them in and blew them out and came off
the ropes and was Ali the Magnificent for the next minute and
thirty seconds. The fight turned. The troops of Ali's second corps
of energy had arrived, the energy for which he had been waiting
long agonizing heartsore vomit-mean rounds. Now he jabbed
Frazier, he snake-licked his face with jabs faster than he had
thrown before, he anticipated each attempt of Frazier at coun-
terattack and threw it back, he danced on his toes for the first
time in rounds, he popped in rights, he hurt him with hooks, it
was his biggest round of the night, it was the best round yet of
the fight, and Frazier was beginning to move into that odd pet-
ulant concentration on other rituals besides the punches, tap-
pings of the gloves, stares of the eye, that species of mouthpiece-
chewing which is the prelude to fun-strut in the knees, then
Queer Street, then waggle on out, drop like a steer.

It looked like Ali had turned the fight, looked more like the same in the tenth, now reporters were writing another story in their mind where Ali was not the magical untried Prince who had come apart under the first real pressure of his life but was rather the greatest heavyweight champion of all time for he had weathered the purgatory of Joe Frazier.

But in the eleventh, that story also broke. Frazier caught him, caught him again and again, and Ali was near to knocked out and swayed and slid on Queer Street himself, then spent the rest of the eleventh and the longest round of the twelfth working another bottom of Hell, holding off Frazier who came on and on, sobbing, wild, a wild hermit of a beast, man of will reduced to the common denominator of the will of all of us back in that land of the animal where the idea of man as a tool-wielding beast was first conceived. Frazier looked to get Ali forever in the eleventh and the twelfth, and Ali, his legs slapped and slashed on the thighs between each round by Angelo Dundee, came out for the thirteenth and incredibly was dancing. Everybody's story switched again. For if Ali won this round, the fourteenth and the fifteenth, who could know if he could not win the fight? . . . He won the first half of the thirteenth, then spent the second half on the ropes with Frazier. They were now like crazy death-march-maddened mateys coming up the hill and on to home, and yet Ali won the fourteenth, Ali looked good, he came out dancing for the fifteenth, while Frazier, his own armies of energy finally caught up, his courage ready to spit into the eye of any devil black or white who would steal the work of his life, had equal madness to steal the bolt from Ali. So Frazier reached out to snatch the magic punch from the air, the punch with which Ali topped Bonavena, and found it and hit Ali a hell and a heaven of a shot which dumped Muhammad into fifty thousand newspaper photographs—Ali on the floor! Great Ali on the floor was out there flat singing to the sirens in the mistiest fogs of Queer Street (same look of death and widowhood on his far-gone face as one had seen in the fifth blind round with Liston) yet Ali got up, Ali came sliding through the last two minutes and thirty-five seconds of this heathen holocaust in some last exercise of the will, some iron fundament of the ego not to be knocked out, and it was then as if the spirit of Harlem finally spoke and came to rescue and the ghosts of the dead in Vietnam, something held him up before arm-weary triumphant near-crazy Frazier who had just hit him the hardest punch ever thrown in his life and they went down to the last few seconds of a great fight, Ali still standing, and Frazier had won.

The world was talking instantly of a rematch. For Ali had shown America what we all had hoped was secretly true. He was a man. He could bear moral and physical torture and he could stand. And if he could beat Frazier in the rematch we would have at last a national hero who was hero of the world as well, and who could bear to wait for the next fight? Joe Frazier, still the champion, and a great champion, said to the press, "Fellows, have a heart—I got to live a little. I've been working for ten long years." And Ali, through the agency of alter-ego Bundini, said—for Ali was now in the hospital to check on the possible fracture of a jaw—Ali was reported to have said, "Get the gun ready—we're going to set traps." Oh, wow. Could America wait for something so great as the Second Ali-Frazier?

George Plimpton

THREE WITH MOORE

I had two months in which to get a quite questionable apparatus ready for the confrontation with Archie Moore. I am not properly constituted to fight. I am built rather like a bird of the stiltlike, wader variety—the avocets, limpkins, and herons. Since boyhood my arms have remained sticklike: I can slide my watch up my arm almost to the elbow. I have a thin, somewhat fragile nose which bleeds easily. Once, in my military days, I brought up my hand in a smart salute that banged the tip of my nostrils and started a slight nosebleed there in ranks, a bead of blood quivering at the end of my nose, like a drop at a shot bird's beak, before it fell to the dust of the parade ground. A lieutenant colonel stared at me solemnly. He sighed slightly and went on down the line.

Also, I suffer from a condition which the medical profession refers to as "sympathetic response," which means that when I am hit or cuffed around, I weep. It is an involuntary reation: The tears come and there is nothing I can do except dab at them with a fist.

Charley Goldman, Rocky Marciano's famous, gnomelike trainer, once said of fighters built along my lines, "You know them fighters with long necks and them long, pointy chins. They cost you more for smellin' salts than they do for food."

Yet, I knew the first step in getting ready for Moore was to find a trainer like Charley Goldman willing to take me on. I reached a man named George Brown. I had been introduced to him by Ernest Hemingway, who always spoke of him with highest regard—as a boxer who could have been a champion fighter if he had been able to accept the idea that he was going to be hit once in a while. But having classic features better suited, perhaps, to an Irish dandy sitting astride a hunter, he stayed on the periphery of boxing, as the proprietor of a famous gymnasium on Fifty-seventh Street, where he sparred with a fancy New York clientele, if they were of a mind to try it, and where he taught boxing. Hemingway spoke of his skills with awe, saying that he could never remember having landed a good punch during a sparring session with Brown.

So I telephoned Brown. After I had explained what I wished of him, he said no, he was taking a job on the Isle of Pines, off Cuba, and wouldn't be able to help me train for the fight. He admitted that the idea of preparing a "tiger" to go against the light-heavyweight champion intrigued him, but frankly, and he hoped I didn't mind his saying so, he felt that in his future he'd be better off in Cuba—despite the fact that Fidel Castro's forces were beginning to work down from the Sierra Maestra and the place was in a political uproar. He was very polite about it and jocular at the same time.

"Well, what am I going to do, George?" I asked. I told him I had been advised by Martin Kane, of *Sports Illustrated*, to go down to Stillman's Gym, on Eighth Avenue, and get myself a trainer—I mentioned Charley Goldman and Joe Fariello—and work out in that crowd for at least a month.

Brown was appalled. "Stay out of Stillman's," he said. "You'll get some awful disease fooling around there. Stillman and his people don't know what a *mop* looks like, much less how to push such a thing through the crud in that place. . . ."

"How about the trainers?" I asked.

Brown sounded very concerned on the other end of the phone. "Listen," he said, "most of the trainers you'll find in Stillman's don't have the brains God gave a goat. Maybe they'll give you one lesson—how to lace on the gloves—but then they'll get you up there in the ring for their bums to maul you around so you 'learn experience.' You'll get ruined. Listen," Brown said, "if you have to go to Stillman's, go and work on the light bag, the heavy bag, but don't get yourself pushed into the ring if anyone else is fooling around in there. Go into the ring when it's empty—*alone*— shadowbox, get the feeling of the canvas, and *get out* if anyone starts climbing through the ropes. I don't care if it's Lou Stillman himself, or someone who looks like your grandmother . . . get out!"

"They'd really tee off on me?" I asked.

"In the ring with those guys you're fair game," Brown said. "Those guys'll hit anything moving—the timekeeper, if he got in there; a handyman sent in to check the ring posts; anybody. And as for a writer, those guys'd smack a writer on the beak just to see what would happen."

Brown heard me whistle softly over the phone; he said, "Don't forget, in the ring friendship ceases, and as for fooling around with Stillman's crowd, you'd be better off jumping into a bear pit. Wouldn't smell as bad."

With George Brown warning me sternly away from physical contact with the trainers in New York's gyms, I fell back on the theory that I could teach myself what to do from books and a self-imposed training program. I paid a visit to the library of the Racquet Club, on Park Avenue, where a small section of the shelves was devoted to boxing. I looked through the titles for a manual and arbitrarily selected one of a number—a thin volume which produced a fine aroma of mold when removed from the shelf. *The Art and Practice of English Boxing*, the volume was called, first published in 1807. I took it off to one of the library's large leather chairs, settled myself down, arranged a wooden footrest under my feet, reached up then and switched on a reading lamp—all this with a genuine sense of accomplishment, of getting underway. Around me, unaware that a fellow member was starting his preparations to fight the light-heavyweight champion of the world, quite a few members dozed in their chairs. One of them, in an adjoining chair, slept with a thin page of the *Wall Street Journal* over his face, the paper rising and falling barely perceptibly to his gentle snores. The library is used for sleeping as much as for reading. But it was peaceful that afternoon, some of the leather chairs occupied but quiescent, a fire murmuring in the grate the loudest sound in the room, and so I opened up *The Art and Practice of English Boxing* and began.

The first paragraph, devoted to some general remarks, included a reassuring sentence: "Both parties," the line read, referring to contestants in the ring, "should keep in the best humours possible." How this was to be done was not specified, but at least the inference was that George Brown's dictum that friendship ceases in the ring was not inflexible. I shifted comfortably in my chair and read on:

"One of the chief studies of a pugilist of character is to know where he can most successfully plant his blows. The parts of the body in which a blow is struck with the greatest probability of terminating the battle, are on the eye, between the eyebrows, on the bridge of the nose, or the temporal artery, beneath the left ear, under the short ribs, and in the pit of the stomach . . . a blow under the left ear forces back the blood which proceeds from the head to the heart [I shifted uneasily in my chair] . . . so that the vessels and sinews of the brain are overcharged, particularly the smaller ones, which being of too delicate a texture to resist so great a change of blood, *burst* . . . and an effusion of blood succeeding from the apertures of the head completes his business. . . ."

In my preparation for Archie Moore, I passed up sending for any Charles Atlas material. I recalled it had not wrought any discernible changes in my eleven-year-old body. Besides, there were other advertisements in the boxing magazines that seemed more suitable. I was especially drawn to one that showed an item referred to as the Killer Karate Krusher. It seemed to be some sort of leather gripper (the illustrations were always very dim in advertisements of this sort, as if the picture of the device had been taken through a keyhole by a spy on the run). The hyperbolic come-on for the Krusher was in the best tradition of such notices: MAYBE YOU DON'T WANT TO BREAK A BRICK IN TWO WITH YOUR BARE FISTS OR RIP A PHONE BOOK IN HALF—BUT WOULDN'T IT BE GREAT IF YOU COULD! The text went on to say that the exercises with the Krusher had been developed from the centuries-old secrets of Japanese Killer Cults and were quite capable of turning the user into a "two-fisted tank of power." I ordered the Krusher. I also ordered the 007 "Twister"—a piece of steel tubing, ribbed like a length of vacuum-cleaner hose, which was being bent double in the hands of a broad-chested blond youth with two girls leaning in on him from either side, their heads resting on the slopes of his shoulders. The "Twister" came ready-made—it could be used "right out of the box for musclebuilding fun"—and gave its user after almost no time at all "the power to lift girls over your head with one arm." The headline at the top of the page read MUSCLE UP AND MAKE OUT!

Very heady stuff. I also ordered a nutritional "wildcat" drink named Crashweight Formula #7 that was guaranteed in vibrant prose "to put an end to your hungry-looking muscle-poor body." There were before-and-after photographs showing what happened to somebody who had quaffed the Formula #7—in the "before" picture a thinnish fellow standing almost hidden in the shadows with his hands on his waist, holding up a pair of oversize boxer trunks, with the "after" picture showing a cataclysmic change to someone of such muscled proportions that his arm could hardly hang naturally at his side.

Odd. I cannot remember the 007 Twister's arriving, or the Krusher's, but I recall the Crashweight Formula #7's arriving. I certainly do not remember drinking the stuff. I suppose it arrived and sat on a shelf somewhere. What took my mind off these devices was that the phone rang one morning and it was George Brown on the other end. He said that the job on the Isle of Pines had not worked out, and that as long as he was back in New York, he was willing to take me on. What had I been doing to get ready, he wanted to know.

Well, I had ordered some equipment, I had been doing a lot of reading. Not much else. I heard him grunt. Reading!

I told him that some of it had been interesting. I wanted to tell him about ordering the Killer Karate Krusher and the 007 Twister, but I thought I'd wait.

George Brown went to work. The reading tapered off. He got me to stop smoking—from two or three packs to nothing, cold turkey, pointing out that it was not likely that I would ever find a better reason for quitting (short of lung disease) than having to get into condition to fight the light-heavyweight champion. In the Racquet Club gymnasium he began showing me the boxing fundamentals themselves—how to throw the jab and duck slightly behind the right to protect oneself from the counterpunch. Though he taught me one or two combinations, and we worked on the heavy bag, he said we would "rely" mostly on the jab. "No man, I don't care who he is," Brown explained, "likes to have a glove flicking around his eyes. It's like a fly up there. So we're going to stick him—peck, peck, peck; just keep that glove floating in his face."

He worked me hard. I learned what an extraordinary length of time three minutes of effort in a ring is; that even holding one's arms extended, especially with the gloves on, requires considerable stamina and strength. I could understand the extensive exercises Albert Speer reported Hitler went through to hold the fascist salute while reviewing the long columns of troops. Much of the work was simply conditioning—working with weights, strengthening the stomach muscles so I wouldn't get "sick," as George Brown put it, when I was hit there. At the end of the workout I would work at the heavy bag, circling it, peppering it for three-minute stretches, and finally, to conclude things, I would face the light bag that hung from its swivel under the bangboard. Along with skipping rope, it was the traditional boxer's exercise—the *rat-a-tat-tat* you could hear out in the street from the innards of Gleason's or Stillman's. It seemed symbolic in my case; though the bag was easy enough to hit four or five times, it then escaped the rhythm and slued violently around on its swivel, as independent as a balloon losing its air.

Brown arranged things for me to do outside the gym. He ordered me out into Central Park to run in the early morning. I hated getting up to do it. It was certainly one of the burdens of a fighter's life. In my Racquet Club reading I had read that Willie Pep once caught Jake LaMotta spiking his premorning-run orange juice with a jigger of brandy to make the exercise more palatable. "Hell, Willie," La Motta explained, "I don't run good, but I'm the happiest guy in the world."

Once out there, though, I enjoyed it. I told Brown how lovely it was in the park, with the light of the sun coming up, making the façades of the buildings on the West Side shine like a theater curtain in the footlights; and if one ran down by the zoo, the lions were grunting and the keepers were getting ready for the morning feedings. The seal pond was very lively at that hour.

Brown made a face and said I was not tending to business. Always I had to remember why I was out there—and that I should try to work up a controlled rage against Archie Moore, seeing him always in my mind's eye, shadowboxing as if his presence were just beyond reach, and to hell with what was going on in the seal pond. He told me that when Gene Tunney was training for Dempsey, he would take off time to play golf, but even on the course he would tag after his drive, shuffling and feinting and shadowboxing, and his caddy, hurrying after him, could hear him muttering between his teeth, "Dempsey . . . Dempsey . . . Dempsey."

So I tried it while running through Central Park on those cold mornings, whispering between my teeth, "Moore . . . Moore . . . Moore," but the picture that hastened into my mind was not a reassuring one at all: a mental vision of Archie Moore glowering down over his gloves, and *enormous*, dwarfing the ring as if he had been pumped up with helium and steadied in his corner of the ring with guy ropes. He swayed and looked down at me. "Moore . . . Moore . . . Moore!" No, I could not cook up much rage against him. It was best to let the mind go blank and run mindlessly past the tree trunks and under the footbridges, where the echo of my sneakers against the vaulted ceilings was sharp.

We began sparring sessions with a friend, Peter Gimbel, who had been coached for the Golden Gloves by George Brown when Gimbel was an undergraduate at Yale. Peter was a stockbroker (he left the brokerage business not long after to pursue his great love, which was ocean diving, and to make films about it, most notably one on his search for the great white shark), and he would arrive at the Yale Club with his attaché case to meet me and George Brown. We would change and spar in the gym, a high-ceilinged room which was being used as a temporary storage area for scores of stuffed-animal heads from the walls of the bar and lounge—an antlered spectator row of moose, elk, and deer under whose dull agate stares Peter and I shoved and belted each other around. The room seemed very crowded. Sometimes members came in and exercised in the rowing machines in the corner, and one afternoon, glimpsed over Peter's shoulder during a clinch, I saw an elderly man in a gym suit lying on his back and straining to lift a tiny barbell—it didn't seem much bigger than two golf balls impaled on the opposite ends of a cane.

Peter and I sparred on a large blue wrestling mat—Brown off to one side, watching, calling out "peck! peck! peck! come on now! come on now!" keeping us at it for three minutes at a time, sometimes more if he felt I could take it, until finally the breath whistled out of me with calliope shrillness, the arms and body sagging, and Brown would say, "twenty more seconds, come on now! peck! peck! peck!" as the knees would begin to flutter, and Peter's face blur behind his gloves, and then Brown would stop it. I would stumble off the wrestling mat to crouch down among the moose heads; he'd call out, "No, no, on your feet, take big breaths, fill your lungs . . . only forty-five seconds to get your breath back," and I would stand ashen-faced and gulp in sweat-tainted draughts of gymnasium air.

There seemed no respite. Once, just as the rest time was expiring, two men in Yale-blue sweatsuits strode in and threw themselves down on our mat, where they began to wrestle—furiously and with long sad gasps of exertion. I was relieved. There wasn't enough room on the mat for the four of us to compete; the wrestlers' innocent usurpation of our mat meant a halt. But Brown led us quickly into an empty squash court just off the gymnasium and set us at it again—our gym shoes shuffling across the tiles— and I remember the sharp echoes in that white chamber, and how the walls seemed to perspire in the heat.

We usually spent an hour in the gym, and then, after showering and having a drink in the dressing room, the three of us would ride uptown in a taxi—Peter with his attaché case at his feet, Brown holding the equipment bag with the boxing paraphernalia on his knees—and the two of them would argue about boxers, most often about the relative merits of Joe Louis versus Jack Dempsey. George Brown said that Dempsey could have licked anybody in the modern era easy as pie; he was just the greatest tiger there had been, "except for this tiger we got sitting here in the cab," and he would laugh and dig me in the ribs. "Why, this tiger could take Dempsey and Louis in one afternoon and chew up Gene Tunney in the evening time," and I would look out the window at Third Avenue in the rain and think how much I enjoyed being called "Tiger."

Once, George Brown motioned out into the street and he told me that I now knew enough to take on just about 95 percent of the people out there—wouldn't have no trouble with them at all—and I looked out at the pedestrians, innocently hurrying along in the rain with their shopping bags, and I thought, "Fancy that." I felt like a substantial piece of weaponry being transported in the back of the cab. I hoped they'd refer to me as a "Tiger" again. There wasn't a more satisfactory word.

The fight, or exhibition, or what people later called "that time when you . . ." took place in Stillman's Gym, the famous and rickety boxers' establishment on Eighth Avenue just down from Columbus Circle. A dark stairway led up into a gloomy vaultlike room, rather like the hold of an old galleon. One heard the sound before one's eyes acclimatized: the *slap-slap* of the ropes being skipped, the thud of leather into the big heavy bags that squeaked from their chains as they swung, the rattle of the speed bags, the muffled sounds of gym shoes on the canvas of the rings (there were two rings), the snuffle of the fighters breathing out through their noses, and, every three minutes, the sharp clang of the ring bell. The atmosphere was of a fetid jungle twilight. When Gene Tunney trained at Stillman's, he wanted to open the windows, which were so caked that it was hard to pick out where they were in the wall. "Let's clear this place out with some fresh air," he had said, and everybody there had looked at him astonished. Johnny Dundee, the featherweight champion at the time, made an oft-quoted remark: "Fresh air? Why, that stuff is likely to kill us!"

The proprietor was Lou Stillman himself. His real name was Lou Ingber, but he had managed Stillman's so long—it was originally opened by a pair of philanthropist millionaires as a charity mission to bring in kids off the street—that he found himself named for the gym that he made famous. His attitude about his place was as follows: "The way these guys like it, the filthier it is, the better. Maybe it makes them feel more at home." He announced this in what Budd Schulberg had once described as a "garbage-disposal voice." He sat up on a high stool under the automatic timer that set off the ring bell.

I remember him for leaning forward off the stool and delivering himself of a succession of tiny spits—oh, the size of BB shots— and though there were signs nailed up everywhere that read NO RUBBISH OR SPITTING ON THE FLOOR, UNDER PENALTY OF THE LAW, Stillman himself expectorated at almost every breath. Perhaps he felt that he was exonerated by the infinitesimal size of his offerings.

I had gone in there to ask him if we could take over the premises for an hour or so; I told him about Archie Moore and what we hoped to do. *Sports Illustrated* would pay him a small sum for the inconvenience. He did not seem especially surprised. An eyebrow might have been raised. It turned out that he condoned almost anything that would break the dreary tedium of the workouts—the never-ending three-minute doomsday clang of the ring bell, the mind-stupefying slamming of the punching-bag equipment—and that in the grim steerage-hold atmosphere much more hanky-panky and joking went on, perhaps as a sort of therapy, than one might have expected. For years the fall guy for practical jokes had been a huge scar-faced black fighter known as Battling Norfolk, employed by Stillman as a rubdown man, who became such a target for a hotfoot, or a bucket of water on the nape of the neck, that as he moved around the gym he *revolved*, turning to make sure no one was coming up on him from behind. They never let up on him. When he answered the phone, an explosive charge would go off; a skeleton was set up in the little cubicle in the back reaches of the gym where he gave his rubdowns, and when he saw it there, glistening in the dull light, he gave a scream and was said to have fainted, crashing up against the wood partition.

Perhaps Stillman saw me as another in the line of Battling Norfolks. He agreed to turn over his premises, though he told me what a businesslike establishment he was running there, and what a considerable inconvenience it was going to be to stop operations for the hour or so of the exhibition. Couldn't *Sports Illustrated* come up with more scratch? I said that I would see what I could do. I told him that, frankly, it was the least of my worries.

As the day of the fight approached, I began to get notes in the mail. I don't know who sent them. Most of them were signed with fighters' names—aphorisms, properly terse, and almost all somewhat violent in tone. I suspected Peter Gimbel, my sparring partner, but he would not fess up.

One of them read, "If you get belted and see three fighters through a haze, go after the one in the middle. That's what ruined me—going after the other two guys."—MAX BAER.

Another, on the back of a postcard that had a cat sitting next to a vase of roses on the front, announced succinctly, "Go on in there, he can't hurt us."—LEO P. FLYNN, FIGHT MANAGER.

Another had the curious words Eddie Simms murmured when Art Donovan, the referee, went over to his corner to see how clear-headed he was after being pole-axed by Joe Louis in their Cleveland fight: "Come on, let's take a walk on the roof. I want some fresh air."

Joe Louis's famous remark about Billy Conn turned up one morning: "He can run, but he can't hide." So did James Braddock's description of what it was like to be hit by a Joe Louis jab: ". . . like someone jammed an electric bulb in your face and busted it."

One of the lengthier messages was a parody of a type of column Jimmy Cannon occasionally wrote for the New York *Journal-American* in which he utilized the second-person form for immediacy and dramatic effect. "Your name is Joe Louis," a column might start. "You are in the twilight of your career . . ." The one I received read as follows: "Your name is George Plimpton. You have had an appointment with Archie Moore. Your head is now a concert hall where Chinese music will never stop playing."

The last one I received was a short description of a fighter named Joe Dunphy, from Syracuse, a fair middleweight, who became so paralyzed considering his prospects against a top mid-

dleweight Australian named Dan Creedon that he stood motion-
less in his corner at the opening bell, his eyes popping, until
finally Creedon, carefully, because he was looking for some kind
of trick, went up and knocked him down, much as one might
push over a storefront mannequin.

Occasionally, someone of a more practical mind than the mysterious message-sender would call up with a positive word of
advice. One of the stranger suggestions was that I avail myself
of the services of a spellcaster named Evil Eye Finkel. He possessed what he called the "Slobodka Stare," which he boasted
was what had finally finished off Adolf Hitler.

"Think of that," I said.

"Evil Eye's got a manager," I was told. "Name of Mumbles
Sober. The pair of them can be hired for fifty dollars to five
hundred dollars depending—so it says in the brochure—on the
'wealth of the employer and the difficulty of the job.' "

I wondered aloud what the price difference would be between
saving my skin in the ring against Archie Moore and what it had
cost to preserve the western democracies from fascism.

"I don't know," I was told. "You'll have to ask Mumbles."   ·

As it was, I picked corner men who were literary rather than
evil-eyed, or even pugilistic—composed of the sort of friends one
might have as ushers at a wedding (or perhaps, more appropriately, as someone pointed out, as bearers at a funeral) rather than
at a boxing showdown in a gymnasium. They were Peter Matthiessen, the novelist and explorer (he appeared on the day of
the fight and gave me the tibia of an Arctic hare as a good-luck
token—the biggest rabbit's foot I had ever seen); Tom Guinzburg,
of the Viking Press; Blair Fuller, the novelist; Bob Silvers, then
an editor of *Harpers*; and, of course, George Brown, the only
professional among us, who of course had literary connections
because of his friendship with Ernest Hemingway. None of them,
except Brown, had anything to do, really. I asked them if they
would have lunch with me the day of the fight. They could steady
me through the meal and get me to eat something. They could
distract me with funny stories.

We had the lunch at the Racquet Club. My friends stared at
me with odd smiles. We ordered the meal out of stiff large menus

that crackled sharply when opened. I ordered eggs benedict, a steak Diane, and a chocolate-ice-cream compote. Someone said that it was not the sort of place, or meal, one would relate to someone going up against the light-heavyweight champion of the world, but I said I was having the meal to quiet my nerves; the elegance of the place, and the food, arriving at the table in silver serving dishes, helped me forget where I was going to be at five that afternoon.

I took out Matthiessen's enormous rabbit foot. "How can I lose with this thing?" I said. We talked about good-luck charms and I said that in the library down the hall I had read that when Tom Sharkey was preparing for a fight against Gus Ruhlin, he was sent a pair of peacocks by Bob Fitzsimmons, the former heavy-weight champion. Sharkey was somewhat shaken by the gift, because he said he had heard from an old Irishwoman that an owner of a peacock never had any good luck. But Fitzsimmons was such a good friend that Sharkey didn't want to insult him by sending the birds back. So Sharkey kept them around, walking past their pens rather hurriedly, and indeed when he lost his fight to Ruhlin in the eleventh round, he blamed it on what he called his "Jonah birds."

"You trying to tell me you feel awkward about that hare's foot?" Matthiessen asked.

I had the sense that he had been reluctant to give it up in the first place. It was a *huge* foot, and it probably meant a lot to him.

"Perhaps you could hold it for me," I said.

"You better keep it," he said.

During lunch I kept wondering what Archie Moore was up to. I knew that he was in town, not far away. I thought of him coming closer all the time, physically moving toward our confrontation, perhaps a quarter of a mile away at the moment, in some res-taurant, ordering a big steak with honey on it for energy, every-body in the place craning around to stare at him, and a lot of smiles because a month before he had won an extraordinary fight against Yvon Durelle, a strong pole-axer French Canadian, in which he had pulled himself up off the canvas five times, even-tually to win, so that the applause would ripple up from among the tables as he left the restaurant; then he would turn uptown feeling good about things, people nodding to him on the avenues, and smiling, and then he might duck into a Fifth Avenue shop to buy a hat.

Later I discovered what he *was* doing. At the same time I was having lunch with my entourage, he was sitting in a restaurant with Peter Maas, a journalist friend of mine. Over dessert, Archie Moore asked Peter who I was—this fellow he had agreed to go three rounds with later that afternoon. Maas, who knew about the arrangements—I had invited him to Stillman's—could not resist it: he found himself, somewhat to his surprise, describing me to Moore as an "intercollegiate boxing champion."

Once Peter had got that out, he began to warm to his subject: "He's a gawky sort of guy, but don't let that fool you, Arch. He's got a left jab that sticks, he's fast, and he's got a pole-ax left hook that he can really throw. He's a barnburner of a fighter, and the *big* thing about him is that he wants to be the light-heavyweight champion of the world. Very ambitious. And confident. He doesn't see why he should work his way up through all the preliminaries in the tank towns: he reckons he's ready *now*."

Moore arched his eyebrows at this.

"He's invited all his friends," Maas went on gaily, "a few members of the press, a couple of guys who are going to be at the McNeil Boxing Award dinner tonight"—which was the real reason Moore was in town—"and in front of all these people he's going to waltz into the ring and *take* you. What he's done is to sucker you into the ring."

Maas told me all of this later. He said he had not suspected himself of such satanic capacities; it all came out quite easily.

Moore finally had a comment to offer. "If that guy lays a hand on me I'm going to coldcock him." He cracked his knuckles alarmingly at the table.

At this, Peter Maas realized that not unlike Dr. Frankenstein he had created a monster, and after a somewhat hollow laugh, he tried to undo matters: "Oh, Arch, he's a friend of mine." He tried to say that he had been carrying on in jest. But this served to make Moore even more suspicious—the notion that Maas and the mysterious man with the "pole-ax left hook" he was describing were in cahoots of some sort.

At the time, of course, I knew none of this. I dawdled away the afternoon and arrived early at Stillman's. George Brown was with me, carrying his little leather case with the gloves, and some "equipment" he felt he might have to use if things got "difficult" for me up in the ring.

We went up the steps of the building at Eighth Avenue, through the turnstile, and Lou Stillman led us through the back area of his place into an arrangement of dressing cubicles as helter-skelter as a Tangier slum, with George Brown's nose wrinkled up as we were shown back into the gloom and a stall was found. George sat me down in a corner, and, snapping open his kit bag, he got ready to tape my hands. I worried aloud that Archie Moore might not show up, and both George and I laughed at the concern in my voice, as if a condemned prisoner were fretting that the fellow in charge of the dawn proceedings might have overslept. We began to hear people arriving outside, the hum of voices beginning to rise. I had let a number of people know; the word of the strange cocktail-hour exhibition had spread. Blair Fuller arrived. He was the only one of my seconds who seemed willing to identify himself with what was going to go on. The rest said they were going to sit in the back. Fuller was wearing a T-shirt with THE PARIS REVIEW across the front.

Suddenly, Archie Moore himself appeared at the door of my cubicle. He was in his streetclothes. He was carrying a kit bag and a pair of boxing gloves; the long white laces hung down loose. There was a crowd of people behind him, peering in over his shoulders—Miles Davis, the trumpet player, one of them; and I thought I recognized Doc Kearns, Moore's legendary manager, with his great ears soaring up the sides of his head and the slight tang of toilet water sweetening the air of the cubicle (he was known for the aroma of his colognes). But all of this was a swift impression, because I was staring up at Moore from my stool. He looked down and said as follows: *"Hmm."* There were no greetings. He began undressing. He stepped out of his pants and shorts; over his hips he began drawing up a large harnesslike foul-protector. I stared at it in awe. I had not thought to buy one myself; the notion of the champion's throwing a low blow had not occurred to me. Indeed, I was upset to realize he thought *I* was capable of doing such a thing. "I don't have one of those," I murmured. I don't think he heard me. The man I took to be Doc Kearns was saying, "Arch, let's get on out of here. It's a freak show." Beyond the cubicle we could hear the rising murmur of the crowd.

"No, no, no," I said. "It's all very serious."

Moore looked at me speculatively. "Go out there and do your best," he said. He settled the cup around his hips and flicked its surface with a fingernail; it gave off a dull, tinny sound. He drew on his trunks. He began taping his hands—the shriek of the adhesive drawn in bursts off its spool, the flurry of his fists as he spun the tape around them. During this, he offered us a curious monologue, apparently about a series of victories back in his welterweight days: "I put that guy in the hospital, didn't I? Yeah, banged him around the eyes so it was a question about could he ever *see* again." He looked at me again. "You do your best, hear?" I nodded vaguely. He went back to his litany. "Hey, Doc, you remember the guy who couldn't remember his name after we finished with him . . . just plumb banged that guy's name right out of his skull?" He smoothed the tape over his hands and slid on the boxing gloves. Then he turned and swung a punch at the wall of the cubicle with a force that bounced a wooden medicine cabinet off its peg; it fell to the floor and exploded in a shower of rickety slats. "These gloves are tight," he said as he walked out. A roll of athletic tape fell out of the ruin of the cabinet and unraveled across the floor. Beyond the cubicle wall I heard a voice cut through the babble: "Whatever he was, Arch, he was not an elephant."

Could that have been Kearns? An assessment of the opposition? Of course, at the time I had no idea that Peter Maas had built me up into a demonic contender whom they had good reason to check.

"What the hell was that?" I said. I looked at George Brown beseechingly. He shrugged. "Don't let it bother you. Just remember what we've been doing all this time," he said, smoothing the tape on my hands. "Move, and peck at him."

"At least he didn't find out about the sympathetic response," I said.

"What's that?" Brown asked.

"Well, it's that weeping you've noticed when I get cuffed around."

"Maybe he'll think it's sweat," Brown said cheerfully.

After a while he reached for the gloves and said it was time we went out.

The place was packed; the seats stretching back from the ring (a utility from the days when the great fighters sparred at Stillman's) were full, and behind them people were standing back along the wall. Archie Moore was waiting up in the ring, wearing a white T-shirt and a pair of knit boxing trunks like a 1920s bathing suit. As I climbed into the ring he had his back to me, leaning over the ropes and shouting at someone in the crowd. I saw him club at the ring ropes with a gloved fist, and I could feel the structure of the ring shudder. Ezra Bowen, a *Sports Illustrated* editor, jumped up into the ring to act as referee. He provided some florid instructions, and then waved the two of us together. Moore turned and began shuffling quickly toward me.

I had read somewhere that if one were doomed to suffer in the ring, it would be best to have Archie Moore as the bestower. His face was peaceful, with a kind of comforting mien to it—people doubtless fell easily into conversation with him on buses and planes—and to be put away by him in the ring would not be unlike being tucked in by a Haitian mammy.

I do not remember any such thoughts at the time. He came at me quite briskly, and as I poked at him tentatively, his left reached out and thumped me alarmingly. As he moved around the ring he made a curious humming sound in his throat, a sort of peaceful aimless sound one might make pruning a flower bed, except that from time to time the hum would rise quite abruptly, and *bang!* he would cuff me alongside the head. I would sense the leaden feeling of being hit, the almost acrid whiff of leather off his gloves, and I would blink through the sympathetic response and try to focus on his face, which looked slightly startled, as if he could scarcely believe he had done such a thing. Then I'd hear the humming again, barely distinguishable now against the singing in my own head.

Halfway through the round Moore slipped—almost to one knee— not because of anything I had done, but his footing had betrayed him somehow. Laughter rose out of the seats, and almost as if in retribution he jabbed and followed with a long lazy left hook that fetched up against my nose and collapsed it slightly. It began to bleed. There was a considerable amount of sympathetic response and though my physical reaction, the *jab* ("peck, peck, peck"), was thrown in a frenzy and with considerable spirit, the efforts popped up against Moore's guard as ineffectually as if I were poking at the side of a barn. The tears came down my cheeks. We revolved around the ring. I could hear the crowd— a vague buzzing—and occasionally I could hear my name being called out: "Hey, George, hit him back; hit him in the knees, George." I was conscious of how inappropriate the name George was to the ring, rather like hearing "Timothy" or "Warren" or "Christopher." Occasionally I was aware of the faces hanging above the seats like rows of balloons, unrecognizable, many of them with faint anticipatory grins on their faces, as if they were waiting for a joke to be told which was going to be pretty good. They were slightly inhuman, I remember thinking, the banks of them staring up, and suddenly into my mind popped a scene from Conan Doyle's *The Croxley Master*: his fine description of a fight being watched by Welsh miners, each with his dog sitting behind him; they went everywhere as companions, so that the boxers looked down and everywhere among the human faces were the heads of dogs, yapping from the benches, the muzzles pointing up, the tongues lolling.

We went into a clinch; I was surprised when I was pushed away and saw the sheen of blood on Moore's T-shirt. Moore looked slightly alarmed. The flow of tears was doubtless disarming. He moved forward and enfolded me in another clinch. He whispered in my ear, "Hey, breathe, man, breathe." The bell sounded and I turned from him and headed for my corner, feeling very much like sitting down.

Lou Stillman had not provided a stool. "There's no stool," I said snuffily to George Brown. My nose was stopped up. He ministered to me across the ropes—a quick rub of the face with the towel, an inspection of the nose, a pop of head-clearing salts, a predictable word of the old advice ("just jab him, keep him away, keep the glove in his snoot, peck, peck, you're doing fine").

He looked out past my shoulder at Moore, who must have been joking with the crowd, because I could hear the laughter behind me.

For the next two rounds Moore let up considerably, being assured—if indeed it had ever worried him—of the quality of his opposition. In the last round he let me whale away at him from time to time, and then he would pull me into a clinch and whack at me with great harmless popping shots to the backs of my shoulder blades which sounded like the crack of artillery. Once I heard him ask Ezra Bowen if he was behind on points.

But George Brown and Blair Fuller did not like what was going on at all . . . I think mostly because of the unpredictable nature of my opponent: his moods seemed to change as the fight went on; he was evidently not quite sure how to comport himself— clowning for a few seconds, and then the humming would rise, and they would grimace as a few punches were thrown with more authority; they could see my mouth drop ajar. In the third round Brown began to feel that Moore had run through as much of a repertoire as he could devise, and that the fighter, wondering how he could finish things off aesthetically, was getting testy about it. I was told Tom Guinzburg, one of my seconds, came up to the corner and threw a towel into the ring . . . but whether he was doing it because he was worried or because he knew it would raise a laugh—which indeed it did—I never discovered. But, long after the event, I found out that Brown had reached down and advanced the hand of the time clock. The bell clanged sharply with a good minute to go. Ezra called us together to raise both our arms, and, funning it up, he called the affair a draw. I can remember the relief of its being done, vaguely worried that it had not been more conclusive, or artistic; I was quite grateful for the bloody nose.

"That last round seemed awfully short," I mentioned to Brown.

He dabbed at my face with a towel. "I suppose you were getting set to finish him," George said.

Much of the crowd moved with us back into the cubicle area. In my stall, I was pushed back into a corner. Moore stood in the doorway, the well-wishers shouting at him, "Hey Arch, hey Arch!" There was a lot of congratulating and jabber about the great Yvon

Durelle fight. I heard somebody ask, "Whose blood is that on your shirt, hey, Arch?" and somebody else said, "Well, it sure isn't his!" and I could hear the guffawing as the exchange was passed along the gloomy corridors beyond the cubicle wall.

The character of the crowd had begun to change. The word had gone around the area that Archie Moore was up in Stillman's, and the fight bars down the avenue had emptied. A whole mess of people came up Stillman's stairs, some of them in time to see the final round, others pushing against the striped-tie crowd leaving. "It's over? What the hell was Arch doin' fightin' in Stillman's?"

"I dunno," one of the others pushing up the stairs said. "I hear he kilt some guy."

"A grudge fight, hey?"

They pushed back into the cubicle area. The cigar smoke rose. I caught sight of Lou Stillman. He was frantic. He had found two women, a mother and daughter, back in the cubicle area, which had flustered him; but the main aggravation was that his place was packed with people who had not paid to come through his turnstile. Someone told me that he had become so astonished at the number turning up for the exhibition, at the quantity of coats and ties, signifying that they *could* pay, that finally venality had overcome him; he rushed to the turnstile and the last twenty or thirty people who crowded in had to pay him two dollars a head. Later, I heard that he had tried to recoup what he had missed by charging people, at least those wearing ties, as they *left*.

I sat on my stool, feeling removed from the bustle and the shouting. While I pecked at the laces of my gloves, suddenly in front of me a man turned—I had been staring at the back of his overcoat—and he said, "Well, kid, what did you get out of it?"

He was an older black man, with a rather melancholy face distinguished by an almost Roman nose; his ears were cauliflowered, though very small.

"So far, a bloody nose," I said.

He smiled slightly. "That's the good way to begin; that's the start."

"I guess that's right," I said.

"There's a lot more to it," he went on.

I must have looked puzzled.

"Stick to it," he said. "You've got a lot to find out about. Don't let it go, hey?"

"No," I said vaguely, "I won't."

I never discovered who he was. I thought of him a couple of times later that evening.

Stillman's cleared out, finally. The fighters, who had been standing along the back wall to watch the strange proceedings, took over the premises again; they climbed up into the rings; the trainers sat down in the front seats, gossiping; things returned to normal.

I was told that at seven o'clock or so the Duchess d'Uzès had arrived. She was not a duchess then (she had a marriage or so to go before she became one) but she had the airs: she was delivered to the door of Stillman's in a Rolls-Royce. She stepped out and hurried up the stairs. She was famous for being late— even at her own extravagant parties, where her guests stood yawning with hunger, waiting for her to come down the long, curved stair and make an entrance—and she paused at the turnstile, a lovely, graceful girl who always wore long light-blue chiffon to set off her golden hair.

She peered into the gloom. "Where's everybody?" she called. She had a clear musical voice, perfect for cutting through the uproar of a cocktail party.

Lou Stillman approached. I don't know if he produced one of his infinitesimal spittles. Let us say he cleared his throat.

"Everybody is not here," he said.

Hugh McIlvanney

Superman at Bay

*Joe Frazier v. Muhammad Ali,
New York, March 8, 1971*

For more than a decade now, whether calling himself Cassius
Clay or Muhammad Ali, the man has sought the whole world as
an audience. The heavyweight champion has always exerted a
fascination that transcends sport, but no previous holder of the
title has been able to invade so many lives at so many levels.
Compared with him, the most vivid of his predecessors are blurred
figures dancing behind frosted glass. When he speaks, he assumes no less than that he is addressing mankind. "I think," he
told me solemnly the other day, "I must have the most populous
face on earth, exceptin' maybe Nixon's. And maybe even more
than his." The word "populous" had a kind of surrealist appro-
priateness, for no one who looks into his face can expect to see
one man. He dreams himself anew each morning.

If anything is consistent in him, it can only be the hunger for
universal attention, his constantly articulated fantasy that when
he puts himself at risk, when he lays his invincibility on the line,
the world holds its breath. On Monday night Muhammad Ali will
go as close as any athlete ever could to making that fantasy a
fact. His fight with Joe Frazier at Madison Square Garden in New
York will be filmed, photographed, described in the spoken and
written word, analyzed and argued over as no sports event ever
has been before or is ever likely to be again. Gross takings from
the worldwide operation should fall between 20 and 30 million

171

dollars, which is not a painful place to fall. This is—as everyone associated with it freely admits—something else, the greatest, the big apple. Muhammad Ali's craving to be center stage in an unprecedented drama is being fulfilled. The fees may be identical ($2½ million each), and his opponent may be billed as the official owner of a championship that he was forced to yield to the politicians, but there is no doubt that Ali is the greater of two undeniable stars. His magnetism, not the vigorous and beautiful talent of Joe Frazier, will draw the thoughts of the world toward that square of illuminated canvas at the Garden on Monday.

Yet the realization of Ali's dream may be flawed by a deep irony. His moment of supreme exposure may be his one moment of profound failure: it could be that all these years he has been accumulating an unimaginable audience to witness his final downfall, to be stunned by the stripping away of the Messianic aura, saddened by the revelation that the child of destiny remains a prizefighter who can be punched apart from his quick wits. "No one has ever worked so hard on the buildup for his own funeral," a Frazier supporter said cynically in midweek. That, blatantly, is the sort of sweeping assumption that can never be made about Ali. His achievement so far in his career has not been to stay unbeaten but, in an almost supernatural sense, to seem unbeatable. Frazier, too, has avoided defeat in his twenty-six professional contests (five fewer than Ali has fought) but while he has done it by dint of fairly conventional prowess, the other man has often appeared to be divinely insulated against calamity. Ali is a magnificently gifted and graceful boxer, the most aesthetically satisfying the heavyweight division has known, but there have been times when his marvelous skills and brimming athleticism might have been insufficient without something that could pass for collusion with the Fates. Adversity, whether created by opponents or the United States draft laws, has been overcome or turned to positive advantage. At the heart of the hypnotic appeal his personality has for so many of us is an irrational suspicion that here is a man capable of willing his own outrageous image of himself into reality. To attempt such a thing is, however, close to the ultimate hubris, and it is fear of the fall that has sunk admirers like myself in nervous gloom this week-end. There is too much of Sophocles in the scenario of this fight.

If Nemesis there must be, Joe Frazier is classically equipped for the part. He is, as they say around the gyms here, "all fighter." Since moving north as a boy from Beaufort, South Carolina, he has lived in Philadelphia, which also happens to be the hometown of Angelo Dundee, Ali's trainer. "Philadelphia," Dundee has said, "is not a town. It's a jungle. They don't have gyms there. They have zoos. They don't have sparring sessions. They have wars." Frazier is true to that background. His work in the ring has a cumulative, percussive urgency, a mounting, destructive rhythm that corresponds to some private music in his head. He is a volume puncher, the most impressive since "Homicide" Henry Armstrong, who is the only boxer ever to have held three world titles simultaneously. Frazier's appetite for training is frightening. In the days when he worked from 4:30 A.M. until six o'clock at night in a local slaughterhouse, he would face a full schedule afterwards. He first went to a police gym in his teens because he was overweight, and he still burdens himself with special clothing to force the sweat out, especially around his huge thighs. Neither these clothes, nor a leaded belt round his waist, can prevent him from maintaining a pace that would kill many fly-weights. Punching the bag, bench exercises, roadwork, sparring, all are done at exaggerated tempo, often to rock music. He is a joyful masochist in the gym, flogging himself without respite in pursuit of the toughness that will make him oblivious of his opponent's aggression, even that of a man who will be four inches taller and—at a predicted 215 pounds—about ten pounds heavier. "I work so hard in camp, punish myself, and then when I get to the real thing it's that much more easy for me. When the bell rings, I'm ready. I'm turned on."

In fact, he is rarely turned on quite enough at the first bell. It usually takes him two or even three rounds to find his rhythm and, since he is remarkably easy to hit in those tentative minutes, he can anticipate a hard time from Ali's sharp punches to the head. Billy "Moleman" Williams, who has long been Frazier's principal sparring help, suggests that the first round could be sensational, with Frazier down and in real difficulties. "But if Joe gets his thing goin', if he cuts off the ring like he does with us in training and gets to Ali's body with both hands, then to the head with that terrific left hook—and forgets his crazy idea of throwin' right leads—then he should take Ali somewhere between the third and the ninth. If Ali gets beyond that point without taking too much, he must be favorite."

Frazier refuses to believe he is in any serious danger. "This is just another man, another fight, another payday," he said in his Philadelphia motel this week. He agrees with his manager, a former railway welder named Yancey Durham, that retirement, at the age of twenty-seven, is something they should consider after the fight. The success of Cloverlay, the organization set up by the syndicate of businessmen who handle his money, has made Frazier financially independent, and he does not have to pretend that singing with his Knockouts pop group offers a genuine alternative career. The main function of his music, he claims, is to soothe the savage breast. Cradling his guitar in his lap and strumming amateurishly, he said: "I play to keep myself calm, to keep from hittin' people or tearing down the wall. I used to have phone bills of $2,000 before I took up music."

He is a paradox not unfamiliar in boxing, a friendly, church-going family man who leaves his compassion in the dressing room. "I like to hit guys and see their knees tremble. I like to feel my strength and go for broke. Clay's a big guy but I've fought big guys before. Movers, too. He says I won't reach him, but that's a broad statement. He will find the ring will get smaller and I will get bigger. I don't see the job taking more than ten rounds. I'll be talking to Clay in there. I always talk in my fights and I've got something special to say to him after all his crap about me being an Uncle Tom. I'll tell you what this fight will be all about—conditioning. And there's no way he's going to be in better shape than me."

Before his compulsory three-and-a-half-year absence from the ring, no opponent could have been optimistic about being in better condition than Muhammad Ali. But, in the two victories since his return, the nine-minute laceration of Jerry Quarry and the fifteenth-round knockout of Oscar Bonavena, the exciting elements of his performances have not concealed a definite erosion of his speed. There has been nothing in his training in Miami

Beach to encourage hopes that he can rediscover the vast overspill of vitality that swept him to the championship. This time he has talked significantly of being twenty-nine, of conserving himself for the night. "Twenty-nine ain't old but I don't want to go usin' up stuff I need in the ring. That's why I'm quieter than I used to be, not leapin' and foolin' around like I did."

The truth is that he has done a fair amount of fooling around, haranguing the paying spectators at his workouts, eulogizing himself and dismissing Frazier as a second-rate street fighter, a short-armed hooker who will never get past his jab. But mainly in these moments he gives the impression of remembering a part he played in another show. One striking exception was the day he took Burt Lancaster, who has connections with the promoters, on a Pied Piper's tour of the black ghetto area of central Miami. As Ali leapt from his Cadillac, five years fell away and he was the compelling, hysterically ebullient champion who had led me noisily through the same district three weeks before his title fight with Henry Cooper. "I bring the greatest movie stars in the world to see y'all," he shouted, thrusting the nervous actor out of the afternoon glare into the dark interior of a bus. As he strode past Moon's Recreation Hall and the barbershops and drugstores, the crowd around him swelled and Lancaster was not the only member of the tiny white minority who was uneasy. An undercurrent of violence eddied through the blacks who closed in on all sides. Two or three of them challenged Ali to spar, and a tall, wild-looking man in an Apache wig who called himself Nicodemus went at the boxer with dangerous briskness. Ali was their hero, but too many of them wanted to acquire glory by the laying on of hands.

Some of us were given a lift back from the ghetto by Smokey the Bear, a large black wrestler who had attached himself to the camp. He agreed that the situation had been delicate for a few minutes, "But Reggie would have taken care of it," he said. Reggie Thomas is a Muslim agent from Chicago who acts as chauffeur and bodyguard to Ali these days. He favors single colors, white or blue, from his flat cap to his pull-on boots. He is small and light-skinned, with the excessively composed features and mobile eyes of the professional bodyguard. Joe Frazier said last week he would never fight in an alley unless he "was dressed." He did not have to draw diagrams. Reggie is almost certainly dressed.

Between five and six o'clock in the morning Reggie was to be found easing the black Cadillac around the three-mile perimeter of Bayshore golf course behind Ali's pounding silhouette. Practically every day in the last six weeks or so breakfast was followed by a sleep in the compact penthouse the fighter occupied in a block of apartments (where two Muslim sisters cooked for him and his privacy was forcefully protected) and he was driven to the Fifth Street Gym at twelve o'clock. The big square room was invariably walled in by the bright Florida noon pressing against the dirty windows and the heat was thick as Vaseline on the skin. Ali worked rather perfunctorily amid a motley of engrossed fighters, adding to their noise, to the drum and swish and smack and scuff and grunt, the melancholy cacophony of a boxing gym. Hanging in the air at such times is a muted apprehension, a quiet dread that all this self-denial may mean nothing when the moment comes. One detects among some of the fighters a longing that everything could stay suspended like this, so that a man just sweated and exhausted himself and then showered and drove home through the heat to flop on a couch and mindlessly watch television. Even Ali may have lost his lust for crisis and maybe that was what was wrong with the atmosphere in the Fifth Street Gym.

Or perhaps he is fooling us once again and we are worrying needlessly. Perhaps Rufus Brassell, the sharpest of his sparring partners, is right when he says the great man's talent is virtually intact and the lazy mauling that has often marred his training is an irrelevant joke. Perhaps Angelo Dundee and his doctor friend, Ferdie Pacheco, are justified in saying that Ali, though he is thicker around the middle, is fit to jab and move for twenty rounds if he has to. They insist that Frazier, for all his record of having destroyed so many previously indestructible fighters, will not be able to invade Ali's territory and will disintegrate at the end of the jab. But neither the paid observers like myself nor the locals and holidaymakers who have crushed into the gym in their colored shirts and dresses, herded in a sweaty cluster like damp confetti, have seen persuasive evidence of all this.

Those of us with an emotional commitment have found more hope in the words of Richard Durham, a black journalist who has been sharing Ali's quarters in Miami to continue the research for a book on him: "He will win because of his morale. He draws strength from the people. They nourish him and he keeps what they give him. Some men cannot take from the people. If the people give to them it doesn't get through or it just seeps away. He has the power to keep it. It strengthens him the way a parent's love strengthens a child. And, when he has enough of that strength, he can do anything the people want of him. If they want him to win, he wins. They do. He will."

Just Another Brother . . .

In the middle of Tuesday afternoon the lobby of the New Yorker Hotel in Manhattan was so crowded that people who wanted to stay on the ground floor were riding in elevators to take a rest from the jostling. One man tried to reduce the crush by elbowing his way through the bodies and shouting warnings. "You're creating a fire hazard," he yelled. "Get back! You'll have to move back. Somebody could get killed here." No one moved and he turned away hopelessly. "All this," he said, "for a beaten fighter."

A few minutes later the door of one of the express elevators opened and the beaten fighter stepped out and attempted to make his way to the street within a straining ring of his black friends and attendants. He was taller than almost anyone else in the lobby, so that his disembodied face rode above the swaying crowd, composed and detached, the lips pursed in a patient expression. He remained undisturbed, signing the pieces of paper that were pushed at him, when his protectors had to give up on their first effort to force him through the main doors. The pressure eased when at last he reached the pavement. Most of the mob fell in behind him, scurrying to compensate for the length of his stride. There were at least 200 people with him when he turned out of Eighth Avenue into the hard wind of Thirty-fourth Street on his way to the basement garage of the hotel. A tiny black boy, thin as a stick, was held high in his mother's arms for a glimpse. "Hey, Muhammad, hey, Muhammad," he called. Then, in desperation: "Hey, Cassius Clay." Ali's eyes rolled round slowly in mock rebuke. It took several minutes for the police and his friends to extricate him sufficiently to squeeze him into a black Cadillac. "Oh, Jennifer," an attractive black girl said to her white friend as the car door closed. "I saw him. I saw him." The white girl laughed. "I touched him," she said.

"Muhammad, you're beautiful," a young white man shouted from the fringe. "You'll be back. You're coming back." Ali turned toward him and winked above the hard ball of swelling on his right cheek. As the car edged out and swung tentatively across to the other side of the street, someone muttered that after all Frazier had won the fight. A big man with red hair and a brown outdoor face spun round on the voice. "He won't win next time. Believe me. Frazier won't win next time."

It was a moment that no one but Ali could have created, a scene that had very little to do with the usual mobbing of a celebrity. Pop singers and film actors can have young girls scrambling to touch them, but they don't make 225-pound building workers tighten at the throat and offer emotional declarations of faith. Perhaps the most remarkable aspect of that utterly remarkable heavyweight championship fight in Madison Square Garden is that defeat, far from diminishing Ali in the eyes of his admirers, has deepened their feelings far beyond the normal limits of public respect and affection. That suggestion will represent sentimental rubbish to many people, but they are the people who have always been immune to Ali. By no means all of them are racists, blatant or latent. Nor are they necessarily so superficial that they can only see him as a loud-mouthed boor. What is common to most of his detractors is a failure to let themselves become attuned to his spirit, to his dream. To those of us who believe in him, such a failure is astonishing. The beauty of his physical performances, his whole impact as a performer, is inseparable from his bizarre but ultimately heroic vision of himself. Arthur Miller's salesman is not the only man who has to dream. Whoever you are, it comes with the territory. The world would be uninhabitable if all of us dreamt on the epic scale of Ali, but it would be a considerably drabber place if one among us had not done so.

That was why all the sadness of last Monday night was diluted, even transformed, by Ali's refusal to let his dream be diminished. Against an opponent of genuine nobility, one of the most honest wills ever put to work in the prize ring or anywhere else, he stayed true to himself and everyone who identifies with him. He fought a unique fight, one that was almost baroque in the intricacy of its stratagems. And when all his elaborate attempts to conceal the deterioration of his leg speed, to reduce some of his weaker rounds to a vacuum of restful play-acting, to "con" Joe Frazier into believing him far stronger and less vulnerable than he was, when all these failed, he took the consequences with magnificent courage.

The white American reporters who screamed, "Kill the sonofabitch, take his head off, his time's here now," were blinding themselves to the truth of what was happening in the ring as much as the hotel maid who said: "So the big mouth got shut good," and offered a smile that was an invitation to dance on a grave. They wanted a crucifixion, but if they think that is what they got they are bad judges of the genre. The big man came out bigger than he went in. He lost. There should be no doubt about that. His own claim that he thought he won nine rounds, and therefore the fight, was a confirmation of continuing pride rather than a logical analysis. Exactly the same interpretation must be put on his opinion that, if he had fought Joe Frazier before the politicians put him out of boxing four years ago, Frazier "would have licked me quicker because I wasn't as strong as I am now." To say otherwise, as I certainly would, clearly would be seen by Ali as an admission that he is in decline. That, for such a man at the age of twenty-nine, is unthinkable. Inevitably, in the midst of all his generous words about Frazier, he finds himself saying that he would have done better with "a referee from England or Scotland, and judges from Japan and Germany" in place of officials appointed by "the authorities that took my title away, guys who are a lot more friendly toward the Veterans of Foreign Wars than the Muslims."

Newspaper stories which gave the impression that he was ranting about having been robbed were ridiculous distortions. During an hour and a half in his hotel suite on the twenty-fifth floor of the New Yorker Hotel on Tuesday, I heard him quietly correct several interviewers who called him champ. "I ain't the champ," he said quietly. "Joe's the champ. I call him champ now. Not before but I do now. I ain't protestin'. He's a good, tough fighter. Not a great boxer but great at his own thing. He puts pressure on you all right, cuts off the ring, and he's the best hitter I ever met. I always thought of him as a nice fella. What I said before, that was to do with the fight. Just the fight. I got to know him pretty good traveling up from Philadelphia before he fought Jimmy Ellis. I was low on money that day and he loaned me $100. He's a nice man with a family, just another brother workin' to make a living."

Ali was lying back low in an armchair that had been placed to suit the television crews who had just left. He wore a fawn and beige wool shirt and blue slacks. His eyes were heavy and his voice was subdued. He said he was sore rather than tired. The worst pain was at the top of his right thigh, where Frazier's lower left hooks had made regular contact. They had hurt him more there than in the body, he said, contradicting those who had concluded wincingly at ringside that he would be "pissing blood for a week." He was suffering less than might have been expected from the bruise on his jaw and kept telling us proudly that it was the only real mark on him. His hands were sore and he extended his right one lightly clenched when anyone wished him luck. He would talk quietly for a while and then fall into silence, glancing absently through a newspaper. Three men who said they were from Blackpool, and gave no reason to question it, had come to deliver an obscenely large stick of rock with MUHAMMAD ALI printed through it. "What you tryin' to do?" he asked, smiling. "Give me the sugar diabetes?" "If you had licked this, you'd have licked Frazier," one of the three told him. The line sounded no better than it had at rehearsal.

Ali had more practical explanations of what went wrong. "If I knew then what I know now, I would have done different. If I knew I was gonna lose those rounds when I played about, I wouldn't have fooled so much." This came across as wishful rationalization of something that was forced upon him. Such contradictions, the tendency to submerge yesterday's facts in today's feelings, come naturally to him. He is an existential thinker.

The truth is that the use he made of his equipment in this fight, though inevitably riddled with all kinds of dangerous exaggerations, was basically the approach that offered him the best hope of winning. No one knew better than he did that his legs had lost the elastic agility and inexhaustible fluency they once had. He knew he could not invalidate Frazier's strength and rhythm by the once favorite technique of "surrounding" his man, dancing outside the range of his opponent's punches while using his speed, reach, and precise timing to pour in his own. At his best, the unequaled mobility had made him as secure as a dive-bomber attacking a wagon train. But a long look at his training in Miami had left me sadly convinced that his foot speed was a memory, that against Frazier he would be obliged to fight flat-footed for much of the time.

It was equally obvious that if he allowed this realization to commit him to a straightforward slugging war, there would be only one winner and it would not be Ali. He had always sought, and always previously found, a highly specific solution to the problems posed by each opponent and here he appeared to decide that he had more chance of overwhelming Frazier with his personality than with his pared-down talent. In the past he has concentrated on psyching himself into invincibility. Here the emphasis was on psyching Frazier out of belief in himself. From the moment of entry into the ring Ali set out to persuade Frazier that he was taking on impossible odds. The two corners told a story. Yank Durham, Frazier's manager, brought in the minimum help. Ali had a half-dozen cornermen, all clad in aggressive scarlet uniforms. A lesser fighter might have been unnerved by the sight of such a red army. But this one was content with the knowledge that Ali would be alone when the bell went. He was only mildly irritated when Ali, gliding sideways past his corner, muttered contemptuous predictions.

When the bell did go, the big man started well, exploiting the anticipated clumsiness of Frazier's early moves with accurate jabs and right crosses. As Frazier pressed in close, Ali smothered his attacks, tangling up the arms and employing the advantage in height to lean heavily on the smaller man's neck and shoulders. If the clubbing hooks got home to the body, Ali exposed his mouthpiece and shook his head in dismissal of their effects, implying that the hitter was punching himself out. In fact Ali was being hurt. He simply takes hurt rather well.

Despite a substantial improvement in Frazier's work by the third, he could not, in my judgment, have won more than two or—at the absolute outside—three rounds up to and including the ninth. Ali had avoided draining himself too severely in this early period, especially in the sixth and eighth, by filling in time with some highly calculated comedy. He held a glove against Frazier's forehead, seeking to ward him off with insulting ease, or stood against the ropes with both hands down, eluding many punches and frowning pityingly over those that landed. Occassionally he rapped his man's face with playful little flurries of his right hand. Spectators who felt that his tactics were insanely hazardous did not appreciate how careful he had to be with his energy. Boxing positively is much more tiring than boxing negatively. Ali knew that if he tried to attack vigorously in every round he would burn out fast. He was more confident of his endurance than his destructive strength, so he gambled on breaking Frazier's spirit rather than his body. It was the boldest bluff imaginable.

This strange mixture of sharp aggression and farcical histrionics went very near to winning the fight. Ali had a superb ninth round, drawing traces of blood around Frazier's nose and mouth and adding to the already distinct swellings around the eyes. When Frazier staggered back, his mouth open in an almost drunken grin, after taking jolting hooks and uppercuts to the head, the fight seemed to have swung decisively. But all this time, in his most frustrating moments, one simple statement could be read into everything Frazier did: "My time is coming." Now it had arrived. He rallied in the tenth and in the eleventh he took control. At last the left hook reached Ali, who had wearied himself in the ninth, and soon he was staggering around the ring at a crazily reclining angle, like a surfer before he loses the board. "What surprised me most was how often Joe caught me with the hook, with good ones after the eleventh," he said later. His ability to withstand a punch is prodigious, however, and Frazier could not put him down.

For the next two rounds he was catching but not disastrously, and in the fourteenth, managing perhaps the best footwork he had shown all night, he boxed beautifully and won the round comfortably. But he had done his grandstanding too early. In the fifteenth his legs were leaden. Frazier punished him immediately, and before the round had gone a minute a sickeningly violent left hook smashed across the right side of Ali's face, instantly increasing the swelling that had developed there earlier and hurling him flat on his back with his legs kicking high toward the ring lights. Now came one of his worst and greatest moments. Any possible ambiguity about the result was removed by that punch, but so were the unjustified doubts about Ali's heart. Any man (and especially one so close to exhaustion) would have been entitled to stay prostrate after such a blow, but he rolled over without hesitation, was up at the count of two and when he had taken the compulsory eight he went straight at Frazier to hold on through the rest of a brutal round. I found it impossible to give Ali fewer than six rounds, with probably two even, but the eleventh and fifteenth were won so easily by Frazier that he was undeniably in front at the finish.

Joe Frazier, a thoroughly pleasant and admirable man, is also a champion fit to share a ring with any who have held the world heavyweight title. "I have fought anybody y'all put in front of me and God knows I beat them," he said afterwards. "What more can I do? Now I got to live a little, man. I've been working for ten long years."

Both men say they want to meet again—"All we need is $6 million split evenly down the middle," says Yank Durham—and the odds are that all the objections of lawyers and politicians and wives will not prevent a second collision. "Next time would be different," Ali said in his hotel room. "Myself would make it different. When you get as big as I got in this game you get intoxicated with so-called greatness. You think you just have to run three miles a day. That's all I did for this fight. And I didn't rest properly, didn't train hard as I used to. You convince yourself you'll get by on natural talent, that it will all just explode in there on the night. But it don't. Next time I'd run more, get the legs right. That would make it different." Unfortunately, one remem-

bers the same self-criticism of his preparation for Oscar Bonavena. The signs are that he is no longer capable of driving himself
through the endless training that maintained his unrivaled condition, that he no longer has the obsessive, unsuffering enthusiasm for it. He, too, wanted to get home, to his new hacienda-
style house in New Jersey, and live an ordinary life for a while,
"washing the dishes, putting out the garbage, landscaping the
backyard. We been whupped. Maybe we'll get a little peace now."

But he was not about to abandon those people who were waiting for him down in the lobby. "I've never thought of losing, but
now that it's happened the only thing is to do it right. That's my
obligation to all the people who believe in me. We all have to take
defeats in life. We lose loved ones, or a man loses his property
or his job. All kinds of things set us back, but life goes on. If so-
called great people can take these defeats, whatever they are,
without cracking, the others are encouraged. They feel strong.

"If I lost again, I'd say, 'That's it. I've had my day.' You don't
go mad. You don't shoot yourself. Soon this will be old news.
People got lives to lead, bills to pay, mouths to feed. Maybe a
plane will go down with ninety persons in it. Or a great man will
be assassinated. That will be more important than Ali losing. I
never wanted to lose, never thought I would, but the thing that
matters is how you lose. I'm not crying. My friends should not
cry."

The last time I saw him before he went home he was at the
wheel of a bus that was taking his entourage to New Jersey. As
it pulled away through the crowds he gave a slow little smile and
waved, like royalty. How else would he wave?

Hugh McIlvanney

ONWARD VIRGIN SOLDIER

Lupe Pintor v. Johnny Owen,
Los Angeles, September 19, 1980

Johnny Owen's mother worries when he fights, and so does every other mother who has ever seen him stripped. The British and Commonwealth bantamweight champion has the kind of physique that makes him elusive when he is standing still. His 118 pounds are elongated over 5 feet 8 inches, so that his biceps are scarcely more prominent than his Adam's apple or the veins on his forearm. Indeed, most of Owen's muscles come disguised as skin and bone. His ears protrude endearingly from a face that is small, shy, and much younger than could be expected of a twenty-three-year-old who has been boxing competitively since he was ten. When that appearance is juxtaposed with the thought of what he is asked to do in the ring, hearts that are not at all maternal find themselves melting.

On a recent night in Bedlinog, a South Wales village a couple of valleys away from his home town of Merthyr Tydfil, a friendly man in the crowd turned to the boxer's father. "Dick, you have a lovely son," he said. "And I hope you won't be insulted if I tell you how he makes me feel. When I look at him I want to pick him up, put him in a shawl, carry him home and give him a good basin of broth."

Dick Owen wasn't insulted. He and his wife were accustomed to far more indignant misconceptions about a boy so obsessively dedicated to a fighting career that he has never once allowed

185

himself to be distracted by a girl, has never as much as kissed one in earnest. When her virgin soldier goes off to war, Johnny's mother, stubbornly refusing to watch him take punches, sits at home until she can bear the waiting no longer and then goes to pace around a telephone box higher up the hilly council estate of Gelli-deg in Merthyr, painfully delaying her call until she knows the *Western Mail* sports desk in Cardiff will be able to tell her the result. "The main reason we've never had the phone put in," says Dick, "is that we know we'd be pestered to death by people telling us we should be locked up for letting Johnny fight. Dai Gardiner, his manager, has had to take some terrible stick over that, especially from women. They've called Dai something rotten. He's more like one of the family than a manager, but these characters seem to think he is starving Johnny, then sending him out to get knocked about by sturdier lads. They don't bother to notice that Johnny won more than a hundred amateur fights and lost only eighteen, or that he's unbeaten after seventeen as a professional and has stopped eight of those professional opponents inside the distance."

Around midnight next Saturday, in Almeria, southern Spain, Owen will attempt to effect a dramatic improvement in that already exceptional record by taking the European bantamweight title away from Juan Francisco Rodriguez. A glance might suggest that Rodriguez, with only thirteen paid fights, is even less experienced than the Welshman, but that statistic is deceptive, because the Spanish authorities were so proud of their man's achievements at the amateur level—where he held a European championship and earned an Olympic bronze medal—that for a long time they severely discouraged ambitions of defecting to professionalism. Since joining the harder school, he has kept respectable company, not only making himself head boy on the Continent but putting himself in the way of the world champion, the intimidating Mexican Carlos Zarate. Admittedly, that argument was comprehensively lost after five rounds, but the defeat may be considered less than disgraceful when set against Zarate's record of having stopped fifty-two out of fifty-three opponents and having been beaten only once—and that just recently at the so-called super-bantamweight mark of 122 pounds by Wilfredo

Gomez. Yet, if the form book invites caution in the approach to Rodriguez, it does nothing to make Owen pessimistic. If there is a line of comparison, perhaps it emerges from Owen's latest success, the points victory last November over the seasoned and impressively capable Sicilian Australian Paul Ferreri, who had previously given Zarate plenty of aggravation over twelve rounds before succumbing to cuts. The Welshman's apparent fragility has never looked more like Nature's con trick than it was at Ebbw Vale as he came from behind to subdue Ferreri in the last third of the fifteen-round match.

Rodriguez is known as a boxer of skill and style but one who is inclined to seek rests during rounds and continues to exhibit too many of his amateur habits. He is unlikely to be more slippery than Ferreri and he can forget about taking breathers against Owen, who seems to harbor a deep resentment of the rule that gives him a minute's break between rounds. So the biggest threat to the British champion's challenge may be the eccentricities of scoring in Spain: "We accept that we'll have to stop the fella to get the title and I expect Johnny to do that, maybe after about twelve rounds," says Dai Gardiner. After watching Owen in training last week, it was easy to accept that forecast as merely realistic.

Whether running on the scarred hills around Merthyr or working at the gym above the local Labour Club, where the harsh poverty of the facilities makes the fight emporia of New York or Philadelphia look like suites at the Savoy, his application to work is frightening. When the recent snow and ice made the sheep-paths of his roadwork hazardous, he wrapped rags and old socks around his heavy running boots and did his best to maintain his daily schedule of nine-mile slogs. On the one day a week when he is excused gym sessions, he likes to extend the run to twelve miles. His sparring has the intensity of warfare and a night's business can include as many as fifteen rounds of it. He has used a handful of experienced and active pros in this his second full preparation for a championship match that has been postponed three times. None has been less than nine pounds heavier than he is but all have had trouble coping with his pressure. On Thursday evening it was the turn of Les Pickett, the local featherweight who is due to fight an eliminator for the British championship in the midweek following the Almeria date. Pickett is not naturally accommodating but he was forced rather than forcing through the eight hard rounds and at the end of each he was gulping down extra air while Owen wandered his corner impatiently with hardly a hint of rise and fall about his narrow chest.

His floor exercises gave further evidence of freakish stamina and, through it all, from the moment he began slowly to accouter himself for work with the ritualized care of a bullfighter dressing for the ring, there was something even more remarkable: the sense of a man being stimulated and enlarged by submergence in his true métier. Earlier, in the council-house living room bright with a spreading clutter of trophies and decorated on one wall with a lurid green painting of a skeleton presented by a fan, his personality had come across as diffident almost to the point of being fugitive. But in that incomparably shabby gym, with its makeshift ring, patched punch-bag and medicine ball, wrinkling fight posters and an old bath puddled with spit and littered with dog-ends, he grew and brightened visibly with the knowledge that he was a hero at the game in hand, the certainty that he would go out from there to cause a stir in the world. Win or lose in Almeria, he will be doing what he is happiest doing. "I don't expect to lose," he says, both the accent and the quietness of voice demanding a straining alertness from the listener. "I know they say Spain is a hard place to win but it's just him and me at the finish. I really love boxing and I really love training, too, for itself as well as for the confidence it gives me. I've got a job as a machine setter in a components factory but I'm happy when I take a fortnight off for a big fight. After all the running and the other stuff in the gym, I know I'm not going to fade. I can go all out from the first bell. It's a great feeling."

It's not usually so good for the opponent, who finds Owen coming at him with an incessant variety of sharp, hurtful punches, crowding and hustling, undeterred by any but the most forceful counters. Owen's nose has been thickened and polished by all the years of aggressive attention but he has never been stopped and as a pro he has only once been briefly bemused, by George Sutton, who was eventually beaten out of sight. "The only mark I can remember him getting since turning professional was a tiny one under the left eye in his thirteenth fight," says his father. "His mother played hell when he came home. That was to be the end of it, no more boxing. He wouldn't even let me put something on the bruise. He was so proud about the thought of having a black eye to show."

Dick Owen did some amateur boxing (the family connection goes back at least as far as Dick's own grandfather, who inflicted a bit of damage in the booths) and all five of his sons were so keen that he had to set up an alfresco gym on the drying green of 22 Heol Bryn Padell, Gelli-deg. "The boy older than Johnny was really good but gave it up too early and the one immediately beneath him, Kevin, was a Welsh international until he took to the courting lark and packed in the boxing," he says. "Johnny's different. He lives for the game and has never looked at a girl. There are enough of them coming for him now but there's plenty of time for that." John agrees. "I'd like to be still unbeaten this time next year and we could think about going for the world title. Ferreri's manager said he thought I was near the top class now but we're not rushing. Whatever happens, I think I want to be out of the game by the time I'm around twenty-seven. It seems young but, do you see, I'd have been boxing nearly twenty years by then."

Dai Gardiner, the manager, bearded and still, at thirty-eight, carrying the briskness that took him through thirteen professional fights with only one loss before a detached retina ended his career, acknowledges that the punching strength of someone like Zarate will represent the decisive question for Owen. "Can he take one on the chin from a man like that and keep going? That's the only question he's got to answer for me, and we'll just have to find out about that when it comes along. What is sure is that he won't fail because of lack of fitness or temperament, lack of skill or heart."

In short, Johnny Owen is a legitimate heir to the fighting traditions of South Wales and Merthyr Tydfil in particular. "This was a hard town in the days when the pits and the ironworks were booming," says Dick, himself a former miner. "It had 100,000 people, with Irish, Geordies, Spanish, Italians, and all sorts mixed in. Even the women were hard. They had to be. My grandmother had a job underground in the pit and my own mother handled a wheelbarrow in the Dowlais Ironworks."

The charm of Johnny is that he has inherited that toughness and kept his gentle side. His father again: "He's mine and maybe I shouldn't say this, but he *is* a lovely boy. He still washes the dishes and clears out the ashes to light the fire in the morning. Nothing changes with Johnny." Even the Spaniards may find it difficult to complain if he changes things just a little by taking that title next Saturday.

Johnny Owen's Last Fight

It can be no consolation to those in South Wales and in Los Angeles who are red-eyed with anxiety about Johnny Owen to know that the extreme depth of his own courage did as much as anything else to take him to the edge of death. This calamitous experience could only have happened to an exceptionally brave fighter because Lupe Pintor, the powerful Mexican who was defending his World Boxing Council bantamweight championship against Owen, had landed enough brutal punches before the twelfth and devastatingly conclusive round to break the nerve and resistance of an ordinary challenger. The young Welshman was, sadly, too extraordinary for his own good in the Olympic Auditorium.

Given the basic harshness of boxing as a way of earning a living, no one could blame Owen or his father or his manager, Dai Gardiner, for going after the biggest prize available to them, but some of us always felt that the right to challenge Pintor in Los Angeles was a questionable privilege. Making some notes about the background to the fight on Friday morning, I found myself writing: "Feel physical sickness at the thought of what might happen, the fear that this story might take us to a hospital room." This scribble was not meant to imply any severe criticism of a match which, on the basis of the relevant statistics, could not be condemned as outrageous. Indeed, the apprehension might have been illogically excessive to anyone who set Pintor's career figures of forty-one wins, seven losses, and a draw against the fact that Owen's one defeat had been a blatant case of larceny in Spain and the further, impressive fact that he had never been knocked off his feet as a professional boxer.

Yet it is the simple truth that for weeks a quiet terror had been gathering in me about this fight. Perhaps its principal basis was no more than a dread that the frailty that the boy's performances had hitherto dismissed as illusory would, some bad time in some bad place, prove to be terribly real. There is something about his pale face, with its large nose, jutting ears and uneven teeth, all set above that long, skeletal frame, that takes hold of the heart and makes unbearable the thought of him being badly hurt. And, to my mind, there was an ominous possibility that he would be badly hurt against Pintor, a Mexican who had already stopped thirty-three opponents and would be going to work in front of a screaming mob of his countrymen, whose lust for blood gives the grubby Olympic Auditorium the atmosphere of a Guadalajara cockfight, multiplied a hundred times.

No fighters in the world are more dedicated to the raw violence of the business than Mexicans. Pintor comes out of a gym in Mexico City where more than a hundred boxers work out regularly and others queue for a chance to show that what they can do in the alleys they can do in the ring. A man who rises to the top of such a seething concentration of hostility is likely to have little interest in points-scoring as a means of winning verdicts. So it was hard to share the noisy optimism of the hundred-odd Welsh supporters who made themselves conspicuous in the sweaty clamor of the hall and brought a few beer cups filled with urine down on their heads. But they seemed to be entitled to their high spirits in the early rounds as Owen carried the fight to Pintor, boring in on the shorter, dark-skinned champion and using his spidery arms to flail home light but aggravatingly persistent flurries of punches.

The first round was probably about even. Owen might have edged the second on a British scorecard and he certainly took the third, but already Pintor's right hooks and uppercuts were making occasional dramatic interventions, sending a nervous chill through the challenger's friends around the ring.

It was in the fourth round that Pintor's right hand first struck with a hint of the force that was to be so overwhelming subsequently, but this time it was thrown overarm and long and Owen weathered it readily enough. He was seen to be bleeding from the inside of his lower lip in the fifth (the injury may have been inflicted earlier) but, since both Pintor's eyebrows were receiving attention from his seconds by then, the bloodshed seemed to be reasonably shared. In fact the laceration in the mouth was serious and soon the challenger was swallowing blood. He was being caught with more shots to the head, too, but refused to be discouraged, and an American voice behind the press seats said incredulously: "I don't believe this guy."

Pintor was heaving for breath at the end of the fifth but in the sixth he mounted a surge, punished Owen, and began to take control of the contest. The official doctor, Bernhard Schwartz, checked the lip for the second time before the start of the seventh. Pintor dominated that one but Owen revived heroically in the eighth, which made the abrupt disaster of the ninth all the more painful.

Pintor smashed in damaging hooks early in the ninth but their threat appeared to have passed as the round moved to its close. Then, without a trace of warning, Pintor dropped a shattering right hook over Owen's bony left shoulder. The blow hurled him to the floor and it was here that his courage began to be a double-edged virtue. He rose after a couple of seconds, although clearly in a bad condition. There was a mandatory eight count but even at the end of it he was hopelessly vulnerable to more hooks to the head and it took the bell to save him.

By the tenth there was unmistakable evidence that the strength had drained out of every part of Owen's body except his heart. He was too tired and weak now to stay really close to Pintor, skin against skin, denying the puncher leverage. As that weariness gradually created a space between them, Pintor filled it with cruel, stiff-armed hooks. Every time Owen was hit solidly in the eleventh the thin body shuddered. We knew the end had to be near but could not foresee how awful it would be.

There were just forty seconds of the twelfth round left when the horror story started to take shape. Owen was trying to press in on Pintor near the ropes, failed to prevent that deadly space from developing again and was dropped on his knees by a short right. After rising at three and taking another mandatory count, he was moved by the action to the other side of the ring and it was there that a ferocious right hook threw him on to his back. He was unconscious before he hit the canvas and his relaxed neck muscles allowed his head to thud against the boards. Dai Gardiner and the boxer's father were in the ring long before the count could be completed and they were quickly joined by Dr. Schwartz, who called for oxygen. Perhaps the oxygen might have come rather more swiftly than it did but only if it had been on hand at the ringside. Obviously that would be a sensible precaution, just as it might be sensible to have a stretcher immediately available. It is no easy job to bring such equipment through the jostling mass of spectators at an arena like the Auditorium, where Pintor's supporters were mainly concerned about cheering its arrival as a symbol of how comprehensive their man's victory had been. The outward journey to the dressing room, with poor Johnny Owen deep in a sinister unconsciousness, was no simpler and the indifference of many among the crowd was emphasized when one of the stretcher bearers had his pocket picked.

There have been complaints in some quarters about the delay in providing an ambulance but, in the circumstances, these may be difficult to justify. Dr. Ferdie Pacheco, who was for years Muhammad Ali's doctor and is now a boxing consultant with NBC in the United States, insists that the company lay on an ambulance wherever they cover fights, but no such arrangements exist at the Auditorium and the experienced paramedics of the Los Angeles Fire Department made good time once they received the emergency call. Certainly it was grief and not blame that was occupying the sick boy's father as he stood weeping in the corridor of the California Hospital, a mile from the scene of the knockout. A few hours before, I had sat by the swimming pool at their motel in downtown Los Angeles and listened to them joke about the calls Johnny's mother had been making from Merthyr Tydfil on the telephone they had recently installed. The call that was made to Mrs. Owen from the waiting room of the California Hospital shortly before 7 A.M. Saturday, Merthyr time (11 P.M. Friday in Los Angeles) had a painfully different tone. It was made by Byron Board, a publican and close friend of the family, and he found her already in tears because she had heard that Johnny had been knocked out. The nightmare that had been threatening her for years had become reality.

She can scarcely avoid being bitter against boxing now and many who have not suffered such personal agony because of the hardest of sports will be asking once again if the game is worth the candle. Quite a few of us who have been involved with it most of our lives share the doubts. But our reactions are bound to be complicated by the knowledge that it was boxing that gave Johnny Owen his one positive means of self-expression. Outside the ring he was an inaudible and almost invisible personality. Inside, he became astonishingly positive and self-assured. He seemed to be more at home there than anywhere else. It is his tragedy that he found himself articulate in such a dangerous language.

(The doctors' struggle to rescue Johnny Owen from deep coma proved to be hopeless and he died in the first week of November 1980. His body was brought home to be buried in Merthyr Tydfil.)

Leonard Gardner

ROBERTO DURÁN AND THE WISE OLD MEN

As a child I had no doubt that Joe Louis was a greater man than Franklin D. Roosevelt, and in the tales I heard of great heroes, Corbett, Jeffries, Gans, Ketchel, and Dempsey ranked right along with Perseus and Daniel Boone. I put myself to sleep reciting the order of champions, and to the end of my father's life the subject of boxing kept the two of us from ever reaching that lonely gulf where child and parent no longer have anything of passionate interest to say to one another. My father's last words to me, in fact, an hour or two before his death, were, "Do you think Big Train Liston can win the title again?"—a confusion of two heavy-weights, Amos Lincoln and Sonny Liston, that was as definite an indication of his failing powers as any medical test could have provided. In his mid-seventies he had a speed bag in the attic he could still punch into a rhythmic blur, and in his early eighties he had his last fight, on State Street in Santa Barbara, with a panhandler who put his hand in my father's pocket. "I gave him the Fitzsimmons shift," my father said. His hands were badly bruised.

The shift was the arcane maneuver with which Bob Fitzsimmons had conquered Jim Corbett in 1897 and won the heavy-weight championship, and which had apparently become lost to the body of modern boxing technique. In my childhood we practiced it with the gloves on in the backyard, and my father, no longer a young man, executed it with confusing speed. He would feint at my head with his left, feint with his right, shoot his right foot in front of his left foot and let go a left hook he would pull up short at my solar plexus, reenacting a turning point in history.

The idea was to put the same weight of the body behind the left as you got behind the right, through a sudden shift to south-paw. Sometimes the punch wasn't pulled quite short enough, and I got a sense of how Corbett was undone by the gangly, baldheaded Fitz, who my father swore weighed only 157 pounds. It was a peculiar series of moves, that shift, and a little alarming when the whole works came swirling at you. But nobody I saw at that time used it, and I don't recall having seen a version of it until Roberto Durán came on the scene and tore through a decade of lightweights.

I first saw Durán in 1972, on television, when he won the lightweight title from Ken Buchanan with an electrifying attack. It was unfortunate that the bout ended after the thirteenth round, with Buchanan on the floor from a low blow. Buchanan was ruled unable to continue, and so Durán became champion.

It was a sour ending to the bout, but Buchanan had been overwhelmed from the opening bell and there was no doubt of Durán's superiority. He had fought as if possessed. Over the years Durán acquired finesse, but without losing any of that unrelenting aggressiveness that gave his fights such excitement. In his final defense of his lightweight title he showed fine ring skills, knocking out Esteban DeJesus in twelve rounds. Durán then retired as undisputed lightweight champion, in an era so overpopulated with WBA and WBC champions that the concept of a true world champion is eroding.

Durán had epitomized the old-fashioned hungry fighter, but with wealth he ate too well and his appetite cost him his title. He had to move up to the welterweights, and now he was getting a shot at a media hero and new champion, Sugar Ray Leonard. Leonard was a 9-to-5 favorite. The consensus, when the bout was announced, was that a lightweight's frame couldn't stay in there with a welterweight's frame, especially if the welterweight had the fastest hands in the business and could punch.

Before leaving for Montreal I called a friend who for many

years had contributed to the cultural stature of the city of Stockton, California, by matching the right Mexican with the right Filipino. We talked over the old argument that a good big man beats a good little man.

"What about Fitzsimmons?" he said.

In the restaurant of the Hotel Bonaventure, I was eating an early supper when Durán appeared. With him were his Panamanian bodyguards, some Panamanian friends, and one of his two elderly trainers, Freddie Brown, who is seventy-three and was smoking a cigar and looking disgusted. They were accompanied by a terrific din of Latin music out of Durán's tape deck, which was the size of a small suitcase. Trumpet blasts, voices, thumps, clacks, strums, ringings, and high-pitched whistles poured from the box at a volume close to that favored by campaign cars cruising neighborhoods before election day.

Durán put his tape deck on the table, sprawled in a chair, and began loudly beating time on the table. He was bearded, wore a T-shirt in praise of Panama, jeans, a white cap, and a pair of rainbow suspenders. His black eyes gazed vacantly, his head and shoulders rocked, and he appeared a captive of his own restless energy. He let out a few sharp cries, then took up a knife and spoon, beating them together even as the waitress took the orders. When he spoke his voice filled the room.

At the table next to mine a couple was speaking with raised voices.

"Why do they let people like that in here? Why don't they throw him out?"

"They must be some of Durán's crowd," the man said.

"That *is* Durán," I told him.

"Is *that* Durán? Is that really Durán?" he called back. "Then I've just decided who I'm pulling for. The other guy."

When Durán's steak arrived, Brown intercepted it and with a look of scorn dumped the french-fried potatoes onto his own plate. Durán cut the steak into large chunks which he held up on his fork and gnawed hastily. Within a very few minutes he had finished his meal and was walking out with his bodyguards and his music.

Out in the lobby, Durán was signing autographs with careful block printing, while Brown stood gazing into space, chewing his cigar. Slightly stooped, he wore red and gray checkered trousers high over a small paunch, and a multicolored sport coat with a zigzag pattern. Brown had worked with Marciano and many other champions, acquiring a degree of immortality as the cut man who closed the rip in Rocky's nose in his second bout with Ezzard Charles. Brown's own nose had been hammered flat. I had heard that fifty years ago he had considered plastic surgery, but then had decided to hell with it.

"Roberto sure looks up for this one," I said.

Brown kept gazing and chewing. "He hasn't been in this good a shape since the second DeJesus fight six years ago."

"Is that why he didn't work out today? Are you afraid of over-training him?"

"Overtrain?" he said, staring at me with utter exasperation. "How can you get overtrained? You're either in shape or you're not. What does overtrained mean? I never heard of such a thing. You got to work hard. If you don't you're not in shape to fight. This is the most talked about fight of all time." He relit his cigar. "Let me tell you something," he said. "There's a lot of tension in this fight. But it favors experience. Durán's been through all this before. But the tension's getting to Leonard. He's worried. Leonard didn't want this fight. The commission made him take it. He wanted to fight Cuevas."

This was a source of confidence for the Durán camp, which included Don King. King was copromoting the bout with his rival, Bob Arum, whom he has been known to call The Snake. Arum's headquarters were across the street in Le Régence Hyatt and he always managed to appear without King at press conferences, where he predicted record-breaking sums from the closed-circuit telecast. King had been trying to make the match for some time. Leonard had been ordered by the WBC to defend against Durán, the number one contender, or risk being stripped of his title. Negotiations began, instead, between Leonard and Pipino Cuevas, who holds the WBA version of the title. But Durán is such a national hero in Panama that the president himself is his friend, and so officials in the government of Panama, specifically Colonel

Rubén Paredes, a commander of the Panamanian national guard, interceded with the WBA, whose president, Rodrigo Sanchez, is Panamanian.

The result was that negotiations broke down between Cuevas and Leonard, who was then forced to sign with Durán. Arum claimed Leonard would gross $8 to $10 million. As the bout drew near he was calling it "the dream fight of the century." And Don King declared himself "ecstatic with delight."

"Dundee didn't want this fight," Brown said. "They did everything they could to avoid this fight."

Angelo Dundee, Leonard's manager, gave me his line on Durán in the bar at the top of the Hyatt. A singer was singing as he spoke. "Durán's a heel-to-toe guy," he said. "He takes two steps to get to you. So the idea is don't give him the two steps. Don't move too far away. The more distance you give Durán, the more effective he is. What you don't do against aggression is run from it, because then he picks up momentum. My guy won't run from him.

"Durán waves at you with his hand. He gives you movement of his body, slipping from side to side. He won't come straight in. He'll try to feint you. He misses you with an overhand right. He turns southpaw, comes back with a left hook to the body. My guy's going to be moving side to side. And he's going to go to the body. Nobody ever hit Durán in his weak spot." Dundee poked his fingers under his ribs. "He doesn't do his homework on the table. He's soft. Leonard's the puncher in this fight. I think Leonard's going to knock him out in ten or eleven rounds. Because Durán hasn't destroyed anybody as a welterweight. The reason being that he's hitting on bigger guys and the bigger guys are able to absorb it more than the little guys. He was devastating as a lightweight, but he never was one of those one-punch knockerouters. He was a grinder. Ray's going to nail him. Ray's going to stop him in his tracks with the jab. Leonard's got so much talent they haven't seen it yet."

Dundee, who has the manner and appearance of a gentle professor, didn't like the singer's moves. He pointed out her whole repertoire of mechanical gestures. He liked her songs well enough to sing a few lines himself, but he particularly disliked the way she kept handling her hair. As we rode down to the lobby, Dundee went into a reflective mood often observed in elevators. "I got the greatest respect for Durán," he said. "I've known him for years. I talk Spanish with him and I know what kind of a guy he is. He's a sweetheart and he's a great fighter. I don't take anything away from him. He's great at what he does, but he's a heel-toe guy."

Both Durán and Leonard worked out at a hockey arena converted to a gym. Leonard boxed brilliantly, hitting on the move, slipping punches and countering with combinations that seemed to flow from him effortlessly. Once he knocked down a sparring partner so picturesquely that the young man, from Leonard's hometown boxing club, got up with what seemed a smile of aesthetic appreciation. At intervals, while Leonard skipped rope, a trainer would mop his sweat from the floor with a towel. Sweating in the dressing room, he talked with newsmen, some of his statements sounding rehearsed, with an eye toward boosting the gate. At the close of the session he took up a newspaper and looked it over while an aide knelt and removed his boxing shoes.

Durán held few press conferences, and his dressing room was filled with noisy friends from Panama. He was indeed a heel-toe man, but he got around the ring quickly, occasionally sending a sparring partner reeling from a right hand thrown with an authority and form that stirred memories of great right-hand punchers of the past. He tugged and hauled, bulled his man into the ropes, and swung viciously to the body. He clowned, beating the speed bag with his head, skipping rope like a drunk, then leaping high, then hopping while in a squat, whirling the rope flamboyantly. And all through the workout, in the ring and on the bag and rope, he emitted strange shrill cries. They were not snorts and grunts many boxers make when punching. They were oohs and aahs, wailed in a sharp, high-pitched staccato, like cries of birds, and seemed to strike an emphasis, set a rhythm or express exuberance. He was an appealing eccentric.

Three days before the fight Durán shadowboxed two ten-minute rounds, and energy poured from him. Joyously he prowled the ring, swaying and bobbing. He squatted, leaped high, and turned. He punched the ropes, the corner pads, circled the ring and, like a child or a cat, tapped the hands of the men grasping the ropes. Brown leaned on the top strand, trying to smile as punches shot past his face. Weaving and punching, emitting his cries and shrieks, exchanging insults with his friends in the bleachers, Durán seemed possessed by the wild joy of his own vitality. After nine weeks of training, the nearness of the fight seemed to fill him with happiness. He ducked through the ropes, and just as he was about to jump to the floor, his eighty-one-year-old co-trainer, Ray Arcel, stepped quickly over and reached up and lifted him down from the ring.

"He gets so excited he doesn't know what he's doing," said Arcel. "I had a fighter jump out of the ring once and he hurt his leg and couldn't fight."

I remembered Arcel from my childhood, when he handled a long procession of Louis's victims.

Back in the lobby of the Hotel Bonaventure I found Arcel relaxing in a chair. His eyes are dark and impenetrable, his mouth set, his prominent nose well-shaped despite fights in New York streets and rings that preceded his career as a trainer. He wore a dark tie, a striped shirt, and a navy blue sport coat, and had the stern, dignified appearance of a retired judge. He had trained Ross, Braddock, Zale, and more than a dozen other champions, and had been in Charles's corner the night he sliced up Marciano's nose. But Benny Leonard was the gem of all his fighters. He had worked with Leonard in 1931 and 1932 when the stock market crash forced the great lightweight champion out of retirement.

I asked his opinion of the new Leonard.

"We'll find out what this guy has to offer in the first round," Arcel said. "Leonard's a master craftsman. I don't underestimate him, but I'm going to find out early how much stamina he has. I want to see if he can take a body beating and stand up for the first six or seven rounds. He looks good but who's he fought? Durán was in against good opposition in the lightweights. Guys like Buchanan and Lampkin and DeJesus were good boxers. That guy Bizzarro was like a deer. But could they keep it up for fifteen rounds?

"The only reason Durán was ineffective as a welterweight was because he wasn't in condition. The fights meant nothing to him, except Palomino. He could still be a lightweight. He won't listen. A fighter's got to have some kind of self-control. He can't just eat every kind of crap. He's like a kid. He didn't have to be a welterweight but now that he is, he's still good enough to beat everybody. He's strong enough to handle the bigger men."

"Mickey Walker did it," I said. "He even beat heavyweights."

"Mickey Walker was a drunk," said Arcel. "Jack Kearns made a drunk out of him. Tunney was a terrible drunk, too, after he retired. Disgusting. Liquor is a terrible thing. Did you know it was Benny Leonard who taught Tunney how to beat Greb? I was right there in the gym and I saw what he showed him. Leonard was a great student of boxing. He could do it all."

"I've wondered about the no-decision bouts in those days," I said. "You take a look at Benny Leonard's record and he's got a lot of knockouts in the important bouts but a lot of the no-decision bouts went the limit. Did they go all out in those no-decision bouts or did they have an understanding to go easy?"

In an instant Arcel came out of his chair and was facing me, his eyes combative.

"The fighter never lived that Benny Leonard would have to ask to go easy on him!"

"I didn't mean it that way," I said. "I meant did *he* go easy on *them*?"

"He *had* to go easy! He couldn't get anybody to fight him if he didn't agree to carry them."

In the men's room of the Hotel Bonaventure, sports pages with the daily fight news in English and French were tacked on a bulletin board above the urinals. Panamanians crowded the lobby. When Durán passed through they went along with him and sometimes Arcel had to shove them away. "If you love this guy so much, leave him alone!" he yelled.

Arcel and Brown were upset. Carlos Padilla had been named referee by Jose Sulaiman, president of the WBC, who was staying across the street in Leonard's hotel. Padilla had been the referee who stopped Wilfred Benitez with six seconds to go when he lost the championship to Sugar Ray Leonard. More recently, he had worked the first Antuofermo-Minter middleweight title bout.

"He breaks you before you get in there," complained Arcel. "Remember what he did to Antuofermo? He prevented a man from defending his title successfully. Then what recourse do you have? You lose a fight, then two days later it's all forgotten. I want a referee in there that'll let my fighter fight, that's all."

To a tremendous roar, Durán came up the steps and through the ropes. As he moved restlessly around the ring he appeared loose and confident and charged with a predatory intensity. The rain that had fallen during the preliminaries had stopped now, but many of the ringside spectators still sat encased in the black plastic rubbish bags distributed by the Olympic Stadium staff.

Although the ring was under a canopy, wet spots showed along the apron of the blue canvas. Holding the ropes, Durán worked his feet in the resin box and Brown and Arcel had a moment to speak to Padilla before the roar came up again and Leonard approached the ring, surrounded by a large entourage of friends and his cornermen—Dundee and the two trainers who have been with him since his first amateur fights, Dave Jacobs and Janks Morton.

The instructions took place without delay. The seconds ducked out through the ropes and the fighters stood facing one another across the ring. When the two came out at the bell, Durán looked short by comparison, with short, powerful legs and the thick neck that helps a fighter absorb the force of blows to the head. As he advanced on Leonard, feinting with his head and shoulders, his disadvantage in reach was evident. Yet he stepped in almost immediately to hit Leonard solidly to the head with his right and left. Standing flat-footed, both men landed hard jabs. Then Durán attacked with a rush, driving Leonard to the ropes, where he hit him some terrible blows to the body and established what was to be the pattern of the fight.

Leonard fought back and when he had punching room, drove in his jab. But Durán was fighting with the fierceness of a man whose whole being willed one thing. He swarmed over Leonard with startling violence. When his right missed he banged in with his head and he kept Leonard on the ropes with the fury of his attack. When Leonard covered up, arms tied against his body and gloves shielding his face, Durán beat on his arms as if in a frenzy to take something out of him, some resilience or sense of control, and in that first round he took some of his strength, too. He landed a hook to the liver that might've put another fighter on the canvas in a knot of pain.

Through the first five rounds Durán overpowered him. With quick and unpredictable moves he hit hard at long range. In close, he grabbed and mauled, chopping hooks to Leonard's ribs and head, grappling and hitting, while Leonard covered and fought back in flurries. But Leonard was taking heavy punishment. His jab, so quick and accurate in other bouts, seemed to have deserted him. Often, at long range, he stood flat-footed as Durán stalked him, and he hesitated until Durán led and was swarming over him again, and then he would open up and trade with him, but this was Durán's kind of fight and he excelled at it.

Arcel and Brown had no more worries about Padilla. He stood back and let the battle rage in the clinches. Sometimes, instead of separating the two, Padilla would simply slap away a grasping hand, allowing the infighting to go on. When he did push them apart, Leonard would move toward him, putting him in the line of Durán's charge and gaining a moment of respite. Durán came in without fear of Leonard's power, and took what he had to take, but his feints were deceptive and he was ducking and slipping and rolling with punches. He had moves Leonard was unable to solve. Again and again Leonard's back was against the ropes. He seemed unable to slip and sidestep as he had against the twenty-seven professionals he had fought previously. Durán, with the experience of seventy-one bouts, was showing him the roughest secrets of the trade.

Leonard proved to have extraordinary durability and gameness in those rounds. There were times when I doubted he could survive them. In the middle rounds Leonard began to come back. He fought head to head with Durán, slamming him with hard combinations that had no apparent effect. Durán kept coming. Between rounds, Dundee, his face grave, was shouting at Leonard to move and box, but Leonard went on slugging as if unable to move.

It became a contest of fighting heart, and resulted in exchange after fierce exchange, a slugfest between two men with great speed and punching skills. Leonard was hurt on the ropes in the eleventh, a round of bitter trading, and in the thirteenth his knees were buckled by a left hook. Still he fought back, taking lefts and rights on the jaw and coming back with hard, quick flurries in a round of almost constant exchanges. With disregard of danger, their bodies steaming in the misty, humid air, both fighters traded punches in the fastest and most stubbornly fought round of the fight. Drawing on the depths of his stamina, Leonard finished strong enough to win the last two rounds. In the final seconds, Durán dropped his arms and stuck out his chin in a taunt that may have come from frustration over the unyielding toughness he had encountered in Leonard.

The fight was Durán's, although the judges made it close. One scored ten rounds even. With that kind of judging, there seemed the possibility of a draw, but the voting, after a correction in addition, was unanimous: 145–144, 148–147, 146–144. Durán had taken the title, but both men had fought with such fire that the fight would rank with the great ones.

The ring filled with excited fans and security guards. Several fights broke out and it appeared Durán was scuffling with somebody, too. His interpreter, Luis Henriquez, was squared off with Wilfred Benitez, the former champion, who was asked by Howard Cosell to comment on the fight, and had abandoned his post to yell insults at Durán. A security guard picked him up and was about to throw him over the ropes into the press section when I convinced him that Wilfred was a valuable commodity.

Afterward, in the press room, a jubilant Durán, his chest bare, was asked what had made the difference for him, and he placed his hand over his heart.

His heart indeed had been indomitable. However, there was enough controversy in the press room to ensure that the lawyers and promoters would be talking about a rematch. Dundee was displeased with the refereeing. He called the fight a wrestling match. There were debates over why Leonard had slugged and not boxed. The opinion was offered that he had chosen the wrong strategy. But I believed what I had seen—a good man giving his best while outfought. By pressuring him, crowding him and hurting him, Durán had taken away Leonard's advantages.

At three o'clock that morning, Arcel was leaving the hotel with Carlos Eleta, Durán's manager, and other friends to look for an all-night restaurant, and I walked along with them. We talked about the fight, and I asked Arcel if he was satisfied with the refereeing.

"Yes, I thought Padilla did a good job," he said. "Freddie and I had a talk with him. I told him the whole world was watching. This was the fight everybody wanted to see, and he should let the fighters fight."

Someone asked if Durán was the greatest fighter he had ever trained. For a while Arcel didn't answer, as if unwilling to compromise his devotion to the legendary Benny Leonard, whom he considered the greatest he had ever seen. But then the past seemed to give up its hold on him. He was tired, and he told me that Benny Leonard was all used up by the time he had worked with him. At last, Arcel said, "Yes," and a moment later added, "Durán is the best fighter in the world."

John Schulian

ON ROBERTO DURÁN

Montreal, June 15, 1980

The legend does not serve Roberto Durán well. He has soared to the heavens of boxing, a sport in which simply escaping the gutter is an accomplishment, but the spotlight has done little beside capture his shadow. To people who should know better, Durán has remained a runty Panamanian savage who can drop a horse with one punch and has suffered loss after loss to the English language. And no doubt he would have gone to his athletic dotage neglected and misunderstood were he not where he is now, blinking in the reflected glory of Sugar Ray Leonard.

It shouldn't be like this, of course, this stealing into the public consciousness because a fighter five years his junior, with less than half his experience, deigns to give him a shot at the World Boxing Council's welterweight championship. Life isn't always fair, though, and the fight racket never is. So Durán must squirm indignantly while Leonard, headed back to Montreal, the scene of his Olympic triumphs, plays the lord of the manor.

Most of the time, the Sugar Man handles the role with consummate grace and intelligence, but every now and then the temptation to gloat and preen becomes too much to resist. Witness his act in New York at the press conference announcing the fight that will earn him $10 million and Duran $2 million.

Durán-Leonard, Montreal, 1980

He stood tall on the dais and glared down at the opponent everyone in the room expected him to respect grudgingly.

"I want to kill you," Leonard said.

Durán did not need a translation.

Even now, two months later, with the fight just five days away, he bristles at the thought of such insolence, such macho posturing. There is no calming him with Leonard's innocent plea that he was only trying to speak the little assassin's language. Indeed, there is nothing to do but flinch at the thought of vengeance those ill-chosen words have aroused.

"If he wants to kill me" Durán says, "he has to stand up and fight."

A cold smile twists Durán's face into a death's-head. It is the same smile so many of his victims have seen before he sent them reeling to the canvas, jaws unhinged, senses unraveled.

"How in hell is Leonard going to stand up and fight?"

Now Durán's eyes dance crazily.

"He'll be running once he feels my punch."

It is not for nothing, after all, that Roberto Durán is called Manos de Piedra. He has just what his nickname says he does— hands of stone—and if you doubt it, you need only think of the damage he has done while winning sixty-nine of seventy fights and knocking out fifty-five targets. "If the foundation crumbles," says the man in charge of demolition, "the building will come down." Lord, how he loves that sight, loves to break his opponents into small pieces and dance on the rubble.

When the once great Carlos Palomino fell before him, he sneered, "Quit. You don't got it no more." When Ray Lampkin got carted off to the hospital, the victor shouted that next he would get in shape and, yes, "kill him." Heartless cruelty, perhaps, but in the Panama City slum where Roberto Durán grew to manhood, heartless cruelty was an impregnable defense against street-corner extinction.

He was a fighter from the start. Fighting went with carving out the turf where he shined shoes, peddled mangoes, and danced in saloons. He played the drums, too, and maybe he would have been the star of his high school band if he had survived that long in academia. But the third grade was it, and his hair-trigger right hand—what else?—was his undoing. He was thirteen years old.

Two years later, he stepped into the ring as a professional for the first time with a jockey as his manager and a zest for violence as his foremost weapon. The jockey soon vanished, selling Durán's contract to a millionaire sportsman named Carlos Eleta for the magnificent sum of $300. The zest for violence remained, waiting for Durán to put together his two-fisted attack and flee Panama for Madison Square Garden. When he finally arrived there, in December of 1971, the crowd belittled him as a skinny fraud until he knocked Benny Huertas still as death for six minutes. From that night on, people began to understand what Durán's hands were made of.

The stone in them destroyed everyone blocking his way, made him the lightweight champion of the world, turned him into his native land's tax-exempt hero. But in the United States, where the money was, the coast-to-coast infatuation with heavyweights proved too much to overcome. "Small guys can't raise any hell,"

Muhammad Ali said. It was poppycock until Durán ballooned into the welterweight division and became the butt of cruel jokes and insidious whispers. Since then, his knockout punch has disappeared and, at times, so has his enthusiasm.

"When you're fighting smear cases and you're the best fighter around," says Ray Arcel, the mouthpiece for Durán's braintrust, "it's hard to be interested."

Now that has changed. At twenty-nine, with the end rapidly closing in on him, Durán finds himself faced with a challenge so all-consuming that he doesn't care whether he steps into the ring as a 2-to-1 underdog or whether he takes home only one-fifth as much loot as Leonard. "I no happy for the money," Durán says. "I happy for the fight." Happy because this is his one real chance to wear another crown, to prove his greatness and to win the love he has been denied throughout his career.

On the surface, the need for love would seem totally foreign to Durán, and yet to see him being honored as one of the two Fighters of the Decade was to see the thing that could get him past Leonard. Never once did he fret that the New York boxing writers were abusing propriety by calling him Ali's equal. He had chills running down his spine, and he let it be known. "I speak English because I am learning from my teacher," he said. "I am glad to be here. I thank you very much for this award." For just a moment, those crazy eyes of his were calm and the room was quiet. For just a moment, you could tell what Roberto Durán will have on his side Friday night. Emotion.

Montreal, June 22, 1980

He was in bed now, his phone silenced by growls to the hotel operator and the hallway outside his room patroled by Panama's answer to the Prussian Guard. The well-wishers who were turned away nodded knowingly, their smiles saying that after a night of fighting and partying, even the strongest of men—even this champion—would have to sleep the sleep of the dead.

What none of them realized was that after he threw his last punch and before he set foot on the dance floor, Roberto Durán cried himself a river.

The tears streamed down his cheeks and into his scruffy beard. They came in rivulets that could not be stopped in the dressing room or in the limo carrying him to the celebration. They came and came and came, and it was not just because Durán had unhorsed Sugar Ray Leonard and been crowned king of the World Boxing Council's welterweights. It was also because he had defeated the demons he couldn't see.

"So much trouble, so much trouble," Luis Henriquez said in a hoarse whisper, and shook his head slowly, as if there were weights attached to it.

This was Saturday morning and Luis Henriquez, honorary Panamanian vice consul and friend of Roberto Durán, nevertheless managed to look impervious to suffering. He was leaning against a lushly papered wall in the Bonaventure Hotel, wearing a sport coat made of raw silk and flashing enough gold jewelry to finance an emerging nation. The only thing that didn't jibe with the rest of him was his line of conversation.

"Did you hear what that television announcer say about Roberto?" he asked. "Even after Roberto win, the announcer is saying he look like a villain and that he was a thief and all that bull. Listen, my friend, in the ghetto in Panama, all of us had to steal to eat."

If those days had a virtue, it was that the poor woke up every morning knowing they weren't going to get a break. After two weeks in Montreal, Henriquez wonders if breaks weren't just as hard to come by for an underdog in a championship fight, even if he was going to earn $2 million.

The underpinning for such skepticism is the five trips Durán was forced to take to the hospital and the three electrocardiogram tests to which he was subjected. "What was that all about?" Henriquez said. "They say Roberto has an irregular heartbeat? Fine. Check it out. But why again and again?" A sad smile. "They only make Leonard go once and then it was to another hospital. How do we know he even go?" That was the maddening, almost paranoid question that drove them into a memorable rage.

Durán's boiling juices were the easiest to spot, of course. The first punch he let fly Friday night caught Leonard squarely on the protective cup, and from that point on, good manners were past tense. "My guy's got lumps all over the joint," said Angelo Dundee, the sweetest thinker in Sugar Ray's corner. Durán hit Leonard with head, fists, and, it is rumored, knees. And the reason he got away with it is that Freddie Brown was equally teed off about the shabby treatment Durán was getting.

"You ever see Freddie happy about anything?" Dundee asked. He had a point there. The three greatest joys in the seventy-four-year-old Brown's life appear to be molding fighters, chewing on cigars, and griping constantly. Next to eighty-one-year-old Ray Arcel, Durán's other trainer and a picture of pugilistic courtliness, Brown comes on like the wrath of God. "You think that ain't for a purpose?" said Dundee. "Hey, those two guys been around. They're as old as water."

No wonder referee Carlos Padilla didn't dare say anything when Brown accosted him in the ring before the fight. Padilla obviously respects his elders, even if they are shouting and waving fingers under his nose. "I seen the guy work before," Brown said. "He wouldn't let my fighter work inside and it cost him the fight. So this time I was straightening him out ahead of time. You know, tellin' him there'd be a Senate investigation if he didn't let these guys fight."

"Did you get what you wanted?" someone asked.

"No. Hell, no," said Brown. "Every time the ref broke 'em up, he pulled Durán away and held him while that damned Leonard sneaked a couple punches in."

Do not get the impression, however, that Sugar Ray overflowed with fistic inspiration. If anything, he waged the most chuckle-headed war of his career. He is an artist at sticking and moving, at attacking from one angle and then another, and yet he was bound and determined to go toe-to-toe with Durán. "Ray got all macho," Dundee said. "He thought he could beat the little mother at his own game." Obviously he was dreaming.

Oh, the three WBC judges scoring the fight did their utmost to keep Leonard in the hunt. Ignoring how cowardly it is to call a round even while using the ten-point-must system, one judge copped out ten times while the other two followed suit a total of nine times. Yet even that couldn't keep Durán from the unanimous decision that moved him to tears and shoved him to the kind of prominence he never had when he was the lightweight champion.

Suddenly, after fourteen years of knocking around the world's rings, he is a hot commodity among the welters. After giving up the battle to keep his weight down two years ago, he has advanced to boxing's new glamour division—a division that features Pipino Cuevas and Thomas Hearns as well as Leonard—and if the WBC won't pay him what he wants, then the World Boxing Association will. As Don King, the polysyllabic promoter, said Saturday: "Roberto will be happy to take on anyone in order to become a notch in the annals of immortality."

Please understand, though, that there are certain segments of society in which Durán's name already has been bronzed and put in the trophy case. In New York, the little drummer boy is very big at Latin music festivals. And at home in Panama, he is the reason for a holiday that began Friday and will run through Monday. Soon Durán will be there himself, dancing all night, eating what he pleases, and washing it down with his beloved Coca-Cola. Soon he will be there reveling in the fruits of his sacrifices, with no more sacrifices to make for the time being. Just let him sleep a while longer before he goes.

Chicago, January 27, 1982

Good times never last long enough and bad ones always last too long. Barbershop philosophers can explain the phenomenon in a minute, but Roberto Durán gives the impression that he doesn't hang around barbershops. He has a head of inky black hair that he combs straight back, hair so wild and shaggy that it must be modeled after his pet lion's mane. The ragged pompadour suggests a man in a hurry, and Durán certainly was that until he got trapped by a moment's indiscretion.

Just a moment, nothing more. Oh, he may have thought about quitting earlier in the fight that rewrote his life. Sugar Ray Leonard was carving the macho right out of him that November night in 1980, hitting him at will and making him swing wildly and laughing with delight. Never in his fierce, crazy life had anyone done that to the urchin revered at home in Panama as Hands of

Stone. But when Durán finally did something about it, when he decided that two minutes and forty-four seconds of the eighth round was as long as he could stand to be humiliated, the good times stopped and the bad ones began.

He meekly waved his right fist and uttered the words that haunt him still: "*No más!* No more!" They echoed through the funky streets outside the Louisiana Superdome and on into boxing's infamous history. True, Durán has argued ever since that he was done in by stomach cramps, not cowardice. But it doesn't matter. He failed himself and his image when the world was watching, and in that fleeting instant, the good he had done for a far longer time in a far lesser light was rendered inconsequential.

Suddenly, he was the fight racket's answer to Roy Riegels, who ran the wrong way with a Rose Bowl fumble, and Tracy Stallard, who got nailed to the cross of Roger Maris's sixty-first home run, and Ralph Branca, who fed Bobby Thomson the gopher ball that cost the Dodgers a pennant. Durán had done something so memorably bad that its brevity didn't matter. And now it has lived so long and thrived so relentlessly that it seems he never did anything else.

How else can you judge your reaction to his assault on Wilfred Benitez's WBC junior middleweight championship? They will fight in Las Vegas Saturday night—age against youth, savagery against subtlety, scowl against smile, Panama against Puerto Rico—and the chemistry should be all you are thinking about. But it isn't, and Durán knows it, and everyone around him knows it. They can tell at a glance that you are thinking about his fall from grace, if you are thinking about him at all.

"A tremendous tragedy, a great tragedy," says Ray Arcel, his trainer. "I don't condemn him for what he did in New Orleans. But it was a tremendous tragedy."

In the fifteen months since then, there has been no place for the tale of how Durán was born to the slums of Panama City and how he shined shoes, caught fish, and fought off the thugs who tried to prey on him. Once, he was a success story fashioned by his fists, a street child whose incomparable punch made him the pet of Panama's president and its richest man. He flattened a horse with a straight right and almost killed the poor devil who opposed him in his Madison Square Garden debut. He was a pro at fifteen, the world's lightweight king at twenty-one, the world's welterweight champ at Leonard's expense. He was truly Hands of Stone and then, in the rematch he sneeringly granted Sugar Ray, he showed his public what it never suspected he had—a heart of mush.

Even Arcel, who guarded him paternally before that debacle and has returned to do so now, wept bitter tears in the long hours afterward. "Durán quit," the old man said, and the quaver in his voice fueled resentment. It was as if Durán had betrayed the people who thrilled at his rage, painted him as the embodiment of violence and bet their ranches on him. Now they were going to get him. They were going to make him pay for not being what they had imagined him to be. And most of them haven't let up yet.

The reaction is human enough—which of us has not dreamed of revenge of one kind or another?—but it fails to take into account that maybe Durán is human, too. He doesn't always show it, of course. Indeed, you can find him in Las Vegas sneering at reporters who ask him about the night he quit and why he thinks Leonard should give him another shot at the welterweight title. The studied surliness is vintage Durán, yet it may also mask the desperation that has come to mark his life.

At thirty-one, eight years Benitez's senior, his powers are slipping away faster than he discovered them. Though he snarls at the suggestion, surely he must know it is true. It has been happening since his insatiable appetite pushed him into the welters, a weight class where his knockout punch lost its authority and his reputation began to lose its lustre. Leonard drove the point home but, lest you forget, so did Zeferino Gonzalez before that and Nino Gonzalez and Luigi Minchillo afterward. Now the lethal Benitez awaits him with a dose of punishment, but no one begs Durán to turn back before it is too late, no one offers him the kindness that soothed Muhammad Ali and Joe Louis and so many other fallen champions.

In one sense, that may be only fair, for Durán never offered anyone mercy. Violence was his key to boxing's kingdom and so it shall also be his destruction. The violence he suffers, however, comes not just from the men he fights but from the public he betrayed on a night that should be nothing more than a line in the record book. For a moment, he forgot he was Roberto Durán and waved the white flag of surrender. He waved it until he realized his mistake, but by then there was no escape. His moment of shame would last him a lifetime.

John Schulian

Nowhere to Run

Chicago, April 1, 1979

It was a glorious place, the Del Prado Hotel was. If you listen closely, you can still hear the echoes of the young lovers and swaggering big leaguers who used to make its lobby so fresh, so vibrant. But to open your eyes in there is to see the other side of midnight. The furniture is cheap and frayed, and the old folks arrayed on it live with a fear dramatized by a sign taped to the front desk: SORRY, NO MONEY ON PREMISES—PLEASE PAY RENT BY CHECK OR MONEY ORDER. Yes, that is what has become of Hyde Park's leading hostelry, and the change is a hurting thing for everybody except the lost soul dozing in the corner, the one the fight crowd used to call Honey Boy.

He lives in a world that skirts reality, a world filled with panhandling buddies and visions of old movies, a world where no one can hurt him. Late at night, when he is alone in the lobby, alone with his jumbled thoughts, he will rise from the couch where he sleeps and slowly walk toward the full-length mirror. He will raise his fists and bend at the knees and, suddenly, he will be Johnny Bratton, welterweight champion, once again. Never mind that his hair is more gray than black or that he is an easy fifty pounds over his fighting prime. You can't take the past away from him.

He bobs and weaves, jabs, recalculates the old combinations—all in slow motion. How sad and yet how perfect for the setting. It is as if you aren't allowed in the front door of the woebegone Del Prado unless you, too, represent faded elegance.

Johnny Bratton showed up one evening last winter, in the middle of his one-way trip to nowhere. A chill ran through the lobby, for its elderly white denizens did not know how to deal with a black drifter who was caked with street grime and whose long silences were punctuated by bursts of unexpected laughter. There was no predicting that he would soon be running errands for new friends, receiving invitations to breakfast, or whistling at Patricia Bock, the hotel's salty manager, and getting away with it. Indeed, Patricia Bock had to be grabbed by the arm and shaken before she would stop looking down her nose at this uninvited guest.

"Don't you know who that is?" asked the man who runs the variety shop.

"No," she said.

"That's Johnny Bratton."

"So?"

"Do you remember Joe Louis?"

"Oh, he was my idol."

"Well, that man there was as famous as Joe Louis."

The point would have been exaggerated anywhere other than the South Side. But on the turf where Johnny Bratton discovered that he could be somebody, however briefly, it was the stone truth. So he found a roof to cover his head during the blizzard of '79 and, no matter how ragged he was, the Del Prado boasted its first celebrity since American League teams declared the neighborhood unsafe for their precious athletes. "The hotel doesn't look like the Astor anymore," Patricia Bock says now, "so why should anyone care?"

Johnny Bratton wasn't supposed to have to rely on charity, though. In the late forties and the early fifties, when he was fighting in Chicago Stadium and on TV, when it was all you could do to escape reading about him getting ready for a fight or winding down from one, he thought he had gone over the wall from hard times. He was a taxi driver's son, a DuSable High School dropout, but he wore zoot suits and gold cuff links and cruised the city in a Cadillac bearing the name "Honey Boy" and a Jaguar bearing the name "Johnny B." And the marvel of it was, the soft life didn't make him a pushover in the ring.

"I could do it all," he says, "but I had to do it under my conditions. You understand? My conditions."

He had a style that would have become a man trying to sneak into the house past his sleeping wife. It was capable of turning crowds venomous even when he was beating Charlie Fusari for the old National Boxing Association's welterweight title in 1951. Still, there was something about Johnny Bratton that endured longer than the memory of his caution. Perhaps it can best be described as courage.

He came to the fore when boxing moved at a relentless pace. A victory meant the loser got another fight, and if the loser won that one, there had to be a rubber match. Just look at Johnny Bratton's record. He fought the brutal Ike Williams three times. He battled Holly Mims twice within twenty-one days, with a lesser bout sandwiched in between. And nobody who witnessed his last chance to regain the championship, when Kid Gavilan carved him up for fifteen rounds, ever will forget his absolute refusal to retreat or surrender. Afterwards, he lay on his dressing room table unable to speak.

The problems Johnny Bratton had always were supposed to be physical—an impacted tooth that led to a fractured jaw or tiny hands that crumbled like potato chips. But what got him in the end was his mind.

He was not punchy.

He was mad.

"I started getting worse after my last fight," he says. "I got beat by Del Flanagan. The referee patted me on my back and told me I was through. I was twenty-six or twenty-seven. A couple years later, I went to the state hospital at Manteno. I had a private room. Do you think they were giving private rooms to psychopaths in 1954? I wasn't no psychopath. I even had my picture in the paper. Do you remember that? They had a picture of me looking out the window. I was in my room."

There were other rooms in other hospitals and, finally, Johnny

Bratton was allowed to step back onto the streets seventeen years ago. He has walked them ever since, refusing to settle at a halfway house or with an older brother. There is always a letter from Hitler or a covered wagon surrounded by Indians to distract him, to let him know he must keep moving. "You don't understand, do you?" he says, and looks for a bus that will carry him to safety. If he is lucky, it will pass a movie theater and he can hop off and take refuge there. Movies give him something to cling to, something he can't seem to find anywhere else.

"That fella next to you kinda looks like Paul Muni, don't he?" Johnny Bratton says. "I seen Paul Muni in a lot of pictures. Him and Errol Flynn. I don't think Errol Flynn ever made a bad picture. But he got in trouble, right? Him and all his women. Me, what I think you got to do is live a good reputation, like James Cagney. Yessir, the Yankee Doodle Dandy hisself."

On Rush Street, that mecca of clip joints and cut-rate love, they say they have never seen anyone who knew as much about movies as Johnny Bratton. Sooner or later, he makes it up there every day to win his daily bread—and drink—with his vast knowledge. And if that fails, there is always out-and-out panhandling. "He can put the arm on you pretty good," says one old fight guy. "I figure it's good for a sawbuck if he sees me." To be sure, Johnny Bratton is always looking, always moving. He pauses only to gaze at his reflection in the windows of a disco.

What he sees is a slightly stooped figure cloaked in a dirty overcoat; rising up out of the coat's collar is a face on which scar tissue and a goatee fight for prominence. What he sees is what the conventioneers and the swinging singles don't always want to see. The pattern is never altered: a handout here, a turndown there, and don't scare any well-dressed women. He can get by that way, Johnny Bratton can. He won't get rich, but another day will be done and he will have bus fare back to Hyde Park, back to the Del Prado.

The septuagenarians who live there worry about him on those nights when he doesn't show up, and he seems to sense it, even enjoy it. But just as he is getting comfortable, perhaps for the first time in a long time, some hotshot outfit is pumping $4.5

million into the Del Prado to gussy it up again. When the old furniture goes, Johnny Bratton will have to go, too. You can say time is running out on him if you like, but of course that really started long, long ago.

Bill Barich

NEVER SAY NEVER

Ray Mancini's Last Fight

On a cold winter morning in Youngstown, Ohio, Ray "Boom Boom" Mancini, who had once been the lightweight champion of the World Boxing Association, said good-bye to his mother and father and left home for Nevada to begin training for the most important fight of his career. His final training camp was at the El Dorado Hotel, in downtown Reno, and when he arrived he found large cardboard cutouts of himself propped against slot machines in the casino. There were banners that said "Welcome, Boom Boom!" and "The El Dorado Welcomes Ray Mancini!" and several gamblers in polyester gathered around to wish him luck. Mancini was used to such treatment. In boxing circles, he had always been a big star, and he knew how to smile and make small talk, and also how to accept a handshake without doing any damage to the instruments that had helped him to earn almost six million dollars in purse money.

Mancini had an executive suite of rooms in the El Dorado, closed off from public view. Like most veteran boxers, he despised the discipline and routine of getting into shape, so he was glad to be meeting a boxer for whom he had genuine dislike—Livingstone Bramble, a complex and worldly wise Rastafarian from the Virgin Islands. Bramble had taken Mancini's title away in Buffalo, New York, in June of 1984. Mancini had not been himself that night. He'd felt sick and out of sorts, as if he were coming down with the flu. He thought that Bramble had proved to be an unworthy champion. This had less to do with Bramble's talent than with his comportment. He had insulted the Mancini family and had done stupid things, like messing around with voodoo and boxing with a chicken. These antics had grated against Mancini's own love of the fight game, his respect for its rituals and institutions, and had increased his desire for revenge.

He did his roadwork in the high desert country, running along paths that skirted the base of snowcapped mountains. He skipped rope, tossed around a medicine ball, and kept tabs on his weight. Almost every afternoon, he sparred with his sparring partners in a full-sized ring at the El Dorado. He was a compactly built man, thickly muscled. He had a broken nose and a scarred face, but he still dreamed of becoming an actor someday. Among his friends he counted Playboy bunnies and movie stars. He knew Mickey Rourke and Sly Stallone. He knew Frankie Avalon well, and Avalon had told him that whenever you do a film you leave a chunk of your life behind. That made sense to Mancini. He was twenty-three years old, and his brief and sometimes tragic time in the ring was drawing to a close.

Mancini started his career as a pro by fighting in and around Youngstown. He told local reporters that he was dedicating himself to winning a lightweight title in honor of his father, Lenny, the original Boom Boom, who had been a contender himself until he was wounded on a French battlefield during the Second World War. This made for good copy, and Mancini soon picked up a canny, ambitious manager, David Wolf, a former sportswriter who knew the value of a property. With Wolf guiding him, steering him away from potentially dangerous opponents, Mancini followed a cautious path to the top, and in May 1982, after a vicious loss to Alexis Arguello, he beat a shopworn fighter, Arturo Frias, to become the WBA champ.

Mancini was still handsome and relatively unmarked when he knocked out Frias, and his good-natured personality had made him very popular with fans. He was white, Italian, and eminently marketable. The television networks loved him because he had crossover appeal and attracted both men and women. Mancini had never been a stylish boxer; there was little art to his hooks or jabs. He had won twenty-three of his twenty-four pro bouts simply by giving better than he got, by being more courageous and intense than his opponents. The only drawback to his flailing approach was that it had cost him dearly. In swarming over other fighters, he'd left himself open to blows, and he'd been hit more often, and with better shots, than less aggressive men.

He had his first title defense in November 1983 against the South Korean boxer Deuk Koo Kim, in a match that CBS televised. There were more qualified fighters around, but Mancini was kept clear of them. Deuk Koo Kim was a mystery man. Though the WBA ranked him first in the lightweight division, he had never fought in the United States, and he spoke no English. Apparently he saw himself as a warrior going into battle, defending the flag of his nation. On a lampshade in his motel room he scrawled "Kill or be killed." In the ring, he turned out to be a fierce but unskilled brawler, and he lasted through thirteen brutal rounds before Mancini dropped him. Deuk Koo Kim did not get up again, nor did he ever regain consciousness. He died in a Las Vegas hospital of a cerebral hemorrhage, and his mother donated his vital organs to science. A month later, she killed herself by drinking poison.

In boxing, there is an ample history of accidental death, but Mancini is a sensitive man, and the fight left him devastated. A devout Catholic, he spent months consulting his family and his parish priest before deciding to go on. He acquitted himself fairly well in four subsequent bouts, including a promotion held in Italy, but then he came up against Livingstone Bramble, who—unlike Mancini—had risen through the ranks without a management team to help him. Mancini was a heavy favorite to win the fight, but Bramble surprised him. He is a wicked counterpuncher, and he sliced through Mancini's attack and took him apart. Mancini bled so badly from cuts around his eyes that the bout had to be stopped in the fourteenth round. He spent the night in a Buffalo hospital, under observation. He had lacerations in both eyelids. One took eight stitches to close; the other took six.

Mancini had received such a beating that boxing insiders were concerned about his health. Bob Arum, a promoter who had worked with him, stated publicly that Ray should retire, and some other people agreed. Mancini was rich and famous, and since he had achieved his goal, he had no real reason to go on. He just wasn't giving as good as he got anymore. Home Box Office had done a computer analysis of the Bramble fight that showed that Mancini had thrown an amazing fourteen hundred and eight punches— more than a hundred per round. But he had landed only three hundred and thirty-eight, or 24 percent. Bramble had landed 53 percent of his punches. In spite of such evidence, Mancini pushed for a rematch. The truth was that he didn't like being a loser. Already his market value had begun to decline. A publishing company had shelved his autobiography, and a magazine had canceled its plans for a feature.

The idea of a rematch was fine with Bramble and his manager, Lou Duva. Mancini still had drawing power, and he would ensure that the fight would be sold to television. (Without the money and legitimacy that television grants, boxing would not survive as a major sport.) Bramble, on his own, held no interest for the networks. He had no fans, except among reggae lovers and people from the islands, and advertisers would find it hard to be enthusiastic about a worshipper of Haile Selassie who wore his hair in dreadlocks and spoke of himself as one of the world's oppressed. Also, Bramble's boxing style was too subtle for the medium. He was a defensive fighter, calculating and intelligent, and he seldom got into trouble. In order to appreciate him, a viewer had to understand boxing as a sport, not spectacle. On the other hand, Mancini worked in broad strokes. Action was his métier, and his walloping delivery was perfect for an audience that was used to watching car crashes and cops chasing junkies through the streets of Miami.

Once Mancini had announced his intention, he had to be accommodated in certain ways. According to a WBA rule, a rematch cannot be sanctioned unless each boxer has fought somebody else in the interim—this prevents a boxer from taking a dive in exchange for a guaranteed rematch. Bramble had fought Edwin Curet; the rule was waived for Mancini. In the WBA rankings, Mancini was only third, so Tyrone Crawley, the number one contender, had to be paid off to step aside. Crawley got $150,000 and a contract to fight the winner. To resolve questions about Mancini's condition, Dave Wolf mailed around a packet of letters from private physicians that described the positive results of many tests. In the summer of 1984, Mancini had a CAT scan, and Dr. Jeffrey Schwartz, a Manhattan orthopedic surgeon who was Mancini's chief medical adviser, found no subtle changes or irregularities in his brain tissue.

But Dr. Schwartz was concerned about the delicate skin around Mancini's eyes. It had become a constant problem. The skin was so tender that Mancini suffered subcutaneous cuts whenever he did any sparring; then, by the time an actual fight rolled around, the cuts were primed to burst to the surface, as they had done in Buffalo. Dr. Schwartz advised Mancini to wear a protective mask while he was training, but Mancini was reluctant to do so, fearing that his fans and the media would see it as a sign of weakness.

A WBA site-selection committee chose Reno for the fight. More and more championships are being held in Nevada because casino owners are willing to contribute toward the lavish site-selection fees that the WBA demands. Reno city fathers estimated that five million dollars in ancillary profits would spill over to local businesses, much of it in gambling action. After some negotiations, Dan Duva, Lou Duva's son, signed on to promote the rematch through his company, Main Events. He shopped around the live-broadcast rights and sold them to HBO for more than a million dollars. CBS bought the right to show a videotape no sooner than a week after the fight. That put the promotion into the black, and Duva paid each fighter about three-quarters of a million dollars. It was unusual for a challenger to get as much as a champ, but boxing is a sport in which no point of reference is absolute.

A big-money fight always energizes a gambling town, so Reno was happy to play host to Ray Mancini. His fans began to fly in a few days before the bout and took advantage of package deals at various casinos. There were hometown boys from Ohio, high rollers in spring pastels, blonde women in clingy, nonbrand jeans;

and almost every day they convened at the El Dorado to watch their boy sweat. Both Mancini and his trainer, a fierce-looking man named Murphy Griffith, whose shaved head most often reposed inside a New York Yankees cap, felt that he'd overtrained for the first match with Bramble, losing his edge in the gym, and they were monitoring his progress closely, trying to get him to peak at the right moment. The fans were banking on this, betting heavily on Mancini even though he was a three-to-one underdog, and they offered enthusiastic support.

"Boom Boom!" they shouted. Or, more pointedly, "Whip the freak!"

The last press conference before the fight took place on a balmy afternoon in mid-February 1985. Mancini arrived a few minutes before Bramble. Dressed casually, with his longish black hair combed back in an airy pompadour, he strolled in with some other young man of approximately the same size. They looked like members of a boxing club, clean-cut kids from the suburbs. The press-kit photos of Mancini all dated from the Frias bout, so it was disconcerting to see how much his face had changed since then. He wasn't unmarked anymore. His nose was broader, more splayed, and the skin was stretched tight over his cheekbones, as if it had no give left in it. Around his eyes were masses of scar tissue, areas of pearly flesh that shone under the lights. Only his charm was still intact. He was warm, open, and modest, and around him there gathered a palpable glow. When he smiled, his eyes flashed in their abused sockets, and the joy he took in his trade was manifest. He was glad to be a boxer, willing to accept the grueling dictates of the game, and the press respected him for that and acted as if he, not Bramble, were the champ.

"You going to retire after this one, Ray?" somebody asked.

"I don't make predictions," Mancini said.

Livingstone Bramble entered the room and sat at the other end of the table, playing a street tough to hype the fight. He understood the age-old ring drama of white against black, good against evil, and he handled the villain's role with finesse. In his sunglasses and his Bramble brim—a flat, multicolored pancake of a hat—he brooded on cue and pretended to cast a juju spell

on his opponent. He gave Mancini a ceramic skull made in Tai-
wan, and then, from a little sack, he brought out a voodoo doll
and stuck pins in it. "Your eyes jumping around yet, Ray?" he
asked. "I told you I'd do anything to win." Bramble seemed to
have no sense that he had crossed over an invisible border into
the land of bad taste. Nobody knew what to make of him, not
even his manager. He had a capacity for reinventing himself,
baffling the white folks with his jive.

Bramble had been invited to train at the MGM Grand Hotel,
a monolith out in the desert that had once burned up in a fire,
dealing many gamblers the ultimate bad hand, and he was driving
the security force crazy. He walked through the casino at all
hours with a pet boa constrictor draped around his neck, enjoying
the fact that he was pulling off a stunt that no other black dude
was ever likely to duplicate. The MGM lion, caged on a lower
level of the hotel, caught a whiff of the snake one night and
reverted to jungle genotype, roaring and snorting, but that was
no skin off Bramble's back. He knew that his championship was
provisional, and he took a carpe diem attitude toward it, enjoying
himself while he could.

Bramble seemed relaxed around the Grand, but he had some
secret worries. As an amateur, he'd never won a rematch, and
he thought he might be the one who was cursed. He was angry
at Dave Wolf, because Wolf kept insinuating that Bramble and
his entourage (sunglasses, Bramble brims, black satin warm-up
jackets) were using drugs. Lou Duva was also steamed about the
accusation, and he had charged in return that Mancini's corner
was much more likely to use an illegal substance—Monsole's
solution, a banned medication that quickly closes cuts. (If Monsole's dribbles into a fighter's eye, it can blind him.) In a pact
forged at a WBA rules meeting, Duva and Wolf had agreed that
their fighters would submit to a urinalysis after their match.

In addition, Bramble was upset about the treatment he'd been
getting from the press. He was tired of hearing how wonderful
Mancini was, how Mancini embodied all the traditional (and wonderful) American virtues. All Rastafarians know themselves to be
eternal underdogs laboring under the weight of Babylon culture,
and one night, as Bramble stood outside the Grand waiting for

an attendant to find his car (it was lost in the parking lot) so he could go out to a vegetarian dinner, he spoke of his dissatisfaction.

"It's always the same, man," he said. "Everybody telling you what to do. You know what I'm getting for this fight? Seven hundred fifty thousand. Mancini, he's probably getting more. You call that justice?" Bramble sighed and shook his head. "Boxing, it ain't never going to change."

After the press conference Bramble vanished from sight, gone off to some special chamber to replenish his juices, but Mancini continued to put on a show at the El Dorado. The crowd attending his final performance was larger than ever, and they howled when he bopped in to a Hall and Oats tune blaring from a ghetto-blaster. He took off his robe, climbed into the ring, and did some calisthenics, moving at top speed. He was in superb condition. His legs were solid from the roadwork he'd done, and he was trim and flat through the middle. The fight was fast approaching, so he didn't spar—he had to protect his hands—but he laced on gloves anyway and threw punches at a pair of padded mitts that Murphy Griffith held up as targets. His hooks were powerful, coming from a low center of gravity, but his jabs lacked snap, and bystanders wondered aloud if they'd have any effect on Bramble, whose head was reputed to be as hard as a coconut.

Ray Mancini, wearing a red silk robe, paraded into the arena throwing punches and kisses. The crowd, mostly white, rose as a body and cheered when he slipped through the ropes. Moments later, Livingstone Bramble made his entrance, to Bob Marley's "Buffalo Soldier," a reggae song about black men who'd been conscripted into the Union Army and forced to kill Indians. "I'm just a buffalo soldier, fighting for survival," Marley sang, and Bramble, in black trunks adorned with a yellow skull and crossbones, danced in the ring, eyes closed, while in a front row, his supporters from the Virgin Islands held aloft his infant son. Bramble's dreadlocks were slick with Vaseline, and so were his nose and cheeks. The fans booed him, but Bramble had expected as much. "In America," he'd once said, "if you're different they say you're strange."

Right from the start, Mancini carried the fight to Bramble. Bramble's height advantage and superior reach—he had several inches on the challenger—made things difficult, but Mancini compensated, as always, with courage and daring. He stood toe-to-toe with the bigger man and took three punches in order to land one. Bramble scored points throughout these exchanges, refusing to brawl. Instead, he waited patiently and looked for openings. When he threw a jab, he threw it with authority, in a clockwork way, often aiming for the eyes. Mancini was honed as sharp as he could be, but his scar tissue and the subcutaneous cuts he'd got in training soon betrayed him. In the second round, Bramble sliced a cut into his right eyelid; the skin around his left eye began to swell and turn red. Then, in the fifth, Bramble opened an inch-long gash in the damaged lid, so that blood flowed down Mancini's cheek, as if he'd been slashed with a razor.

Somehow, Mancini kept himself together. He had a fine sixth round, wiping the blood away with his gloves and slowing Bramble with a series of efficient hooks to the body, but Bramble took charge again in the seventh, working the eyes, jabbing at them, widening the cuts. When Mancini returned to his corner at the bell, he complained to his cornermen. "I can't see," he said. His cut man, Paul Percifield, closed the wounds as best he could, but Bramble opened them again in the eighth, and the referee called in the ringside physician, Dr. Charles Filippini, and sought a medical opinion as to whether or not Mancini should continue.

Dr. Filippini is in general practice in Reno. The Nevada State Athletic Commission paid him a pittance for his work, and he looked on it as he might on community service. He had presided at many fights, including four championships, but he'd stopped only one of them. He was aware that he was in a difficult position. There were millions of dollars riding on Mancini, and his fans were desperate for him to finish, since he appeared to be behind on points. Also, Dr. Filippini knew that most boxing people mistrust physicians, and he wasn't sure how Mancini's corner would react to his presence. At other fights, he had been blocked from examining injured men, elbowed aside by irate trainers. "They just want us around to pick up the pieces," he would remark later.

Dr. Filippini had given pre-fight physicals to all the boxers on the card, but the exams were cursory, and he wished he could do more. He had read the AMA research, and it gave him cause for concern. He thought that every boxer should have a CAT scan at the start of his career and then after every bout so he could at least be informed of any change in his brain tissue. But a CAT scan costs four hundred dollars, and Dr. Filippini didn't know where the money was going to come from, except perhaps from the TV networks. He leaned over the ropes, pried open Mancini's closed eye with his fingers, and peered into the bloody socket, determining that Mancini's eyelids weren't split and that his retinas were not detached. In essence, the cuts were a soft-tissue trauma. They might look awful, and impair Mancini's vision to some degree, but they would do him no permanent harm.

So Mancini fought on. But the bout was not the same anymore—it did not seem clean or fair. Now a man with a handicap was pitted against a boxer in his prime. Mancini's talent and bravery were not at issue. His body had just let him down. As he circled the ring, flicking his gloves against his eyes to wipe away the blood, he was reminiscent of many other champs in the final stages of their careers. There was something very moving and very sad about his pursuit of Bramble, something that went to the root of boxing's problems. It was a sport that did not know where to draw the line. The line, such as it was, kept shifting, subject to crude economies—to the demands of networks, boxing organizations, promoters, and the other vested interests in control. On this point the record was clear: only rarely did a fighter get out of the game before it was too late.

Because Mancini had a touch of greatness, he landed punches, even good punches, but the blood still flowed. It spotted his chest and speckled his shoulders and back. Bramble was distressed by what he saw. If the eyes had been his, he would have quit and come back another day. Most boxers do not like to inflict unnecessary punishment, but Bramble had no choice. He had hammered Mancini last time out, and yet he had been behind on the judges' scorecards. So Bramble worked the eyes. In all, he would hit Mancini 674 times. Two hundred and fifty-five of those punches would strike Mancini in the face.

The image of a wounded fighter extending himself beyond reasonable limits has always been integral to the mythology of boxing. Maybe there was a period in history when a fan could have watched in innocence as Mancini got hurt, admiring his competitive spirit, but that period had passed. The scientific evidence was in, and it told the truth about what was happening. When Mancini was hit on the jaw, or on the side of his head, his soft brain swirled and glided within his skull, imperiling blood vessels and nerve endings. His future as a person with charm and charisma—his future as a human being—was at risk.

Mercifully, the fight ended. Among most reporters who had kept score, Bramble was an easy winner, ahead by three or four points, although a few dissenters gave the match to Mancini. The judges, too, scored in favor of Bramble, but only by a point on each card. The HBO computer analysis showed that Mancini had connected with just 28 percent of his punches; Bramble had connected with 55 percent. Once again, Mancini had been beaten decisively, but he was ecstatic to have survived. When he met the press after the bout, he delivered a nonstop monologue fueled by a mixture of oxygen and adrenaline. He wore a maroon towel over his head, like a burnoose. His left eye was purple and almost shut. "I hope I've been good for boxing," he said. "I tried."

Somebody asked him if he were hurting.

"I'm not going to lie and say I'm not," said Mancini. "But to what extent?"

Lenny Mancini—broken nose, shock of white hair—sat next to his son, and a reporter asked him if he wanted Ray to keep fighting. "If it was up to me, I'd say forget about it," Lenny said.

"He always says that," Ray said. "I'm his baby."

Another reporter asked Mancini if he planned to retire. He said he had to think about it. "To thine own self be true," he said. "You guys didn't know I knew Shakespeare, did you?"

He laughed and invited everybody to a big party at the El Dorado. Then he went off to a hospital, where twenty-seven stitches were taken in his eyelids. By midnight, he was back in his suite, eating a dish of chocolate ice cream.

In the morning, at the MGM Grand, Bramble, still casual in jeans and Bramble brim, referred to himself as the lightweight champion of the universe. When somebody asked him why he hadn't used his right hand very much during the fight, he said it was because the glove on it had not come from the belly part of the cow.

"Are you going to honor your contract with Tyrone Crawley?" a reporter asked.

Bramble was going to leave that up to his manager. The chump he really wanted to fight was Hector Camacho, who had been at ringside in a gold lamé suit and a pair of rhinestone-studded sunglasses. WBA rankings aside, Camacho was worth a significant piece of cake.

"With Crawley, you get a guy who's a stinking fighter," Lou Duva said, who has a face like Broderick Crawford. "I don't like a Crawley fight. There's nothing good about him stylewise. It would just stink out the joint." He meant that Crawley had a style that was similar to Bramble's and might give Bramble trouble. He also meant that Crawley had no marquee value and might not sell to television.

Shortly after this, the full weight of Babylon came crashing down on Bramble. The post-fight urinalysis revealed a banned substance in his urine—ephedrine, a crystalline alkaloid commonly used for relief of hay fever, asthma, and nasal congestion. Taken in large doses or injected intramuscularly, it elevates blood pressure and works as a stimulant. At first Bramble was puzzled by how it had gotten into his system. He was a vegetarian, a true health freak, and he avoided chemicals of all description. But every day he did swallow a capsule of Chi Power, a supposedly Chinese herbal concoction that he bought at natural foods stores. Chi Power contained ma huang, or *Ephedra sinica*. The WBA, uninterested in Orientalia, fined Bramble $15,000.

Then his big payday with Hector Camacho dispersed into the ozone. The Crawley fight was scheduled instead, but Bramble broke a hand in training, and NBC canceled its contract. For a time, the fight languished in limbo. When it was rescheduled, Crawley injured himself, and NBC again canceled its contract. More months dragged by, and Bramble, a king without a kingdom, became so depressed that he told one of his handlers that he was thinking about moving to Montana and buying himself a cattle ranch.

In the weeks following the fight, Ray Mancini took it easy. For the first time in five years, he let his body rest. When CBS broadcast its videotape, he appeared on camera live, without Bramble, and offered through puffy lips a revised version of recent events. Now he claimed that he'd won the fight convincingly, and that Bramble's drug use ought to cost him the title. In New York, Dr. Schwartz examined Mancini again and told him that his cuts would be fully healed in a few months. Mancini flew to Florida and played some golf.

For a while, he couldn't make up his mind about retirement. Every few days, he would phone Dave Wolf and ask if any new fight offers had come in. Wolf was getting plenty of them, all for big bucks. Mancini was still white and still popular. Would he be able to turn down a million dollars to go up about five pounds and fight a leading junior welterweight? Mancini himself didn't know for sure. How many Americans could refuse a million bucks for taking a beating? And it wasn't really the punishment that Mancini was concerned about—he had no idea if he could go through another training camp. He was tired of paying dues, and he had other options. *Cosmopolitan* wanted him for a photo session on bachelor hunks, and the William Morris Agency had signed him to a contract.

Mancini decided to move to Los Angeles. He bought a house there and put in time around the swimming pool. His movie star friends understood what he was going through and how a million-dollar deal rumbles around in your head. One day he started working out in a gym at Mickey Rourke's house. He took it slowly, testing himself, but he just couldn't do it anymore. He'd had it with sacrifice and pain, so he called a press conference and said that he was hanging up his gloves to pursue a career as an actor. Probably he would never be a great thespian, but he thought he had it in him to do Rambo-type roles. He believed that he could make a go of it in Hollywood, but he would not rule out the possibility that maybe, in the future, if the circumstances were right, he might return to the ring.

"One thing I've learned," Mancini said. "Never say never."

Pete Hamill

UP THE STAIRS WITH CUS D'AMATO

In those days, you had to pass a small candy stand to get to the door of the Gramercy Gym on East Fourteenth Street. The door was heavy, with painted zinc nailed across its face and a misspelled sign saying GRAMACY GYM, and when you opened the door, you saw a long, badly lit stairway climbing into darkness. There was another door on the landing, and a lot of tough New York kids would reach that landing and find themselves unable to open the second door. They'd go back down the stairs, try to look cool as they bought a soda at the candy stand, then hurry home. Many others opened the second door. And when they did, they entered the tough, hard, disciplined school of a man named Cus D'Amato.

"First thing I want to know about a kid," Cus said to me once on some lost night in the fifties, "is whether he can open that door. Then when he walks in, I look at him, try to see what he's seeing. Most of them stand at the door. They see guys skipping rope, shadowboxing, hitting the bags. Most of all, they see guys in the ring. Fighting. And then they have to decide, do they want this or not? If they want it they stay, they ask someone what they should do. Most of them are shy, for some reason. Almost all fighters. They whisper. You tell them to come back, and you'll see what can be done. They have to spend at least one night dealing with fear. If they come back the second time, then maybe you have a fighter."

Mike Tyson–Cus D'Amato, Catskill, N.Y., 1985

I wasn't a fighter, but I came up those stairs almost every day in the late fifties and early sixties, and in some important ways I learned as much from Cus D'Amato as the fighters did. I was living then on Ninth Street and Second Avenue, working nights at the *Post*, and I'd wake up around three in the afternoon and walk to Fourteenth Street and hang out with the fighters. My friend José Torres was then the hottest young middleweight in the city and one of Cus D'Amato's fighters. He had lost by one point to Laszlo Papp in the finals of the '56 Olympics in Melbourne, and when he came to New York from Puerto Rico he placed his career in the hands of Cus.

"I didn't know anything about New York," he said. "I didn't know very much about boxing. Most of all, I didn't know anything about life. So I learned about everything then from Cus."

Cus, who died last week at seventy-seven after a long struggle with pneumonia, was one of the best teachers I ever met. He was a tough, intelligent man who was almost Victorian in his beliefs in work and self-denial and fierce concentration. For years he'd lived alone in the office of the gym, accompanied only by a huge boxer dog named Champ; there were books on the shelves (he loved the Civil War and essays on strategy and tactics and almost never read novels, although he admired W. C. Heinz's *The Professional*) and a gun somewhere, and a small black-and-white TV set and a pay phone on the wall. After Floyd Patterson became champion in 1956, Cus took an apartment over a coffee shop on Fifty-third Street and Broadway and bought some elegantly tailored clothes and a homburg, but, talking to him, I always sense that his idea of paradise was that room and the cot in the office of the Gramercy Gym.

"You can't want too many things," he said to me one wintry evening after the fighters had gone, the speed bags were stilled, and we stood at the large gym windows while snow fell into Fourteenth Street. "The beginning of corruption is wanting things. You want a car or a fancy house or a piano, and the next thing you know, you're doing things you didn't want to do, just to get the *things*. I guess maybe that's why I never got married. It wasn't that I didn't like women. They're nice. It's nice. It's that women want *things*, and if I want the woman, then I have to want the things she wants. Hey, I do want a new refrigerator, or a big TV, or a new couch . . ."

Cus wanted his fighters to be champions, to have money and glory, but he truly didn't seem to want much for himself. Once a bum made his way to the Gramercy from the White Rose bar across the street and Cus gave him a dollar, the next day five bums showed up, the day after that, almost forty. The fighters laughed as Cus dispensed singles, and then Cus said, "That's it, that's all. You want to come back here, bring trunks!" He was a sucker for old fighters. Once when Cus had the shorts (he had to declare bankruptcy in 1971) Ezzard Charles came around to see him; the great light-heavyweight and former heavyweight champion was a broken man, confined to a wheelchair; he needed a thousand, and Cus borrowed the money, gave it to the old champion, and never heard from Charles again. When Patterson won the championship by knocking out Archie Moore on November 30, 1956, Cus used his share of the purse to make Floyd an elaborate $35,000 jewel-encrusted crown; a few years later,

Patterson wouldn't even talk to Cus. Cus once quoted Gene Fowler to me: "Money is something to throw off the back of trains."

He loved style in fighters and in writers, too. His favorite sports-writers were Jimmy Cannon, Dick Young, and Dan Parker, all of whom took shots at him in print from time to time ("I don't mind, they gotta job to do and I'm not perfect"), but he also said that the sportswriter who moved him most consistently was the elegant Frank Graham of the *Journal-American*. Later, when Torres became friends with Norman Mailer, Cus started to read his work, as if inspecting it for signs of moral decay. "The guy is really good, isn't he? He's like a Robinson, he can box, he can punch. . . ."

He cherished great fighters—Ray Robinson, Joe Louis, Mu-hammad Ali, Sandy Saddler, Willie Pep, Tommy Loughran—but sometimes late at night, sitting over coffee, he'd talk about the fighter that didn't exist: the perfect fighter, the masterpiece. "The ideal fighter has heart, skill, movement, intelligence, creativity. You can have everything, but if you can't make it up while you're in there, you can't be great. A lot of guys have the mechanics and no heart; lots of guys have heart, no mechanics; the thing that puts it together, it's mysterious, it's like making a work of art, you bring everything to it, you make it up when you're do-ing it."

Toward the end, he thought perhaps that he had the perfect heavyweight, at last, in young Michael Tyson, who has now knocked out all nine of his professional opponents—six in the first round. "He's strong, he's brave, he's in condition, and most of all, he's got that other thing, the mysterious thing," Cus said, the last time I saw him. "I have no doubt he'll be a champion. But more than that, he might be a great fighter."*

There were a lot of good fighters at the Gramercy Gym in the late fifties: Joe Shaw, a fierce-punching 140-pounder; light-heavyweight Jim Boyd, who'd won the gold medal in Melbourne; two more light-heavyweights named Sylvester Banks and Paul Wright; a wonderful southpaw featherweight named Floyd Smith;

---

*Tyson is presently undisputed world heavyweight champion.

and some fine amateurs ranging from bantamweight Georgie
Colon to light-heavyweight Simon Ramos. But as Cus became
more involved managing Patterson and Torres, the day-to-day
training was left to Joe Fariello (now educating Mark Breland).
Cus was away at camp with Patterson; he was up at Stillman's
with Torres to find experienced professionals for sparring partners. And during the same period, Cus was waging his wars with
both the International Boxing Club and Madison Square Garden.
Some people thought he grew increasingly paranoid.

"If this goes down instead of up," he said to me one day as we
stepped in the elevator in a midtown office building, "we're in
trouble."

He laughed, but Cus meant it, too. The Mob was all over boxing
when Cus brought his first good fighters out of the Gramercy
Gym. The hoodlums cut into fighters, arranged tank jobs, fixed
judges. Frankie Carbo was called the underworld's commissioner
of boxing, a vicious punk who lived off other men's sweat and
controlled a number of managers. Carbo was friendly, sort of,
with Jim Norris, a rich bum with a hoodlum complex who ran
the IBC out of the old Garden on Eighth Avenue and Fiftieth
Street. There's no room here to relate the details of Cus D'Amato's
sustained contest with Norris, Carbo, and the Garden. Certainly
he was on the moral high ground, but the terrible thing was that
his personal crusade also hurt his fighters.

We'll never know how good Patterson and Torres might have
become if they'd been fighting more often, battling those fighters
who were controlled by the IBC and the Garden. Certainly Torres
would have made more money. I remember one main event he
had to take in Boston when he was still a hot fighter in New
York. The total purse came to $28.35. Joe Fariello said, "Joe, you
take the twenty dollars, I'll take the eight dollars, and we'll send
the thirty-five cents to Cus." Patterson did get rich, and Torres
did become champion years later than he should have, and in
the wrong division (he was one of the greatest middleweights I
ever saw, but had to settle for the light-heavyweight championship in 1965). But the competitive fire of Shaw withered from
lack of action; the others drifted away.

"It breaks my heart sometimes, thinking about those kids

not fighting," he said to me once. "But I don't see any other way."

That was the problem. From 1959 on, Cus never worked a corner for any of his fighters; he didn't even hold a manager's license, as a result of the botched promotion of the 1959 Patterson-Johansson fight, when it appeared (but was never proved) that Cus helped bring Fat Tony Salerno in as a money man. The fighters did their best, and for some fights Cus would come to camp, work with them, talk strategy and tactics. But Patterson broke with him, and Torres was forced to go with another manager (Cain Young) to get his chance at a title. Around the time Torres retired, Cus moved upstate, far from the gyms of the city. "I like it up there," he said once. "I like the clear skies, the lake, where I go fishing. It's beautiful. Beautiful." Did he miss the gym of Fourteenth Street? "Yeah," he said. "Sometimes. . . ."

The last time I saw him, in 1985, was on the fifty-seventh floor of the World Trade Center. We were there to watch Torres be sworn in as chairman of the New York State Athletic Commission, the first professional fighter and the first Puerto Rican ever to hold the job. "I'm so proud of José, I can't explain it," Cus said. We talked about Tyson and other things. And then I asked him if he'd ever gone back to the Gramercy Gym since he sold it in the seventies. "No," he said, and looked up at José, who was standing with Mario Cuomo at the front of the room. "No, I don't like to look back."

And so I did the looking back, sitting in the packed, brightly lit conference room, remembering Cus talking to me when I was twenty about the uses of fear, the meaning of courage, the need to concentrate energy and purpose in all things, and how I'd tried and failed so often to follow his lessons. I'd modeled a character on Cus in one of my novels, and he'd liked the book but objected when he saw the TV movie: On the screen, John Cassavetes stood on a ring apron talking to a fighter and smoking a cigarette. "What manager would *do* that? What kind of *example* would he be showing to a kid?" I remembered that conversation, and after

José was sworn in, I turned to Cus and said, "Listen, Cus, I want to thank you for everything." He squinted suspiciously at me. "What do you mean?" he said, and I said, "For letting me climb the stairs."

He nodded, turned away, and said, "You goddamned writers." I'm sorry I never got to explain.

Michael Shapiro

OPPONENTS

The opponent, Obie Garnett, came to Chicago to fight two weeks before Christmas. He took the bus from Cincinnati, where he worked in a mill. He arrived alone, as opponents often do, and that night he boxed in the Aragon Ballroom, a dance hall with stars painted on the ceiling. He did not know the man who taped his hands with gauze and adhesive, nor the man who served as his second. A third stranger was prevailed upon to carry Garnett's water bucket. A white towel was placed over Garnett's shoulders and the three strangers followed him to the ring.

He did not last a round. At the opening bell, Garnett, a flabby light-heavyweight, danced around the local boxer he was being paid to fight. The local fellow measured Garnett and then reached his face with a stiff jab. Garnett crumpled. He rolled onto his side, facing his corner, but he could not see his seconds because his eyes could not focus. His nose ran. His cornermen rushed to him when he was counted out and revived him as the spectators laughed.

Upstairs, in the communal dressing room, Garnett toweled himself dry. Someone offered to buy him a beer. He drank it at the bar downstairs while another opponent, Sylvester Wilder, who, according to *The Ring Record Book* once lost thirty-six fights in a row, took a hook to the belly and was counted out.

Garnett waited for his pay. This was his third professional fight.

N. ALICIA BYERS

He had lost the first two, also by knockouts in the first round. He would fight six more times and lose the same way each time. He was paid $175 for this fight. The man who had been his second asked Garnett why he was taking the chance of being hurt for so little money.

Garnett, who was rushing so he would not miss his shift at the mill the next morning, turned and without a smile or hesitation, replied, "Christmastime, man."

When boxers are known to lose more often than they win they become useful only as opponents. Often they are called less flattering names; but without them the sport, according to those who understand it best, could not exist. Pragmatic opponents, aware of their roles, see no harm in fighting and losing so long as they are not damaged. The romantics among them are sure that someday their true worth will be recognized and they will fight for championships. Boxing purists lament that their sport is not as it was decades ago when there was a club to watch boxing in most every town they visited. But, they add, there has always been a call for opponents to smooth the ascents of new, attractive prizefighters who have the financial backing opponents never know.

"This is boxing as it has been known since the beginning of time," says Hank Kaplan, a boxing historian. "There have always been opponents. Ever since the dawning somebody discovered that the way to build a fighter up was to get him someone he can beat up."

There are good opponents. "A guy who don't get knocked out but who'll always lose a decision," says Chris Dundee, the Miami Beach promoter. "An opponent is a fella that is always dependable, that can give a good account of himself and lose."

There are bad opponents. "If a guy goes out in the first round the fans know you got a stiff in there," says Ernie Terrell, the former heavyweight champion and now a Chicago club-fight promoter who does not like a hard hitter as an opponent because "a puncher is always dangerous."

There are opponents with many aliases. "In the older days guys had ten, fifteen different names," Kaplan says of the practice of avoiding identification. "They knew when to get hit and when to fall and when to go into convulsions. They were specialists."

And there have been opponents who, if not necessarily gifted boxers, are still remembered long after they fought. "I'll never forget the Gorilla," says Jerry White, a long-time Miami trainer of his fighter, Gorilla Gould. "They called me up and needed a heavyweight to fight. They were looking for an opponent. The Gorilla owed me a few bucks. I took 4 to 1 odds that the Gorilla would go the limit. I gave him a couple of cloves of garlic and gave him instructions that whenever you get in a clinch, blow in the other guy's face. He blew and the poor guy stepped back like he was punched."

José Torres, a member of the New York State Athletic Commission, says that boxing is entertainment and that is why opponents are necessary. "Promoters get people who can excite the public," he says. "Opponents exist and I'm sure that promoters will try to get them and good managers will always look for them for their fighters—these 'tomato cans' who are just in there to lose."

States with boxing commissions—most have them but some do not—try to keep boxers from fighting and losing too often. Since 1980, for instance, New York has required boxers to carry "passports," documents in which their victories, losses, and suspensions have been printed. Neighboring states like New Jersey and Pennsylvania have a similar system and also supply information to one another on fighters whom they have suspended. New York stores that information in a computer—it regularly receives boxing data from twenty states—that is scanned before a boxer is permitted in the ring. In New Jersey, a fighter who has been knocked out is suspended for sixty days. In New York the suspension is for ninety days. In Pennsylvania the commission has suspended a boxer for ninety days for a "very poor showing."

Still, transgressions exist. Although New York State will revoke the license of a fighter who has been knocked out six times, Torres says, enforcement is difficult. "They change their names," he says.

Torres, once the world light-heavyweight champion, recalls how his manager, Cus D'Amato, was judicious in selecting the men he fought. In his first fight he knocked out Gene Hamilton in the first round. Hamilton had lost ten of his fifteen fights.

"If I was a promoter and I had a fighter to bring up I'd do the same thing," says David Conteh, who has lost fifteen of his nineteen fights. "Look, I've been around. I'm thirty-four and I'm still pugging. I won't be no champ at my age. If I make a few bucks I'll be lucky. I try to take what I can. A lot of people say I had potential but it never materialized. Everybody wants to use you as an opponent. They say, 'He was a good man when he was younger.' What can you do? What can you say? There's nothing you can do."

Opponents sometimes lose so badly and quickly that it seems as if they lose on purpose. Sometimes they do; often they don't.

"He was supposed to get hit on the chin and he was supposed to fall," says Larry Kent, a Miami trainer for many years, recalling a poorly executed dive he once observed. "Every time he fell he didn't get hit. The referee looked at him and said, 'Get up, you bum, you didn't get hit.' In the fifth round he got hit and he looked up and said, 'Don't tell me I didn't get hit. Start counting.' "

But paying boxers to "take dives" is seldom necessary, boxing elders say. "There's enough bad ones out there to make the really bad ones look terrible," says Joe Mooney, a manager and gymnasium operator in Savannah.

Mooney is a purveyor of opponents. He is not alone in his vocation and maintains that his service is much in demand. "The main reason they call me," he says, "is because I'm dependable."

Mooney takes his fighters to Atlantic City and Hartford and sometimes to Tokyo and South America.

"We go to Bermuda every two months," he says. For these excursions, as well as those to Northeastern cities, he brings only his "main-event quality group." The fortunate ones might make $1,500 for a night's work, which is far more than they could expect to make at home.

Opponents, however, almost always lose on the road; and even a knockout does not assure victory. Terrell tells of one especially unsuccessful opponent—"I never in my life saw him win a fight"— who was shipped to Memphis from Chicago to battle a local hero. The opponent, who was offered few fights because of his thunderous punch, surprised everyone when he quickly knocked the local man senseless with a mighty blow. Then the arena lights went out. They stayed out, Terrell says with a laugh, until the local pug was returned to life. This took perhaps twenty minutes, somewhat longer than the traditional ten-count. Upon his revival, the bout continued to its scheduled conclusion, at which point the arm of the victorious local fellow was raised by the referee.

Promoters call managers like Joe Mooney with specifications

in mind. They tell him who they have and what they need, Mooney says, and he will tell them which of his fighters might be suitable. Then he tells them, "Take your pick." "Usually," he says, "they don't get beat up."

Mooney might drive fifteen hours to bring his boxers to their fights. And if need be, he will step in himself. "Mainly who I fight is the guy no one else will fight," he says. This often means oversized heavyweights against whom Mooney, at 275 pounds, seems a reasonable foe. He has fought thirty-eight fights, he says, and lost thirty-two. But he is never too hard pressed for boxers. "There's a new guy walking in the gym every day," he says.

Opponents enhance the careers of those who might be champions. Consider the rise of Gerry Cooney, who amassed nothing but victories, twenty-one of the twenty-five by knockouts, until Larry Holmes finished him in thirteen rounds in 1982. Cooney first knocked out Bill Jackson, who had been knocked out in his first eight fights and never got past the third round. In his fourth he beat Matt Robinson, who had lost fourteen of sixteen. Cooney knocked out Joe Maye in his fifth. That was on November 18, 1977, the beginning of a hectic Thanksgiving-Christmas season for Maye who, in the next thirty days, fought and lost three more times. Maye's entry in *The Ring Record Book* shows that he lost eighteen fights in a row; the streak would have reached twenty-five but for a draw against Joe Vellmure, who beat him twice before.

Successful opponents are in demand and this sometimes makes their handlers prosperous. "I used to get calls from all over, from Pensacola to Key West, anyplace you can mention," Jerry White says of his halcyon days. "I used to bring the opponents for half the show. We used to make up the show the week before."

Shrewd opponents know the workings of their sport. "You get in shape, you get a fight and it's canceled," David Conteh says. "Another fight is next week. Do you want to take it or leave it? You need the money." But others do not understand why they are being invited to fight. When Johnny Davis, a New York welterweight, became a professional in 1973 he fought four times between July 18 and August 20 of that year, and five more times between November 5 and December 17. He lost each time. In his next twenty-two bouts, Davis won three by knockouts, drew twice, lost a decision and was knocked out sixteen times. Twelve of the knockouts were consecutive.

"I know I'm not a bad fighter," says Davis who, at the age of thirty-four, wants to win just a few so that he will not retire a loser. He sits on a couch in Gleason's Gym on Thirtieth Street near Madison Square Garden. He has thick shoulders and arms but there are wisps of gray in his hair. He has sweated through his blue T-shirt. He finished his workout at the speedbag where he did not sustain a rapid tempo the way most fighters do. "I try so hard at something I like doing," he said. "I love boxing. I dream of being a fighter. I see myself winning the title. I don't know which one. I see myself being picked up, getting carried around, getting my belt. Sometimes I see it in slow motion. I was telling my wife I had a dream last night. I was winning and getting the title. Sometimes she says, 'That's nice.' But she really wants me to quit."

Davis did not think he was an opponent for a long time. He fought a lot and lost most every time but did not question his manager's plan, he says, because he did not think it a fighter's right. He fought the same man twice in Baltimore in his first two fights and, after the second loss, fought in New York three days later and then again, against the same man, two days afterward. "I don't remember," he says. "See, I was fighting every week. I just took them fights. I was new at boxing. I was exhausted. I got knocked out. I tried to get up but I was exhausted."

He paid bills with his first paycheck. Then he bought himself a present. "I think I bought me a suit at a store on Fourteenth Street," he says. "I also bought a hat to go with it, a nice big-brimmed, black hat. I felt big. I felt like I was a big fighter, like a big man. I had a few dollars in my pocket. I had a nice suit, a pinstriped suit. I felt like a big gangster. People would say, 'You got on such a nice suit.' Everyone see you looking better. I felt like I was getting somewhere."

He has promised his wife that he will not fight beyond this year. He made the promise once before. He has a job—many opponents do; they run before work and train afterward—as a carpenter but cannot bring himself to stop.

When he boxes, Johnny Davis shows off a part of himself that he can express no other way. "I don't talk too much," he says. "I'm always alone. But when I'm inside the ring I show them something different. People are cheering for me. I feel good about myself, now I can be outside of the ring. I have people stop me in the street—doctors, lawyers, cab drivers—and they've seen me fight. They say, 'You didn't get a fair deal.' And I say, 'I'm not such a bad fighter.' "

Jackson Cope

PINSTRIPES

It is hard to explain a nearly fifty-year love affair with the fights because I lack expertise. Those who would instruct tell me now as they told me then to look at the feet to predict the immediate futures market, to look into the eyes, the way they telegraph the hands. And I end up focused on the hands. I always looked at their hands. As a consequence, one night a boy with an Italian name, large ears, and inscrutable features (where have you gone, Pete DiSimone?) knocked me down at the U.S. Naval Station in Gary, Indiana, seven times—a record later tied by Floyd Patterson. I visited Patterson at his camp in the Catskills when he was preparing for hari-kari with Sonny Liston as the fatal instrument. I was old then, maybe forty, or about half the age at which one surmised Patterson must have been born, in one of nature's especially heightened comico-tragic confusions of profession and person. I wasn't into numerology, but recent experience made me doubt the efficacy of his assertion that he had climbed seven miles in the hills just the day before. The recent experience had been watching Liston's march through Texas, taking out hopefuls north and south of the border in a round or two: Peron's Willie Besmanoff, Cut-and-Shoot's only schoolteacher, Roy Harris; and the "Big Cat," Cleveland Williams, whose heart was generously purported to be housed mostly in the cathedral he was building out of Popsicle sticks. Liston wore black trunks with red stripes, just discernible below a short white robe without lettering, reminiscent of nothing so much as a surgeon about to operate. Ah, the visual art of understatement. After the ritual slaughters, Patterson assumed a baroque disguise appropriate to Clouseau: moustache and beard, and very dark glasses. It was his way of showing most of us (most of us share it with him) that he hated trying to be professional, with all the quiet that implies. Which is always the issue.

No exaggeration, rebellion against the uniform when you know your business. They both wear pinstripes, the fighters perhaps in submerged psychodrama defying the pusillanimity of the stock brokers, urchins of Wall Streets in glass offices all over the world now, eerily similar in size and structure to what we still strangely call "the ring." Lots of risk in both arenas, of course. But no anonymity for fighters. They covet the uniform as a symbol of singularity, like paratroopers or Roman clerics. A sort of counter-dramatic gesture to so much staged tension. The scene setting is always the same: eighteen feet to twenty-four on each side of the square, according to cajoling or wisdom on the part of the cadre—managers, trainers, matchmakers. And the uniform: vulnerability and nakedness just covered by the little shorts with the pinstripe down both sides. Just a little businesslike scene: a shrug of the shoulders, shaking of the neck; a little scheme for improbable progress into forever being *there*, caught in a grace never repeatable through a lifetime of losses. Just once being unostentatious when the glory clouds gather. Just a pro being there, what the Greeks called a *daemon*, a hero mediating the god and man we all think came together in the immediate and limited environs of our body. And once in awhile we believe it— seeing, sensing (even in ourselves) the movement that cannot be improved, the stage without props (*we* the proprietors finally), just legs and life and everything that will be lost dancing along in little pinstripe shorts as quiet and mortal as skill.

They go about their business in pinstripes, professional men, sometimes amazing boys who are quick studies. Some go crazy in themselves, wear leopard spots, sequins (Joe Frazier under-valued classical drama and his own talent enough to wear Bermuda shorts when he was up against the busiest of all, Ali). But mostly they are all business.

Just those little blood lines running along the thigh before the loneliness begins in there. I watch the angle of the noses while they receive the ritual instruction. Such faces, such lines of achievement they can't even read. But everybody knows the fight has begun here, just before the action. Someone rubs your neck, your back, and you know it is a ritual and you are the symbol of something, and so you smoke.

It is similar to others where you are not permitted a mistake without consequences, a life that can be designated a profession. Red Allen must be world champion of danger.

But fighters can, of course, when we reconsider, afford a margin of error which only bursts nasal veins or cartilage less significant than a shortstop's knee. So many mistakes per round, and nothing costlier than pain. Probably. But naked, except for that little stripe up the thigh, metonymy for all the angles: the ropes, the rope burns across the back, the straight right; ultimately for the choice to be caged on a twenty-foot-square stage with another auditioner for the big part.

You see their eyes fixated upon one another at the pre-fight instructions, but like snakes, cobras, all those nicknames they take, there is always the flicker, sign of the pro examining the real matter: What do you harbor in that little business suit? Let's get busy.

George Garrett

MY ONE-EYED COACH

With Joe Brown at Princeton I encountered an artist, a sculptor, and a coach who had once been a great athlete. Never defeated as a professional fighter. And *just* missed being a world champion. Missed because he lost an eye in an accident while training for a championship fight. As a coach, pure and simple, he had much to teach me. Or, better, there was so much to learn from him. For one thing, he was able to show me that there were things, particularly habits derived not from poor coaching but from experience, which it was already too late to unlearn. Things I would have to live with. There were things, beginning with my basic stance as a fighter, which were "wrong" and less than wholly efficient and effective. I fought out of a kind of sideways stance which allowed for a good sharp left jab and even a left hook and was an effective defensive stance, but limited the use of my right hand except in very close. He taught me how to analyze that stance (and other habits) and how, rather than discarding it and disregarding all the experience which had gone into forming it, to modify it slightly so as to take best advantage of its strengths and at the same time to compensate for its more obvious weaknesses. Compensation, that's what he showed me. How to compensate for what is and what isn't. Compensation for injury; compensation for inherent physical defect or bad habits.

What was happening, then, was the introduction of mind, of

thinking, into a complex process which had been, until then, all intuition and inspiration, all ritual and mystery. He did not seek to eliminate these things, but he added another dimension to them.

The practical values were immediate. For instance, I soon discovered that I was in far better physical condition than I had known. Learned that professional fighters planning on ten round fights did not spend any more time than I was spending in the gym or doing roadwork. Why, then, was I completely worn out, exhausted, after three rounds? Because I was . . . not using my head. Thinking, being aware of what was happening as it was happening, was in fact relaxing. With thought you could not so much coast as control your expense of energy. Which did not mean that you spent any less of yourself. It became, though, a question of how and when you spent your energy. The ideal was to expend exactly what you had, to be exactly on empty at the moment a given round (or the whole fight) ended.

This required a deeper, more objective consciousness of self. It also demanded a greater awareness of what was happening outside and around yourself. Football, at least serious football, was limited after my freshman year because of a serious knee injury. But, even so, I began, thanks to Joe Brown and the introduction of thinking into performance, to be aware of the wholeness of the game, of other things going on even as I was doing what I was supposed to do. With mind came choice. Vision was joined and fulfilled by revision.

From Joe Brown, both by teaching and example (he was still, close up, the best fighter I had ever seen), I began to learn the habits of professionalism, the kind of professionalism which would be demanded of me as an artist. Never mind "good" artist or "bad" artist. I even learned, through the habits of this kind of professionalism and the experience of trying and testing myself and my habits against others who also knew what they were doing, that nobody else, except maybe a critic-coach like Joe Brown who knew what was happening at all levels of his being, could honestly judge and evaluate your performance. I learned to recognize that the audience, even the more or less knowledgeable audience, never really knew what was going on. Nor should they be expected to. One soon had to pass beyond the stage of contempt for the ignorant audience and to recognize that their illusions did not make them contemptible.

I learned that in the end you alone can know and judge your own performance, that finally even the one wonderful coach-critic is expendable. He can solve a practical problem for you, problems of craft, but he cannot and should not meddle with the mystery of it.

I learned something, then, about the brotherhood of fighters. People went into this brutal and often self-destructive activity for a rich variety of motivations, most of them bitterly antisocial and verging on the psychotic. Most of the fighters I knew of were wounded people who felt a deep, powerful urge to wound others at real risk to themselves. In the beginning . . . what happened was that in almost every case, there was so much self-discipline required and craft involved, so much else besides one's original motivations to concentrate on, that these motivations became at least cloudy and vague and were often forgotten, lost completely. Many good and experienced fighters (as has often been noticed) become gentle and kind people. Maybe not "good" people. But they have the habit of leaving all their fight in the ring. And even there, in the ring, it is dangerous to invoke too much anger. It can be a stimulant, but is very expensive of energy. It is impractical to get mad most of the time.

In a sense this was not good training for the literary world. For the good camaraderie of good athletes is not an adequate preparation for the small-minded, mean-spirited, selfish, and ruthless competitiveness of most of the writers and literary types (not all, thank God) I have encountered. They do things which any self-respecting jock would be ashamed of. They treat each other as no fighter would ever dare to.

And all the time they talk about . . . *Art*. With a capital A. With a kind of public and mindless piety and genuflection.

Ever since my youth, since the days of the unforgettable Joe Brown, I have been suspicious of pious amateurs.

Let me put it another way. In anecdote. All through my youth I admired many fighters. Especially Joe Louis. One of the many things I found admirable was that most of his moves (most of

his craft) were so subtle as to be lost on all but the most knowledgeable fans. Once, in those days, I rode the Silver Meteor from
New York to Florida, together with a young heavyweight who
had just that week fought a ten-round exhibition bout against
Joe Louis. I remember (still a fan and an amateur at heart) being
amazed that this young fighter was not overawed. He had great
respect, of course, and some awe. But even though he had been
"carried," he had stood in there and traded licks with the great
man.

"You know what really surprised me?" the fighter said. "His
left jab. He has a very strong, fast left jab. It's his best punch,
really."

Since then I have studied the films and I think that is true.
Louis's jab was so good that it caused pinwheels and cobwebs
in his opponent's heads long before he got around to the right-
hand punches that put them away.

(Try to imagine that kind of professionalism in literature.
Something like: "That Hemingway, he can do a fish story about
as well as anybody around.")

From Joe Brown I also learned something of the permissible
vanity of the professional. Joe had long since outgrown any of
the false and foolish pride of the athlete. But he knew himself
well enough to know that some of the pride was earned and all
right. Once in a great while he would go to the fights in New
York at Madison Square Garden or St. Nick's. If he went, he
would be recognized, starting in the lobby with the old guys
walking on their heels who sold programs. And the ushers. Before
the main fight he would be introduced from the ring. He liked
that moment even when it embarrassed him. It was a homecom-
ing. He wrote a fine short story about it called, as I remember,
"And You Hear Your Name." It was a good and true story about
pride and mixed feelings.

Joe Brown was an artist and he was as articulate about his art
as he was about his sport. He could talk about it, though always
simply and plainly. For those who were tuned in to his kind of
talk it was valuable. R. P. Blackmur, for example, used to discuss
literary matters and matters of aesthetics with Joe. It was from
Joe, Blackmur said, that he got one of his best-known titles—
Language As Gesture. Which was a reversal of something I, my-

self, had heard Joe say: That in sculpture gesture was his language.

Many of his athletes also went, one night a week, to his sculpture class. It was, in those days before coeducation came to Princeton, always a Life Class. The only place you could be sure to see a naked woman on the campus. A powerful inducement. We managed to learn a little about modeling clay and about the craft of hand and eye. For most of us what we learned was that we would never, ever be sculptors even if we wanted to. But, hand and eye, we learned some things that would carry over, despite a lack of natural talent.

Some of the intellectual lessons Joe Brown taught were brutally simple. In boxing, for example, he was fond of reminding his guys that to win in boxing you had to hit the other guy. To hit the other guy you had to move in close enough for him to hit you. No other way. One of the immutable lessons of boxing was that there was no free ride. No free lunch. To succeed you had to be at risk. You had to choose to be at risk. That choice was the chief act of will and courage. After that you might win or lose, on the basis of luck or skill, but the choice itself was all that mattered.

Or a matter of sculpture. Teaching something of the same sort of lesson. At one stage Joe was making a lot of interesting pieces for children's playgrounds. This in response to some Swedish things which were being put up in New Jersey and which, in Joe's view, while aesthetically interesting, had nothing special to do with *play*. He said a piece for a playground should be something you could play on and with. One of his pieces, I remember, was a kind of an abstract whale shape. High "tail" in the air and a slide from the "tail," through the inside of the "body" and out of the "mouth." It was tricky to get to the top of the "tail." There was no one and easy way to climb there. Many different ways as possibilities. Some of them a *little* bit risky. You could fall down. So? You can fall out of a tree, too, or off a fence. Falling down is part of growing up. But worth the risk. Once at the top of the "tail" there was the wonderful, steep S-shaped slide waiting. Only right in the middle it leveled off. The experience of the slide was briefly interrupted.

Why?

"I want these kids to learn the truth," he said. "You can have a great slide, a great experience. But to do it all the way you've got to get up off your ass and contribute at least two steps of your own."

My first lesson in . . . *meaning in Art.*

As I write this, I have news that Joe Brown died recently in Princeton. Thirty-five years and more have passed since he was my coach and teacher. And likewise the half-child, myself, who came to him to try to learn and to improve his boxing skills, is long gone also, even though, by being alive, I can still carry the memory of him, that child, and thus, also, of Joe Brown. I can summon up the sweat and stink of that gym. Pure joy of it when things went well. Pain when they did not.

Ironically, I tend to dismiss most comparisons of athletics to art and to "the creative process." But only because, I think, so much that is claimed for both is untrue. But I have come to believe—indeed I have to believe it insofar I believe in the validity and efficacy of art—that what comes to us first and foremost through the body, as a sensuous affective experience, is taken and transformed by mind and self into a thing of the spirit. Which is to say that what the body learns and is taught is of great significance at least until the last light of the body fails.

Michael Stephens

THE POETICS OF BOXING

Boxing is not so much a sport, not merely a game as it is, like drama itself, a way of life. You must be willing to give your life to this thing. Like drama, too, there is something Aristotelian about it, maybe even an inversion of the dramatic recipe for a poetics; an inversion, because spectacle comes first, not plot, and it is followed by music, or more specifically, *rhythm*, the source of every great fighter's style and content, this rhythm of action. Also, a young fighter learns by imitating other fighters, and in the case of Asian martial arts, they learn by imitating nature (cranes, mongooses, etc.). There is also a diction to this sport, communicating utterances as varied as brute force to animal grace. Thought is quite subtle, a collaborative thing, combining the resources of the fighter with the capabilities of his cornermen; it is strategy, though more checkers, as Larry Holmes once said, than chess, yet still cognitive. If thought were not required of great boxers, an awful lot of lunks and slugs would have been— could have been—as Marlon Brando's Terry Doyle said, "contenda's." Character is almost a too obvious quality in boxing, from the character of the man who does it, his constitutional and genetic imprint, to that subtler characterization of how to develop oneself in a life, given those rawer potentials for aggression with which we are born.

The late Cus D'Amato summed up character quite well when

259

N. ALICIA BYERS

he referred to his fighters as men who should not be fearless—finally an impossible human aspiration—but men living with fear, and using that fear to their advantage. There are actually two characters a fighter must be, and possibly, given fame, even more than those two characters. The first character is that private one, the boiling inner person, the man shaped from heredity (size, speed, stamina, thresholds of pain, etc.), and the second, the most important characteristic for a boxer, that some are born fighters. But then this translates, like an actor in drama, into the persona which the fighter projects. Some terribly gentle men outside the ring are demons inside of it; other aggressive types quail in the public arena. When fighters become celebrities, which the smallest percentage of them do, that is, become known beyond the world of boxing—men like Johnson, Dempsey, Louis, Robinson, Marciano, Ali—they must assume characters that transcend both a private and ring character, and arrive at a rhythm of this invented, public figure. Marvelous Marvin Hagler verges on this type. Then, too, boxing has been, is peopled with what are called "characters," personalities of such a stylized nature,

they assume the regal proportions of rarefied cartoons or cari-
catures. I used to imagine Toots Shor's being wall-to-wall sports
characters, but maybe it was only the late sportswriter Jimmy
Cannon's own character creating them. Certainly Don King and
Lou Duva come immediately to mind as these types of characters.

At times, Muhammad Ali was this sort of larger-than-life character. I remember once, walking near Lincoln Center, a limo
pulled up to a stop at a light, and when the window rolled down,
there he was, the King and Fool of Boxing, and, to my mind, the
finest athlete of his time—The Greatest—Ali! His face was as
large as a mask, eyeballs stretched to bursting, mouth open and
gaping like an Aristophanic clown, all buffo, and really as campy
as a drag queen, he hooted and shouted and waved at us un-
knowns, demanding that we pay homage, and we did. Some
people waved and shouted back; others ran over and shook his
hand, and his hands were enormous like his face, although everything, unlike the Ali of today, was classically proportioned, almost
like statuary, and I could not help think of that Greek notion of
human perfection in the body. Ali, though, bodied forth every
known opposition, and therefore tension, of personality that great
fighters require: the ferocity, the compassion, the intelligence,
the ignorance, the wealth, the poverty, the populism, the elitism,
the buffoonery, and, yes, even the ultimate tragedy, that final
drama.

Aristotle placed plot above character, although as plot is character, and the reverse, it could also be said that a fighter is the
fight, too. A fighter brings his character to a fight, but that character can only be defined in terms of the course of its actions in
the ring. The best fights are not Stallone-like pushes and pulls
of right and wrong, good and evil—Sonny Liston being the exception to the rule—but rather, in the best cases, two rights
colliding, or a right and a left, and so on, until the cumulative
effect of choices unmasks one opponent. In drama it is called the
recognition scene; in boxing it could be called the telling round.
The plot of a good fight breaks down into those scenes we call
rounds, the interchangeability of those words not escaping a pugilistic writer like Bertolt Brecht in *Mahagonny*. Each round, like
a scene, has its peaks and valleys, its goals, objectives, "through

lines," and obstacles, and the result of ineluctable choices creating that rhythm of action. Consider, for instance, an elemental acting exercise in which two people arm wrestle, while reading aloud bits of dialogue, pushing and pulling, according to the tensions in the respective lines. As drama is physicalized this way, as words become actions, boxing speaks to those who want to listen to it; ideas are given actions. Like drama, something happens, and most often the players are never the same as a result of what happens, those various choices; they are changed; they have been transformed.

Most boxers came to the sport early on, either through formal training by a family member or by regulating their fighting aggressions—having fights, I mean—into a more patterned way. Ray Mancini was on a quest from the time he was a child, trying to vindicate the lost crown of his father, whose career was interrupted by the outbreak of World War II. In my own family, for instance, my father and two older brothers were quite pugilistic, and so early on I confronted first violence, and then, more formal fighting techniques. My horde of younger brothers likewise had similar indoctrinations, though, if I am to be honest here, I was perhaps the poorest of all those boys at fighting; it was not in my nature from the beginning, but I will say that I acquired it over the brutal years in my own household and out on the streets of East New York in Brooklyn and in the working-class suburb on Long Island where we later lived. My father was a small, portly dockworker, but he was amazingly fast in the hands and feet, his temper was ferocious, and I think, still today, like many of his sons he liked to fight, not only as a point of honor, but as a kind of entertainment and theatrical enterprise. My mother had seventeen children, ten of us lived, and most of them were boys. My older brothers were great fighters and still are, to a certain degree, today. I remember one of them coming to a play I wrote about six brothers eulogizing their father in a bar, and after the performance, he came backstage to meet the actors.

The owner of this theater bar was somewhat nervous, because it was located on the West Side on Forty-second Street, the home-ground of the Westies, the Irish Mafia, and this brother had certain "connections," if you will, and as I introduced him around, he only had one thing to say.

"Michael may be a good playwright," he said, "but I can still kick the shit out of him any day of the week."

But my brother's declaration aside, it is worth looking at his "intellectual" brother's past by way of explaining how his own ideas about boxing were formulated. Today when I attend boxing matches, I can pass; that is, I might appear to someone like an ex-boxer. My nose is splattered on my face, one eye is lower than the other, and I've always had certain neurological problems associated with fighting: eye-muscle twitches, and, more privately, sleep disorders, occasional blurred vision, a chronic back problem (missing haymakers), and a general personality disorder of—if not starting fights—then certainly never backing away, standing square, with a low center of gravity. The fact is, though never having been either an amateur or professional fighter, I inhabited through the first twenty-six years or so of my life that nebulous world of bar brawls (hundreds) and sparring matches (likewise hundreds) and semiprofessional debacles, known in the old days as "smokers," illegal boxing matches in which you were paid and the audience bet on the outcome. The name derived from the smoke-filled arena, the bettors drinking and talking all the time— a smoker was to boxing what vaudeville probably was to drama. The bouts were held in Queens and Brooklyn, out on the Island, upstate in cities like Albany, Syracuse, and Troy (a good fighting and betting town), and even in cow towns like Cortland, New York. Sometimes they ventured into the south, places like Georgia, especially near military bases, the opponents usually black and lifers.

All this said, I add hastily that I did not resemble a fighter, was six feet tall and thin, though wiry and immensely belligerent in my youth. My hands and feet were small, not good things for a fighter, but as a friend once pointed out, himself a boxer, I have rolled shoulders, which he thought immensely noteworthy for boxing; I have long arms, powerful legs, and my fighting heart being something like that of a bull terrier. I've never actually lost a fight in my life, and in those circumstances where it appeared that a decision would go against me, I made sure to KO or TKO my opponent, no thing in the ring beyond my ken once I started. Head butts, elbows, using the strings on my gloves to open a cut on the eye—that which was most vicious in my personality often was personified in my ring character. Like everyone else in my family, I had a bad temper; I was, and probably still am, incapable of being knocked out—our father taught us to die first—and what may seem strange to someone who knows nothing of this sport, outside of the ring I was, and still am, modest, polite, and even shy.

All of my early boxing matches were with friends much better than myself, we used no mouthpieces or headgear, and we fought until the other person was knocked down or out, or called it quits. In a Catholic prep school we had boxing classes, where I did fairly well, until I had to meet my down-the-street neighbor, an Irish superathlete, to whose blows I fell immediately. Some friends lost teeth; it was the first of the sixteen breaks to my nose. His victory was more psychological than anything else, because I was impressed with his basketball and football prowess, and forgot, momentarily, that he did not have as much of a killer heart as I had. Today, I think, he would stand no chance. My other adversaries were a bunch of brothers across the street, perhaps the finest athletes I ever encountered in my life, but again it was their physical strength, not their mental prowess, which defeated me. Once, in high school, socking the best of these brothers square in the nose during one of these improvised matches, I made him cry, and that made it hard for him to intimidate me ever again.

There was the vaguest chance that I could have gotten into boxing; through a Catholic youth agency for troubled children, I even once met Floyd Patterson, but these things were not to be. I left home when I was fifteen, and although I never fought in the Golden Gloves, I did spar occasionally, usually for money, with people who were, and even several good professionals. My fighting weight was 155 pounds, though if I had done more roadwork, I would have been a welterweight, something I never thought about being at the time. My mind was on the middle-weights, to me the most dangerous, beautiful, and exciting class in this so-called sport. They had the speed of the lighter classes, and some of them possessed the punches of heavyweights. You have to be very good to advance, as an amateur or professional, in this weight division. During this younger period, on my own, I often went to the gym on Fourteenth Street, and even though some people were impressed with me—good lateral movement from playing basketball, hard to hit, a jab and combinations—I could not muster the discipline necessary to commit myself fully to boxing. Becoming a writer, anyhow, had a much higher priority, even then, and though the superficial qualities of writing and boxing can't be denied—the isolation, the training, the discipline—they are two very different activities. In those days I mostly knew writers, and only a few boxers, although among the writers I was considered a fighter, while the fighters did not exactly consider me one of their own. Still, there were any number of fighters I met who had genuine interests in reading, and some who even wrote themselves, not so rare a thing when you consider Ali's once-articulate witticisms and doggerel.

Even when I was not in a gym boxing, I was getting into fights everywhere—in bars, on the street, outside of diners, in the city, and upstate where I attended college for a while. After I quit college and worked on ships, there were also fights at sea and in ports, some of them battles to the death, and luckily I was not one of those combatants. The last bar fight I ever had was in a writers' bar in New York. I was blindsided by a punch, and then I went to town on this journalist. The aftermath was so ugly, I decided right there never to fight again, and I also stopped going to gyms to spar. I've more or less kept that promise to myself, the one exception being a time several years back when a couple of young fighters in the Bronx suckered me into a ring, ostensibly to do me damage, and I was so enraged by them that I tore apart their friend in one round, and walked out of there quickly.

This is not to say I have not "almost" gotten into brawls: that time in front of Columbia University after an evening of teaching, when this jock hit me in the head with an iceball and, without throwing a punch, mentally I put together five punches, and he knew I had him knocked out, and so apologized; I stood talking to him sideways, my right hand gesturing in a way so that it could be turned into a punch; I stood outside the arc of his right hand, presuming that is where he was going to punch from. I write this, not as an excuse, but as an explanation for why I watch boxing on television or at live matches. More than any other sport, I understand boxing; I know what it feels like to be in a ring, to be hitting another human, or being hit by him. It both elates and disgusts me. It is atavistic, even at times barbaric. Long afterward, this "sport" creates problems with the liver, kidneys, spleen, eyes, breathing. Some of the neurological problems are devastating.

It is probably the worst type of exercise for the memory, for remembering; short-term memory is especially affected from the blows to the head. I am the first to note the pathetic lives of old boxers, these afterlives of living legends, falling asleep and drooling at matches. Still, I go to these matches. Had I not been born into a family with so many brothers and a bellicose father, probably none of this would interest me one bit. Had I not boxed, I doubt that any fascination would be there. If I see a poetics in boxing, it is because I have an archetype from early childhood still hovering around my head. There is nothing abstract about the pain involved in this sport; sometimes my empathy is so great at a match that I go home aching in my stomach, bruised all over, one eye half shut. In the morning, I am forever kidded by my wife and daughter for the way I noisily breathe at night, all the results of those constant breaks to my nose. But then as a writer I see boxing today as a durable metaphor for a craft, and when it is done well, I recognize it as an art, and that these brutal men are artists. As Aristotle said, we humans are fascinated by imitation, and boxing's mimesis is a structured, patterned imitation of certain lives, those that were poor and tough, full of pity and terror, and capable of catharsis. This, too, is what Antonin Artaud might have meant by a theater of cruelty, the actor totally sacrificing himself to a deadly craft—the boxer boxing.

Jeanne Wilmot Carter

KISSING THE WILD HORSE'S MANE

The first time I really "considered" boxing was the night Cassius Clay fought Sonny Liston. I was fourteen, sitting in the Kansas City Country Club with my boyfriend, whose great-grandfather, the grandson of the first white man west of the Mississippi, had built the club. Or that's how the story went. No blacks. No Jews. Except guests and workers. My boyfriend was a nice guy. He was talking to an old wrinkled black waiter about the upcoming fight.

By the time war had become a part of my generation's childish consciousness, Cassius had become Ali and was showing us the way. Ali had already lost the championship once. Our king. A true martial artist. He'd be back. Sting-like-a-bee Aleeeee. He had the Supreme Court of Amerika on his side. He'd entered the Garden. Madison Square in 1971. Everybody was there, in reds and blacks and greens. *Life* magazine made it one of the events of the year. It was a Black Event. Maybe the nation divided would meet in a boxing ring instead of fighting it out on the streets, over dead men's bodies. Only four years since Dee-troit. That was our rhetoric at any rate, those of us who were devastated by Orangeburg and Jackson State long before Kent State flickered on the hot tube.

With the Zaire fight, when there were those of us who believed our king could even move world politics by diverting the insurgents with the spectacle of world championship, I was learning to kiss the wild horse's mane. In those days, politics, martial arts, and boxing were one and the same for some people. Especially in New York. It was long enough after '68 that I bristled when even the old standbys asked me about my priorities: international or domestic, which are you into? Translated, that meant Vietnam or blacks—which made your glory days? Sure, we had a duty to give more than a nod to the horror threading those boys from the Pentagon to Saigon to My Lai, but what did I know about boys? I knew a man who had once been a boy, who had won two Navy Crosses for his country in '45. He was my blood, and he fathered a son who helped get the boys out of 'Nam. I knew enough about "the fact" that there was something out there called power, and that it was not within my reach and that it was not all bad. I knew about blacks and I learned to hate what they hated. That was my power.

I learned to kill in the softest of all ways. "Kissing the Wild Horse's Mane" was my elaboration of a real tai chi move called "Parting the Wild Horse's Mane." In my version, the fluid motion of my arms and legs emulates those quick flutters of the dragonfly as its lips lightly brush a single hair of an imaginary golden Oriental horse I named the Sha-Hamai, to pluck from that strand a sweet sweat before the Sha-Hamai can retaliate with a swat of its tail. I made up my own moves because the beauty of the form—and its deadly power—became a metaphor for what I perceived to be a nobility in any endeavor. This process corporealized those things we normally judge too quickly, and provided space for knowledge before attack, patience and bending before or after aggression. The quick departure required of the dragonfly was not cowardice; rather it demonstrated the necessity for the warrior to be prepared to face any attack from one of the eight directions as defined in the *Treatise on the Thirteen Kinetic Movements As They Relate to Mental Comprehension*. The talons of a hawk about to capture a rabbit are recreated by the fingers of a martial artist "Grasping the Bird's Tail." The spirit of the cat as it is about to spring is always present, especially for some in the "Jade Girl (Angel) Works at the Shuttle." The prescribed number of movements in tai chi can vary from 24 to 108 or more depending upon the school or master.

Walking the streets of New York with my friends Beku and Hector was like being given a pair of X-ray vision glasses so that I could see what others did not. Others unlike us, anyway. I had never noticed how men nodded to each other with a regularity. A greeting. Where had all these people been when I had hit the streets of New York before? These people, walking around in full view yet fading into crowds so that their oddness would not be apparent to the typical New Yorker, stood higher on the balls of their feet. Their knees bent just ever so slightly more than the knees of their gray-flanneled counterparts. They were of many colors and sizes. They moved with a grace not common to most westerners, and lived behind locked doors that lead into large spaces, glistening with clean angularity and symmetry. Only mats were scattered about the floors.

Each dojo was a world unto itself and there were rules of each which slowly I learned as I grew accustomed to the animal world, the animal presence in me. There were blacks and Burmese and Japanese and whites. The Chinese would stay to themselves, except for those who taught people like myself just the movements. No non-Chinese could be privy to certain of the secrets, like the Touch of Death. As pop culture welcomed Bruce Lee into its celebrity, the books in the stores in Chinatown began disappearing and the Chinese with their mysteries went underground.

The softest, most melodic and smooth of the styles, tai chi chuan, had as its backup the most brutal form of death. From the flowing arms of the artist could come a swipe of the hand so quick and accurate as to reverse the "chi" flowing through the meridians of the body, like a life's blood coursing through its veins, so that in one week, three weeks, or, depending on the placement and intensity of the "touch," within three months that person's liver or kidneys or very heart would explode from the energy turned back upon itself, reversing the natural order of things. We all figured that's how Bruce Lee got his. Someone got closer, perhaps even handshake close, than that space between the tops of two bowed heads, and Bruce was on the receiving end.

On the way to the uptown showing of the Zaire fight—I was with Beku and Hector—our car turned the corner of 104th and Amsterdam and got no further. Seven cop cars and two unmarked cabs swept around us. Guns were drawn to each of our heads. Patty Hearst had been sighted with two black guys driving east in a car with a midwestern license plate. The wiry, dressed-down black man holding a gun to my sensei's head had jumped from a cab we hadn't even seen. I told the dude that what he'd done was unconstitutional, but it didn't matter, because before I finished speaking a second .44 Magnum was jammed up under my chin. We three sat stiffened with iron rods forcing our faces forward.

This guy with one foot on Beku's leg, holding two guns, one on me and one on Beku, was going to make lieutenant before he was thirty. He calmly shot out staccato orders to the other two undercover cops holding two other guns on us. You could see that this commander was a "down" street dude who, as it turned out, had been an artist since growing up on those streets near 118th and Lenox. I imagined he remembered the wars between the Mighty Disciples of Bed-Stuy and the Rosedale Bombers when he was in a junior ace gang in Harlem. The Disciples were the gods in those days. They knew karate better than anybody on the street. They boxed like a motherfucker. "We're the *Migh*ty Dis*cip*les from *Cham*bers *Street*, and be *de* be da *baba* baa baa baa *baa*." There's words to that riff, but I'm not one of the ones who has the privilege of their use. Another kind of constitutional right, not recognized *unless* you're on the street. The Disciples would chant as they hit the street ready to rumble. Their eyes would tear in anticipation. They chanted, they created rap, they danced through their opponents, until their foes got better and they got "dugie." And then they died. This guy with a gun to our heads wasn't going to die. He'd been the youngest black on the force to make detective. He'd become a real artist. He was smart like Ali. The irony was that it was Beku—my sensei—who had taught him his moves. At the police academy. Their eyes clicked recognition. I was immobilized. Hector figured we were dead, so quick like a cat, moving like a "Snake Creeping Down," Hector ducked the gun, slithered from the car and rolled to the gutter, holding a door of the empty car behind us, in front of his face. This cop wasn't about to fuck with Beku, and he knew Beku wasn't about to fuck with any whacked-out white girl who could change her name from Patty to Tanya and become a revolutionary within weeks. The cars disappeared before I even realized the Magnum no longer held up my head. In and out, and nobody knew the difference but us. This cop had his style down.

Ali ran in like a bomber pilot that night, like a King, but then he didn't do the Ali shuffle. He played it against the ropes with Foreman, taking in the punches with his body in such a way that their impact was lessened. He laid back. Foreman weighed in at 220 and Ali weighed in at a trim 216½. Foreman had six years on him. Ali wasn't worried. He was just as powerful, just as beautiful a boxer as ever. He had a plan. He didn't run. No place to hide, right Joe? But after taking Foreman with rights, Ali decided he didn't want to duke it out from the gitgo. Couldn't. He wanted to do something different. He was cool. A little like junkie cool, where that kinda cool comes from—the language that is—but not so cool he was icebox cool. He didn't feel a thing, or at least it looked that way, but his subtle body punches pushed Foreman back eventually and Sweet Ali's pretty face hadn't been touched. He waited. Somebody said that if you wait ten years and you're still hot, you haven't begun the wait. The third round. The fourth round. Then in the fifth round something happened. Ali took a pummeling that should have hurt him real bad, but in the last thirty seconds of the round he got down to business. Ali hit Foreman with maybe twenty of the hardest punches of boxing history. We saw his game. He shuffled once to let us know. The sixth round was a power round for Ali, but in moderation. What the fuck was happening? The seventh round was the same. The eighth had Ali against the ropes again, yet it was not the same Foreman who entered the fifth round holding him there. Then in the last twenty seconds Ali whaled. He rose up like Jonah and whipped his regal head around, ready for the mantle to be replaced—and it was. Ali KO'd Foreman in the *eighth round*. The King could not be stopped.

And he kept on keepin' on. Maybe that little police lieutenant did the same. Or maybe that lieutenant got even smarter, before Sugar Ray Leonard showed us how to be "young, gifted, and black"—*and* rich. I'll never know about the lieutenant, but I know something about Sugar. In '76, Sugar burst forth as the New Man—and he was a boxer. He was every little girl's dream— black or white. The color boundary was down, at least in the media ring. The King began dying a slow black death, still alive but punch-dead. We never expected *that* of him. And here was Sugar, a beautiful boy who wore a picture of his little girlfriend on each of his boxing socks. He didn't boast. With sugar in his mouth and fire in his eyes he did back flips across the ring after a win. He was the pioneer, spirit of nature and youthfulness of our young country, which had aged only slightly through the sixties.

Sugar fought three glory fights after the Olympics, the one against Benitez that got him the title, the *"No más"* Durán, and then the fight against Hearns that said he wasn't just a pretty boy. It was only a hop, skip, and jump to the reported $40 million. That was good. I liked that politically. Stop while you're ahead and then work another show. Your body, your mind, your plea-sures to come. I *believe* in that—for the normal man, the black man, the white man, the children of the eighties who have not been unaffected by the privacy, individualism, and separateness of Ray's Kingdom. He didn't have to be Our Prince. But I don't believe in all those things for the fighting man—not the artist. The privacy is not my business and I embrace it . . . but to give up the fight, Sugar?

The fighting man *is* an artist. The fighting man who is not a team player, that is: the boxer, and a few others. He is not rea-sonable, except within his own form. His form is not a system. Picasso was not restricted by his forms, because they were his. Nor Borges. Picasso and Borges were boxers—but artists of the mind are luckier than artists of the body. The binary mind at a certain age evolves from the spongelike quality it is born to and by the age of twenty becomes a more analytical muscle. It has less capacity for rote memorization, more for complications and creations. It is at this age the artists of the ring peak. But their remaining years are numbered. So what does the fighter, the fighter who is an artist do? He keeps on fighting. Like Picasso kept painting and Borges writing. Ali had no choice but to con-tinue, then.

But there is an irony here. The fight, in the West, is still primitive. There are two challenging, one the other. We are of the jungle, all sinews, movement, and opposition. But sometimes we are not compatible fighters. We would be better both on one side. We are not opposite enough. In other parts of the world the fight is not between *any* two, only the most opposed two. The body and mind are often not so readily damaged; rather they are extended because the teaching of the fight is everything. It is the tool, not the end. The end rarely comes. These, of course, are some of the ones who first called themselves martial artists.

Yet I am a child of the West, and I know we are the artists of this century. Ali can still believe that all it takes is that one shot—that one last shot, but there's always one more waiting out there. He is the praying mantis. He fights to the death, over and over, and now it is over, but for all that is the urge to fight, in that space where there is no light or dark, no good or evil, for all that, Ray Leonard came back, too. He came back to the Fight.

Born in the USA, we'll fight to the death, like the artist who cannot give up his art no matter what toll it takes on his body, his mind, his people. The fight is primitive in the way the best of art comes from the primordial. We *are* the world's barbarians, but there is charm and greatness to us—our barbarism. We don't stand back like the Taoist and see the "yin and yang" and the ways the Tao's oppositeness moves all things. No. We take stands. We go right in there and fuck it all up. Or make it all okay. We are either yin or yang, depending on the object "tuned in" upon. Argument in search of reasonable compromise is torture for the artist. He is alone and will do what he must do. Standing back and reflecting is indulged only as a momentary fix before returning to the arena.

Ray Leonard didn't give up the Fight; he came back. But he came back only to fight Hagler, a compatible fighter who was opposite enough. Ray Leonard showed my generation something about the Will, as opposed to rhetoric. If there *is* a foe out there for him, Ray will again return; but the energy that would otherwise be expended on boxing insignificant opponents is spent on developing his Will. In this way he resembles the original martial artists.

I believe, if he owed us anything, he owed us one more fight—against Hagler. Leonard had not completed his career, he had left us hanging, waiting for that last round that would attest to his greatness. That one last glory shot. And like the true artist, he was compelled to complete this unfinished business. Ray could not leave unfinished business any more than a storyteller would leave untold the end of the tale, a painter the brush stroke that repeats how the painting emerged in order to complete the circle. Will Ray return from yet another retirement? The announcer will hit the ring. The names will be a trill to the tongue. And the boys will be ready to rock 'n' roll.

Daniel Halpern

DISTANCE & EMBRACE

> If they cut my bald head open, they will find one big boxing glove.
> That's all I am. I live it.
>
> MARVELOUS MARVIN HAGLER, former middleweight champion of the world

1. Their names are as colorful as their robes and trunks—colorful and suggestive as the names of race horses, speedboats, and racing cars, those objects of grace and speed. In the ring the announcers quiet the unquiet crowd and call out these muscled nouns in their bright, accented voices that hover under the glare and heat of the lights: In this corner John "Hollywood" Materi, Ray "Boom Boom" Mancini, Jimmy "Bang Bang" Harrison, Thomas "The Hit Man" Hearns, Johnny "Bump City" Bumphus, "Rockin' " Robin Blake, James "Hard Rock" Green, Al "Earthquake" Carter, Hector "Macho" Camacho, Frank "The Animal" Fletcher, Donald "The Cobra" Curry, Ricky "The Mongoose" Clements, Gregg "Zion Lion" Edelman, "Tiger" Jack Fox, Rick "King Kong" Kellar, Tyrone "The Butterfly" Crawley, Johnny "Honeyboy" Bratton, Alvin "Too Sweet" Hayes.

2. The first officially covered fight, promoted by Achilles, the Don King of the pre-Hellenic world, was Homer's assignment back in 1100 B.C.:

> Both men, belted, stepped into the ring and, toe to toe, let fly at one another, hitting solid punches. Heavy fists then milled together as they worked in close with a fierce noise of grinding jaw. Their bodies ran with sweat. Then Epeios leapt out with a long

left hook and smashed the other's cheek as he peered out through puffed eyes. He could keep his feet no longer, but his legs gave way and down he went . . .

(translation by Robert Fitzgerald)

3. Was it on Wednesday nights that Pabst Blue Ribbon beer sponsored their television fights? My father and I would make ourselves chocolate malteds, clear the living room of my mother and three sisters, and sit down to an evening of boxing. Watching a fight on TV is like listening to Fred Astaire tap-dancing in tennis shoes, but neither my father nor I were aware of what we were missing, and it would be another twenty-five years before I witnessed firsthand the impact of a punch thrown by a 220-pound man in good shape.

On one particular evening back in 1955, my father and I sat in front of our Philco radio and listened as a game Archie Moore rose three times from the blows of Rocky Marciano. In that late September evening Moore failed in his heroic attempt to move up from the light-heavyweight ranks to capture the heavyweight crown—and I became a boxing fan.

4. It is the English who invented boxing as we know it. The father of modern boxing, James Figg, became England's first champion in 1719. Figg's pals were Jonathan Swift and Alexander Pope. In 1743 the first rules were set out by boxer Jack Broughton, a disciple of Figg who worked toward developing the "art" of boxing—blocking, parrying, slipping, and hitting on the retreat—until he was blinded by the "cleaver" punch of butcher Jack Slack. With Broughton's defeat boxing fell from public favor, eliciting from a bemoaning Dr. Samuel Johnson, "I should be sorry to see prizefighting go out. Every art should be preserved, and the art of defense is surely important."

Johnson, Swift, and Pope weren't the only men of letters affected by "the Sweet Science." Byron was taught to spar by "Mr." John Jackson, a lapidary figure who, it was rumored, was capable of signing his name with an eighty-four-pound weight dangling from his little finger. Thackeray and Dickens attended the first world title bout between English Tom Sayers and Californian

John Camel Heenan. After forty-two rounds the police arrived and a draw was declared. And the poet John Clare, retired to an insane asylum, at times imagined he was the well-known prizefighter Ben Caunt, at other times "Boxer Byron." He addressed the art of defense in his poem "Badger":

> When badgers fight, then everyone's a foe.
> The dogs are clapped and urged to join the fray;
> The badger turns and drives them all away.
> Though scarcely half as big, demure and small,
> He fights with dogs for hours and beats them all.

The longest heavyweight fight took place in 1833. James "Deaf" Burke, after ninety-nine rounds and three hours and sixteen minutes, finally killed Irishman Simon Byrne. However, the longest recorded fight in the history of boxing took place in 1893 between lightweights Andy Bowen and Jack Burke: seven hours and nineteen minutes, 110 rounds.

The era of bare-knuckle fighting was ushered out by John L. Sullivan. "On 8 July 1889," writes boxing historian Harry Carpenter, "Sullivan, miraculously fit again having survived typhoid, jaundice, and whiskey, fights Jack Kilrain at Richburg, Mississippi, under a blazing sun." After seventy-five rounds Sullivan was victorious. This was to be the last bare-knuckle championship. As the nineteenth century drew to a close, boxing was brought back on track by the Queensberry rules. They state a round lasts three minutes, with a one-minute rest between each round. Fighters must wear gloves. There's a ten-second count after all knockdowns, and a referee has the right to stop a fight if the fighter has no chance of winning, or can't defend himself.

5. There are currently two primary boxing organizations that rank boxers: the WBA (World Boxing Association), whose title fights go fifteen rounds, and the WBC (World Boxing Council), whose title fights run twelve rounds—three rounds were recently dropped to help ensure the safety of the boxers after Deuk Koo Kim died following his title fight with Ray "Boom Boom" Mancini.

6. The Riverview Ballroom, Cobo Hall, Detroit. 10:00 A.M. 1984. The boxers begin to drift in for the weigh-in. Alvin "Too Sweet" Hayes arrives with entourage. A lightweight, Hayes stands a bent 6′1″ and weighs 135 pounds. Professional record: 21–0 (eighteen KOs). He removes his shirt and holds out his arm so an official can tape his reach. He's like a great bird, bony and elegant, powerful and graceful, standing in his underwear being measured. He'll be fighting Jesús "Chu Cho" Lozano, a quiet, self-contained unit with a record of 28–6. He watches Hayes sadly. He will be knocked out in the second round with a looping overhand right.

The North American Boxing Federation champion, David Braxton, arrives. A junior middleweight carrying a record of 26–1 (eighteen KOs), he's coming off a major victory over James "Hard Rock" Green, won in spite of a broken hand suffered early in the fight. He's dressed casually—blue jeans, white shirt, and black tennis shoes. He sits alone and speaks to no one. Thirty, his face is chiseled and tough, nearly mean until he gets up to be weighed, when something kind rolls across his expression— something momentary and quick, like his movements from the chair to the scales. He is the star of the weigh-in. The gestures of the other boxers as they move around him authorize this position.

Every fighter is intensely aware of his own body, the way he takes up space. Each stands around, working a particular repertoire of moves. There's constant head movement in the room, side to side, down, back and away, weaving, weaving and bobbing, one or two quick, short, inside rights. Twenty shoulders dipping, turning, squaring off. There's an abundance of street presence here, both facile and serious. One of the Latin fighters turns suddenly at me and, pointing to the river out the window, says, "There was ice on that river last time I was here." Muscled, the steely Detroit River rolls on.

Braxton's as soft-spoken as his face is hard-edged. He got into boxing because he discovered he could get away from the punches thrown at him. He sees boxing as an art as well as a way of life. "It makes me different. One-on-one competition—like archery. I meet people because of boxing. I guess they like my personality.

They like the way I carry myself. I'm the kind of guy who stays to himself. I don't mingle much. I'm a homebody guy. But boxing is something else, though. I enjoy the ring and the lights. People come to you. I like to entertain people because I feel people entertain me, you know?"

Back at the hotel, a few tough blocks from Cobo Hall where Braxton and Hayes will fight tonight, we try, without success, to track down Emanuel Steward, head of the Kronk Gym. A religious man with a chauffeured gold limo, Steward is also a man of many moves. He's ubiquitous yet elusive. But once reached there's not another man in the fight game who's warmer, more charming and accommodating. "We've put together a pretty good family organization," he says of his work with the Kronk fighters. "It's a family thing, we go fishing on weekends, we play softball— some of these kids go back ten years. If you spend time with kids they grow up. Milt McCrory first came to see me when he was twelve. Most of my boys, contrary to what people think, are not really that poor. They come from good areas around the country."

Everywhere I go with Steward he's greeted with a sober respect, by the church elders we dine with at Carl's Chop House as well as by black kids on the street outside Kronk Gym. I ask him how he feels about the punishment the members of his "family" must undergo as fighters. It's not a question you'll get a direct answer to in the boxing world. He said, "It's a tough sport. The human body is like an automobile. It's got so many miles on it and that's it. Of course some will go more miles than others."

His stable of boxers includes such notables as Thomas Hearns, WBC junior middleweight champ, who fought Roberto Durán this past June. (Durán, the Panamanian pugilist who went the distance with Marvin Hagler and is the only fighter to defeat media star Sugar Ray Leonard; Durán, who knocked out horses as a teenager and is called "The Little Killer" by fighting promotor Don King.) Hearns knocked out Durán convincingly in a quick round and a half.

Another Kronk fighter, Milton "The Iceman" McCrory, sporting a record of 23–0, is the WBC welterweight champion. And David Braxton, who is looking to find his way into a junior middleweight championship ring as soon as Hearns steps up in weight to pursue middleweight champ Marvin Hagler.

7. "He was dapper, handsome, and Chicago's own. He drove a pink Cadillac with the name of 'Honeyboy' on the side. There was plenty of money and beautiful women." So runs the description in *The Ring* magazine, "the bible of boxing," of Johnny "Honeyboy" Bratton, one of the sport's many colorful figures. This is a sport with a plethora of heroes: Jack Johnson, the first black champion, who developed the art of defense. John L. Sullivan, the infamous Irish-American drinker, remembered for pounding the bars of Europe and America bragging, "I can lick any son-of-a-bitch in the world." Gentleman Jim Corbett—"Pompadour Jim"—a jaunty bank clerk and boxing's first dandy. The triple world champs Henry Armstrong and Bob Fitzsimmons. Jack Dempsey, the Babe Ruth of boxing. The beloved Joe Louis ("The Brown Bomber"). Rocky Marciano, Muhammad Ali, Sugar Ray Robinson, Jake La Motta, Carmen Basilio, Sandy Saddler.

8. It's the *spectacle* of sporting events that makes sport in America—perhaps in the rest of the world as well—the great classless pastime. Tonight it's fight time in Detroit's Cobo Hall, the home ring of the Kronk boxing team. The crowd is restless, but the ring, so named for the group of people that gathers around a fight, takes on a presence of its own. The red corner post and the blue, the neutral corners, stationed. The red and purple velvet-covered ropes and the stained canvas. The referee. The cornermen and fighters stepping through the ropes.

I'm sitting at ringside watching a preliminary fight. Tyrone Trice and Teddy "Hook 'Em" Hatfield. Seated next to me is the boxing commissioner. A pleasant man of about forty, he turns to me and says, "I can see you've never sat at ringside." I attempt a look of surprised irritation. "You wouldn't be wearing a light-colored sports jacket," he adds. By the end of the first fight, stopped prematurely because of a deep gash over "Hook 'Em's" left eye (which later required twenty-six stitches), the commissioner's meaning becomes clear.

Suddenly the lights snap on and the cable TV cameras begin

to roll somewhere in their dark chambers. Rap music comes alive over the loudspeakers—a song called "Breakin': There's No Stoppin' Us"—and in dances Alvin "Too Sweet" Hayes in high theater, earning his nickname. Yellow satin shirt and trunks, a yellow silk mask, high yellow sneakers bedecked with black pom-poms. At 6'1", 135 pounds, he is a gold thread, "breaking" to the cheers of the crowd. Standing ovation. Two rounds later he's back in the dressing room, changing. His record changed from 21–0 to 22–0.

And now David Braxton enters the ring. Hard, serious, no play in him—one of Goya's very own. Within five rounds he's broken Miguel Sepulveda's arm and the fight is stopped. In the dressing room he signs a few autographs, slips into an immaculate white suit, mauve shirt, and purple tie, and disappears into the inelegant Detroit night with the city's most beautiful woman on his arm.

9. When fighters start at each other there seems to be, to the untrained eye, chaos in the ring as the exchange of blows starts up. The punches are fast, and it's difficult to determine who's getting hit regardless of how close you may be sitting. The sound of the gloves can't help you. And the response of the crowd is the least informed; they've come to get rid of a few thousand verbs, for knockouts, for blood, for something unrefined—certainly not for boxing at its most artful. One need be present at a fight only once to know in what way this is true. Boxing crowds can be moblike, and with *them* lies the essence of violence. The fighters practice an atavistic art; they attempt to make a decent living one of the rougher ways. "They have a dream," boxing referee Larry Hazzard told me. "And if the dream is gone, well, then it's a payday." Typically, $300 the match.

At its best a fight is fast and thoughtful, a series of calculated movements around the ring. To get to the top a fighter must exhibit some combination of boxing essentials. He must have good speed and movement, stamina and balance, an ability to cover up when he's been hurt. He must be able to slip punches (i.e., avoid getting hit) and make good and constant use of the jab. He must counterpunch (i.e., punch when getting punched) and punch in combination, using a full arsenal: overhand rights, left and right hooks, straight rights and lefts, lead rights, and uppercuts (a punch invented by an early nineteenth-century Jewish fighter by the name of Dutch Sam). And it's best if a fighter has a good chin (i.e., in the words of A. J. Liebling, "an unlimited absorptive capacity for percussion").

10. Their varied personalities are as hearty as the bodies they represent. In boxing, personality is money in the bank, their investment in the future. If their boxing skills equal their talk, it will pay off in media attention and big money fights. Ali, Leonard, and Hagler (who alone made $7.85 million in 1983) are three of the most visible boxers in recent years. And those who can't compete in *this* ring suffer what fighters like to call "lack of respect and recognition." It was heavyweight champ Larry Holmes's complaint for years, although by now he's certainly proven himself. In any case, he's made his money. He expresses an attitude toward the dollar in this way: "It's hard being black. You ever been black? I was black once—when I was poor." He has chosen to lead a quiet, family life in his hometown of Easton, Pennsylvania, contributing generously to the town and its local charities. Perhaps he'll even retire before it's too late. In his own words, "Your mind makes a date your body can't keep."

There's a lot of *psych* in the fight game. It can occur anywhere, but in the ring it begins when the fighters are brought together by the referee. This is how Ali began to knock out George Foreman in Kinshasa. When they met in the center of the ring Ali said to Foreman, "You've heard of me since you were young. You've been following me since you were a little boy. Now, you must meet me, your master!"

If there are aspects of the sport not overly pleasing to watch, it's precisely this fact that contributes to the spectacle of boxing. Boxing is nothing if not direct, for fighter and fan alike. When boxers are in the ring viewers experience them completely. Unlike baseball, football, and basketball players, they have no uniforms to hide in, no dugout to turn into—they are never off camera. We see the sport and we see what's behind the sport, willing or no.

11. It's 6:00 P.M., 1984, Cotillion Ballroom, Atlantic City. I'm waiting in line with a press pass to watch a night of boxing at Resorts International. The man in front of me is of medium height, black, and stocky; he's wearing a Hawaiian shirt and is being turned away for lack of a ticket. He tries to explain that he's come with one of the boxers, but the woman at the gate appears underwhelmed with this piece of information, and as he turns back I see that it's Smokin' Joe Frazier. I quickly explain to the avid ticket taker that this man is the ex-heavyweight champion of the world and is working with me. She backs off and Joe and I enter the ballroom. "I don't think we've met," he says. "Halpern." "Thanks," he jabs, clenching my hand, which disappears in his large, warm handshake. "Let me know if there's ever anything I can do for you."

I find my seat at ringside, next to the boxing writers. To my left is a youngish man whose name I'm never given. He's got a patch over one eye and has secured for himself a half-pound sack of sunflower seeds, a few of which he offers me. On my right is Ted Larve, editor of *Neutral Corner* and a respected presence on the New Jersey boxing scene. Fighters in street clothes nod grimly to him, the judges joke with him, and at one point a man who introduces himself as being from the state Attorney General's office appears, discusses increased funding to help promote boxing, and disappears.

Larry Hazzard, one of the more elegant and careful referees in the business, is moving in the ring. He's restless, but then he's a dancer in the ring, moving between the boxers and out again as if the fighters' moves were choreographed to his. "I treat fighters the way I liked to be treated when I was fighting," he told me earlier. A serious middleweight pro, and two-time Golden Glove middleweight champion, he finally gave up boxing to become perhaps the most impressive "third man" since Ruby ("Jewel of the Ghetto") Goldstein. Hazzard's also a family man and a high school principal, whose life has been boxing since he was thirteen. I asked Hazzard why he thinks so many club fighters continue to enter the ring only to get beat up each time out. "Well, you see, to them they have a dream. These are young men with dreams."

Throughout the evening Hazzard *conducts* the boxing, ne-gotiates the ring, moving in, circling, walking, looking—*Let him go! Hold it. No. No! Come on, punch out! You cut that out, Jimmy!*—constantly watching the participants for buckling legs, rolling eyes, and lack of defense.

The main event is about to begin. The ring announcer, Michael Buffer, who pays more attention to the syllables of proper nouns, their duration and texture, than any man west of the Boardwalk, is Resorts' answer to Efrem Zimbalist, Jr. Dapper and suave, he introduces the boxing notables present at ringside: Jeff Simms, heavyweight contender; Dwight Braxton, ex-WBC light-heavy-weight champion; Joey Giardello, ex-middleweight champ of the world; and my old pal, Smokin' Joe Frazier, ex-heavyweight champion of the world. Buffer returns to ring center and into his hand-held mike announces, "Welcome ladies and gentlemen to Resorts International. It's time to rumble!"

12. Sure it's a rough sport. Perhaps the roughest. And if, out of the hundred best-paid athletes in America in 1983, the first four are boxers, only five boxers appear in the next ninety-six. Not much room at the top. What is the passion? Is it Hazzard's dream that drives them? That drives them to ignore the kind of damage that might one day alter their lives? Liebling wrote of an old-time fighter buying drinks in a saloon: "As I shared his bounty I thought of all his contemporary lawn-tennis players, laid away with their thromboses, and the golfers hoisted out of sand pits suffering coronary occlusions. If they had turned in time to a more wholesome sport, I reflected, they might still be hanging on as board chairmen and senior editors instead of having their names on memorial pews. I asked Mr. Ray how many fights he had had and he said, 'a hundert and forty. The last one was with gloves. I thought the game was getting soft, so I retired.' "

Artists tend to be passionate about practicing their craft and sullen art, regardless of money and success—amassed *or* unat-tained. It keeps poets writing in obscurity for a pittance. It keeps a boxer like Sugar Ray Leonard, a superstar probably worth over forty million dollars, unable to resist reentering the ring, despite a detached retina that threatens his eyesight. For both poet and fighter the price is willingly paid to pursue the obsession. But perhaps in boxing, more so than with any other sport, we have before us the metaphor stripped down to its bare essentials, the ultimate emblem, for all that can happen to the athlete, to the artist, to us all.

Joyce Carol Oates

ON BOXING

It's a terrible sport, but it's a sport. . . . The fight for survival
is the fight.

ROCKY GRAZIANO, former middleweight champion of the world

They are young welterweight boxers so evenly matched they
might be twins, though one has a redhead's pallor and the other
is a dusky-skinned Hispanic. Circling each other in the ring,
beneath the glaring lights, trying jabs, tentative left hooks, right
crosses that dissolve in midair or turn into harmless slaps. How
to get inside! How to press an advantage, score a point or two,
land a single punch! It seems they have forgotten all they've been
trained to do and the Madison Square Garden fight crowd is
getting noisy, derisive, impatient. Time is running out. "Those
two—what'd they do, wake up this morning and decide they were
boxers?" a man behind me says in disgust. (He's dark, nattily
dressed, neat-trimmed moustache and tinted glasses. A sophisticated fight fan. Knows all the answers. Two hours later he will
be screaming, "Tommy! Tommy! Tommy!" over and over in a
paroxysm of grief as, on the giant closed-circuit television screen
lowered over the ring, middleweight champion Marvelous Marvin
Hagler batters his brash challenger Thomas Hearns into insensibility.)

The young welterweights are surely conscious of the chorus
of jeers, boos, and catcalls in this great cavernous space reaching
up into the cheap $20 seats in the balconies amid the constant
milling of people in the aisles, the commingled smells of hot dogs,
beer, cigarette and cigar smoke, hair oil. But they are locked

286

desperately together in their futile match—circling, "dancing," jabbing, slapping, clinching—now a flurry of light blows, clumsy footwork, yet another sweaty stumbling despairing clinch into the ropes that provokes a fresh wave of derision as the referee helps them apart. Why are they here in the Garden of all places, each fighting, it seems, his first professional fight? Neither wants to hurt the other—neither is angry at the other. When the bell sounds at the end of the fourth and final round the crowd boos a little louder. The Hispanic boy, silky yellow shorts, damp frizzy floating hair, strides about his corner of the ring with his gloved hand aloft—not in defiance of the boos which increase in response to his gestures, or even in acknowledgment of them. It's just something he's doing, something he has seen older boxers do, he's saying *I'm here, I made it, I did it.*

When the decision is announced as a draw the crowd's derision increases in volume. "Get out of the ring!" "Assholes!" "Go home!" Contemptuous male laughter follows the boys up the aisle in their robes, towels about their heads, sweating, breathless. Why had *they* thought they were boxers?

How can you enjoy so brutal a sport, people sometimes ask me.

Or pointedly don't ask.

And it's too complex to answer. In any case I don't "enjoy" boxing in the usual sense of the word, and never have; boxing isn't invariably "brutal," and I don't think of it as a "sport."

Nor can I think of boxing in writerly terms as a metaphor for something else. No one whose interest began as mine did in childhood—as an offshoot of my father's interest—is likely to think of boxing as a symbol of something beyond itself, as if its uniqueness were merely an abbreviation, or iconographic; though I can entertain the proposition that life is a metaphor for boxing—for one of those bouts that go on and on, round following round, jabs, missed punches, clinches, nothing determined, again the bell and again and you and your opponent so evenly matched it's impossible not to see that your opponent *is* you: And why this struggle on an elevated platform enclosed by ropes as in a pen beneath hot, crude, pitiless lights in the presence of an impatient crowd?—that sort of hellish-writerly metaphor. Life *is* like boxing in many unsettling respects. But boxing is only like boxing.

For if you have seen five hundred boxing matches you have seen five hundred boxing matches, and their common denominator, which certainly exists, is not of primary interest to you. "If the Host is only a symbol," as the Catholic writer Flannery O'Connor once remarked, "I'd say the hell with it."

Why are you a boxer, Irish featherweight champion Barry McGuigan was asked. He said, "I can't be a poet. I can't tell stories. . . ."

Each boxing match is a story—a unique and highly condensed drama without words. Even when nothing sensational happens: Then the drama is "merely" psychological. Boxers are there to establish an absolute experience, a public accounting of the outermost limits of their beings; they will know, as few of us can know of ourselves, what physical and psychic power they possess—of how much, or how little, they are capable. To enter the ring near-naked and to risk one's life is to make of one's audience voyeurs of a kind: Boxing is so intimate. It is to ease out of sanity's consciousness and into another, difficult to name. It is to risk, and sometimes to realize, the agony of which *agon* (Greek "contest") is the root.

In the boxing ring there are two principal players, overseen by a shadowy third. The ceremonial ringing of the bell is a summoning to full wakefulness for both boxers and spectators. It sets into motion, too, the authority of Time.

The boxers will bring to the fight everything that is themselves, and everything will be exposed—including secrets about themselves they cannot fully realize. The physical self, the maleness, one might say, underlying the "self." There are boxers possessed of such remarkable intuition, such uncanny prescience, one would think they were somehow recalling their fights, not fighting them as we watch. There are boxers who perform skillfully, but mechanically, who cannot improvise in response to another's alteration of strategy; there are boxers performing at the peak of their talent who come to realize, midfight, that it will not be enough;

there are boxers—including great champions—whose careers end abruptly, and irrevocably, as we watch. There has been at least one boxer possessed of an extraordinary and disquieting awareness not only of his opponent's every move and anticipated move but of the audience's keenest shifts in mood as well, for which he seems to have felt personally responsible—Cassius Clay/ Muhammad Ali, of course. "The Sweet Science" celebrates the physicality of men even as it dramatizes the limitations, sometimes tragic, more often poignant, of the physical. Though male spectators identify with boxers, no boxer behaves like a "normal" man when he is in the ring and no combination of blows is "natural." All is style.

Every talent must unfold itself in fighting. So Nietzsche speaks of the Hellenic past, the history of the "contest"—athletic and otherwise—by which Greek youths were educated into Greek citizenry. Without the ferocity of competition, without, even, "envy, jealousy, and ambition" in the contest, the Hellenic city, like the Hellenic man, degenerated. If death is a risk, death is also the prize—for the winning athlete.

In the boxing ring, even in our greatly humanized times, death is always a possibility—which is why some of us prefer to watch films or tapes of fights already past, already defined as history. Or, in some instances, art. (Though to prepare for writing this mosaiclike essay I saw tapes of two infamous "death" fights of recent times: the Lupe Pintor–Johnny Owen bantamweight match of 1982, and the Ray Mancini–Deuk Koo Kim lightweight match of the same year. In both instances the boxers died as a consequence of their astonishing resilience and apparent indefatigability—their "heart," as it's known in boxing circles.) Most of the time, however, death in the ring is extremely unlikely; a statistically rare possibility like your possible death tomorrow morning in an automobile accident or in next month's headlined airline disaster or in a freak accident involving a fall on the stairs or in the bathtub, a skull fracture, subarachnoid hemorrhage. Spectators at "death" fights often claim afterward that what happened simply *seemed* to happen—unpredictably, in a sense accidentally. Only in retrospect does death appear to have been inevitable.

If a boxing match is a story it is an always wayward story, one in which anything can happen. And in a matter of seconds. Split seconds! (Muhammad Ali boasted that he could throw a punch faster than the eye could follow, and he may have been right.) In no other sport can so much take place in so brief a period of time, and so irrevocably.

Because a boxing match is a story without words, this doesn't mean that it has no text or no language, that it is somehow "brute," "primitive," "inarticulate," only that the text is improvised in action, the language a dialogue between the boxers of the most refined sort (one might say, as much neurological as psychological: a dialogue of split-second reflexes) in a joint response to the mysterious will of the audience, which is always that the fight be a worthy one so that the crude paraphernalia of the setting—ring, lights, ropes, stained canvas, the staring onlookers themselves—be erased, forgotten. (As in the theater or the church, settings are erased by way, ideally, of transcendent action.) Ringside announcers give to the wordless spectacle a narrative unity, yet boxing as performance is more clearly akin to dance, or music, than narrative.

To turn from an ordinary preliminary match to a "fight of the century" like those between Joe Louis and Billy Conn, Joe Frazier and Muhammad Ali, Marvin Hagler and Thomas Hearns is to turn from listening or half-listening to a guitar being idly plucked to hearing Bach's *Well-Tempered Clavier* perfectly executed, and that too is part of the story's mystery: So much happens so swiftly and with such heart-stopping subtlety you cannot absorb it except to know that something profound is happening and it is happening in a place beyond words.

I try to catch my opponent on the tip of his nose because I try to punch the bone into his brain.

MIKE TYSON

Boxing's claim is that it is superior to life in that it is, ideally, superior to all accident. It contains nothing that is not fully willed.

The boxer meets an opponent who is a dream distortion of himself in the sense that his weaknesses, his capacity to fail and to be seriously hurt, his intellectual miscalculations—all can be interpreted as strengths belonging to the Other; the parameters of his private being are nothing less than boundless assertions of the Other's self. This is dream, or nightmare: My strengths are not fully my own, but my opponent's weaknesses; my failure is not fully my own, but my opponent's triumph. He is my shadow self, not my (mere) shadow. The boxing match as "serious, complete, and of a certain magnitude"—to refer to Aristotle's definition of tragedy—is an event that necessarily subsumes both boxers, as any ceremony subsumes its participants. (Which is why one can say, for instance, that the greatest fight of Muhammad Ali's career was one of the few fights Ali lost—the first heroic match with Frazier.)

The old boxing adage—a truism surely untrue—that you cannot be knocked out if you see the blow coming, and if you *will* yourself not to be knocked out, has its subtler, more daunting significance: Nothing that happens to the boxer in the ring, including death—"his" death—is not of his own will or failure of will. The suggestion is of a world model in which we are humanly responsible not only for our own acts but for those performed against us.

Which is why, though springing from life, boxing is not a metaphor for life but a unique, closed, self-referential world, obliquely akin to those severe religions in which the individual is both "free" and "determined"—in one sense possessed of a will tantamount to God's, in another totally helpless. The Puritan sensibility would have understood a mouth filling with blood, an eye popped out of its socket—fit punishment for an instant's negligence.

A boxing trainer's most difficult task is said to be to persuade a young boxer to get up and continue fighting after he has been knocked down. And if the boxer has been knocked down by a blow he hadn't seen coming—which is usually the case—how can he hope to protect himself from being knocked down again? and again? The invisible blow is after all—invisible.

"Normal" behavior in the ring would be unbearable to watch, deeply shameful: For "normal" beings share with all living creatures the instinct to persevere, as Spinoza said, in their own being.

The boxer must somehow learn, by what effort of will nonboxers surely cannot guess, to inhibit his own instinct for survival; he must learn to exert his "will" over his merely human and animal impulses, not only to flee pain but to flee the unknown. In psychic terms this sounds like magic. Levitation. Sanity turned inside out, "madness" revealed as a higher and more pragmatic form of sanity.

The fighters in the ring are time-bound—surely nothing is so excruciatingly long as a fiercely contested three-minute round— but the fight itself is timeless. In a sense it becomes all fights, as the boxers are all boxers. By way of films, tapes, and photographs it quickly becomes history for us, even, at times, art. Time, like the possibility of death, is the invisible adversary of which the boxers—and the referee, the seconds, the spectators—are keenly aware. When a boxer is "knocked out" it does not mean, as it's commonly thought, that he has been knocked unconscious, or even incapacitated; it means rather more poetically that he has been knocked out of Time. (The referee's dramatic count of ten constitutes a metaphysical parenthesis of a kind through which the fallen boxer must penetrate if he hopes to continue in Time.) There are in a sense two dimensions of Time abruptly operant: While the standing boxer is *in time*, the fallen boxer is *out of time*. Counted out, he is counted "dead"—in symbolic mimicry of the sport's ancient tradition in which he would very likely be dead. (Though, as we may recall, the canny Romans reserved for themselves as spectators the death blow itself: The triumphant gladiator was obliged to wait for a directive from outside the arena before he finished off his opponent.)

If boxing is a sport it is the most tragic of all sports because more than any human activity it consumes the very excellence it displays—its drama is this very consumption. To expend oneself in fighting the greatest fight of one's life is to begin by necessity the downward turn that next time may be a plunge, an abrupt fall into the abyss. *I am the greatest*, says Muhammad Ali. *I am the greatest*, says Marvelous Marvin Hagler. You always think you're going to win, Jack Dempsey wryly observed in his old age, otherwise you couldn't fight at all. The punishment—to the body, the brain, the spirit—a man must endure to become even a moderately good boxer is inconceivable to most of us whose idea of personal risk is largely ego-related or emotional. But the punishment as it begins to show in even a young and vigorous boxer is closely gauged by his rivals, who are waiting for him to slip. (After junior welterweight champion Aaron Pryor won a lackluster fight last year, a younger boxer in his weight division, interviewed at ringside, said with a smile: "My mouth is watering." And there was twenty-nine-year-old Billy Costello's bold statement—"If I can't beat an old man [of thirty-three] then I should retire"—shortly before his bout with Alexis Arguello, in which he was knocked out in an early round.)

In the ring, boxers inhabit a curious sort of "slow" time—amateurs never box beyond three rounds, and for most amateurs those nine minutes are exhausting—while outside the ring they inhabit an alarmingly accelerated time. A twenty-three-year-old boxer is no longer young in the sense in which a twenty-three-year-old man is young; a thirty-five-year-old is frankly old. (Which is why Muhammad Ali made a tragic mistake in continuing his career after he had lost his title for the second time—to come out of retirement, aged thirty-eight, to fight Larry Holmes, and why Holmes made a similar mistake, years later, in needlessly exposing himself to injury, as well as professional embarrassment, by meeting with the light-heavyweight champion Michael Spinks. The victory of the thirty-seven-year-old Jersey Joe Walcott over the thirty-year-old Ezzard Charles, for the heavyweight title in 1951, is *sui generis*.) All athletes age rapidly but none so rapidly and so visibly as the boxer.

So it is—the experience of watching great fighters of the past is radically different from having seen them perform when they were reigning champions. Jack Johnson, Jack Dempsey, Joe Louis, Sugar Ray Robinson, Rocky Marciano, Muhammad Ali, Joe Frazier—as spectators we know not only how a fight but how a career ends. The trajectory not merely of ten or fifteen rounds but that of an entire life. . . .

Everything that man esteems
Endures a moment or a day.
Love's pleasure drives his love away,

The painter's brush consumes his dreams;
The herald's cry, the soldier's tread
Exhaust his glory and his might:
Whatever flames upon the night
Man's own resinous heart has fed.

—William Butler Yeats,
from "The Resurrection"

———

Boxing is the sport to which all other sports aspire.

GEORGE FOREMAN,
former heavyweight champion of the world

At least in theory and by way of tradition boxing is a sport. But what *is* sport? And why is a man, *in* sport, not the man he is or is expected to be at other times?

Consider the history of gladiatorial combat as the Romans practiced it, or caused it to be practiced, from approximately 265 B.C. to its abolishment by Theodoric in A.D. 500. In the ancient world, among part-civilized nations, it was customary after a battle to sacrifice prisoners of war in honor of commanders who had been killed. It also became customary to sacrifice slaves at the funerals of all persons of importance. But then—for what reason?—for amusement, or for the sake of "sport"?—the condemned slaves were given arms and urged to defend themselves by killing the men who were ordered to kill them. Out of this evolution of brute sacrifice into something approaching a recognizable sporting contest the notorious phenomenon of Roman gladiatorial combat— death as mass amusement—gradually arose. Surely there is nothing quite like it in world history.

At first the contests were performed at the funeral pyre or near the sepulcher, but, with the passage of time, as interest in the fighting detached itself from its ostensibly religious context, matches were moved to the Forum, then to the Circus and amphitheaters. Contractors emerged to train the slaves, men of rank and political importance began to keep "families" of gladiators, upcoming fights were promoted and advertised as sporting contests are today, shows lasting as long as three days increased in number and popularity. Not the mere sacrifice of helpless individuals but the "sport" of the contest excited spectators, for, though the instinct to fight and to kill is surely qualified by one's personal courage, the instinct to watch others fight and kill is evidently inborn. When the boxing fan shouts, "Kill him! Kill him!" he is betraying no peculiar individual pathology or quirk but is asserting his common humanity and his kinship, however distant, with the thousands upon thousands of spectators who crowded into the Roman amphitheaters to see gladiators fight to the death. That such contests for mass amusement endured not for a few years or even decades but for centuries should arrest our attention.

According to Petronius the gladiators took the following oath: "We swear, after the dictation of Eumolpus, to suffer death by fire, bonds, stripes, and the sword; and whatever else Eumolpus may command, as true gladiators we bind ourselves body and mind to our master's service." Their courage became legendary. Cicero referred to it as a model for all Roman citizens—that one should be willing to suffer nobly in the defense of the Commonwealth. In general, gladiators were slaves and condemned criminals who could hope to prolong their lives or even, if they were champions, to gain freedom; but impoverished freemen often fought as well. With the passage of time, paralleling and surely contributing to what we see as the decadence of Rome, even men of rank volunteered to compete publicly. (Under Nero, that most notorious of Roman emperors, such wild exhibitions flourished. It is estimated that during his reign from A.D. 54 to 68 as many as one thousand aristocrats performed as gladiators in one way or another, in fights fair, handicapped, or fixed. At times even women of rank competed—which matches were no doubt particularly noteworthy.) So drawn to these violent sports were Roman aristocrats that the Emperor Augustus was finally moved to issue an edict forbidding them to train as gladiators.

The origins of gladiatorial boxing are specifically Greek. According to tradition a ruler named Thesus (circa 900 B.C.) was entertained by the spectacle of two matched fighters, seated, facing each other, hammering each other to death with their fists. Eventually the men fought on their feet and covered their fists with leather thongs; then with leather thongs covered with sharp metal spikes—the cestus. A ring of some kind, probably a circle, became a neutral space to which an injured boxer might temporarily retreat. When the Romans cultivated the sport it became extremely popular: One legendary cestus champion was said to have killed 1,425 opponents. Winning gladiators were widely celebrated as "kings of athletes" and heroes for all. By confirming in the public arena the bloody mortality of other men they established for themselves, as champions always do, a kind of immortality.

So it happens that the wealthier and more advanced a society, the more fanatic its interest in certain kinds of sport. Civilization's trajectory is to curve back upon itself—naturally? helplessly?— like the mythical snake biting its own tail and to take up with passion the outward signs and gestures of "savagery." While it is plausible that emotionally effete men and women may require ever more extreme experiences to arouse them, it is perhaps the case, too, that the desire is not merely to *mimic* but, magically, to *be* brute, primitive, instinctive, and therefore innocent. One might then be a person for whom the contest is not mere self-destructive play but life itself; and the world, not in spectacular and irrevocable decline, but new, fresh, vital, terrifying and exhilarating by turns, a place of wonders. It is the lost ancestral self that is sought, however futilely. Like those dream remnants of childhood that year by year continue to elude us but are never abandoned, still less despised, for that reason.

Roman gladiatorial combat was abolished under the Christian emperors Constantine and Theodoric, and its practice discontinued forever. Boxing as we know it in the United States derives solely from English bare-knuckle prizefighting of the eighteenth century and from an entirely different conception of sport.

The first recorded account of a bare-knuckle fight in England—between "a gentleman's footman and a butcher"—is dated 1681 and appeared in a publication called the *London Protestant Mercury.* This species of fight, in which maiming and death were not the point, was known as a "Prize Fight" or the "Prize Ring," and was public entertainment of an itinerant nature, frequently attached to village fairs. The Prize Ring was a movable space created by spectators who formed a loose circle by holding a length of rope; the Prize Fight was a voluntary contest between two men, usually a "champion" and a "challenger," unrefereed but governed by rudimentary rules of fair play. The challenge to fight was put to a crowd by a fighter and his accomplices and if any man wanted to accept he tossed his hat into the ring—hence the political expression with its overtone of bellicosity—and the fight was on. Bets were commonly placed on which man would knock the other down first or draw "first blood." Foul play was actively discouraged by the crowd; the fighters shook hands after the fight. "The Noble Art," as prizefighting was called, began as a lowlife species of entertainment but was in time enthusiastically supported by sporting members of the aristocracy and the upper classes.

England's earliest bare-knuckle champion was a man named James Figg who won the honor in 1719. The last of the bare-knuckle champions was the American heavyweight John L. Sullivan whose career—from approximately 1882 to 1892—overlapped both bare-knuckle fighting and gloved boxing as established under the rules of the Marquis of Queensberry, which are observed, with some elaboration, to the present time. The most significant changes were two: the introduction of leather gloves (mainly to protect the hand, not the face—a man's knuckles are easily broken) and the third man in the ring, the referee, whose privilege it is to stop the fight at his own discretion, if he thinks a boxer has no chance of winning or cannot defend himself against his opponent. With the introduction of the referee the crudeness of "The Noble Art" passes over into the relative sophistication of boxing.

The "third man in the ring," usually anonymous so far as the crowd is concerned, appears to many observers no more than an observer himself, even an intruder; a ghostly presence as fluid in motion and quick-footed as the boxers themselves (indeed, he is frequently an ex-boxer). But so central to the drama of boxing is the referee that the spectacle of two men fighting each other unsupervised in an elevated ring would seem hellish, if not obscene—life rather than art. The referee makes boxing possible.

The referee is our intermediary in the fight. He is our moral conscience extracted from us as spectators so that, for the duration of the fight, "conscience" need not be a factor in our experience; nor need it be a factor in the boxers' behavior. (Asked if boxers are ever sorry for having hurt their opponents, Carmen Basilio replied: "Sorry? Are you kidding? Boxers are never sorry.") Which is not to say that boxers are always and forever without conscience: All boxers are different, and behave differently at different times. But there are occasions when a boxer who is trapped in the ropes and unable to fall to the canvas while being struck repeatedly is in danger of being killed unless the referee intervenes—the attacking boxer has been trained not to stop his attack while his opponent is still technically standing. In the rapidly escalating intensity of the fight only the referee remains neutral and objective.

Though the referee's role is highly demanding and it has been estimated that there are perhaps less than a dozen really skilled referees in the world, it seems necessary in the drama of the fight that the referee himself possesses no dramatic identity: Referees' names are rarely remembered after a fight except by seasoned boxing fans. Yet, paradoxically, the referee's participation is crucial. He cannot control what happens in the ring but he can control to a degree *that* it happens—he is responsible for the fight if not for the individual fighters' performances. In a match in which boxing skills and not merely fighting are predominant the referee's role can be merely functional, but in a fiercely contested match it is of incalculable importance. The referee holds the power of life and death at certain times since his decision to terminate a fight, or to allow it to continue, can determine a boxer's fate. (One should know that a well-aimed punch with a heavyweight's full weight behind it can have the equivalent force of ten thousand pounds—a blow that must be absorbed by the brain in its jelly sac.) In the infamous Benny Paret–Emile Griffith fight of March 1962 the referee Ruby Goldstein was said to have stood paralyzed as Griffith trapped Paret in the ropes, striking him as many as eighteen times in the head. (Paret died ten days later.) Boxers are trained not to quit. If knocked down, they try to get up to continue the fight, even if they can hardly defend themselves. The primary rule of the ring—to defend oneself at all times—is both a parody and a distillation of life.

In the past—well into the 1950s—it was not customary for a referee to interfere with a fight, however brutal and one-sided. A boxer who kept struggling to his feet after having been knocked down, or, like the intransigent Jake LaMotta in his sixth and final fight with Sugar Ray Robinson in 1951, refused to fall to the canvas though he could no longer defend himself and had become a human punching bag, was simply left to his fate. The will of the crowd—and overwhelmingly it *is* the will of the crowd—that one man defeat the other totally and irrevocably, was honored. Hence the bloody "great" fights of boxing's history—Dempsey's triumph over Willard, for instance—are inconceivable today.

It should be understood that "boxing" and "fighting," though always combined in the greatest of boxers, can be entirely different and even unrelated activities. Amateur boxers are trained to win their matches on points; professionals usually try for knockouts. (Not that professionals are more violent than amateurs but why trust judges?—and the knockout is dramatically spectacular.) If boxing is frequently, in the lighter weights especially, a highly complex and refined skill, belonging solely to civilization, fighting belongs to something predating civilization, the instinct not merely to defend oneself—for how has the masculine ego ever been assuaged by so minimal a response to threat?—but to attack another and to force him into absolute submission. This accounts for the electrifying effect upon a typical fight crowd when fighting suddenly emerges out of boxing—when, for instance, a boxer's face begins to bleed and the fight seems to enter a new and more dangerous phase. The flash of red is the visible sign of the fight's authenticity in the eyes of many spectators, and boxers are justified in being proud, as many are, of their facial scars.

If the "violence" of boxing seems at times to flow from the crowd, to be a heightened expression of the crowd's delirium—rarely transmitted by television, by the way—the many restraints and subtleties of boxing are possible because of the "third man in the ring," a counter of sorts to the inchoate wash of emotion beyond the ropes and the ring apron: our conscience, as I've indicated, extracted from us, and granted an absolute authority.

———

I ain't never liked violence.

SUGAR RAY ROBINSON,
former welterweight and middleweight
champion of the world

To the untrained eye most boxing matches appear not merely savage but mad. As the eye becomes trained, however, the spectator begins to see the complex patterns that underlie the "madness"; what seems to be merely confusing action is understood to be coherent and intelligent, frequently inspired. Even the spectator who dislikes violence in principle can come to admire highly skillful boxing—to admire it beyond all "sane" proportions. A brilliant boxing match, quicksilver in its motions, transpiring far more rapidly than the mind can absorb, can have the power that Emily Dickinson attributed to great poetry: You know it's great when it takes the top of your head off. (The physical imagery Dickinson employs is peculiarly apt in this context.)

This early impression—that boxing is "mad," or mimics the actions of madness—seems to me no less valid, however, for being, by degrees, substantially modified. It is never erased, never entirely forgotten or overcome; it simply sinks beneath the threshold of consciousness, as the most terrifying and heartrending of our lives' experiences sink beneath the level of consciousness by way of familiarity or deliberate suppression. So one knows, but does not (consciously) know, certain intransigent facts about the human condition. One does not (consciously) know, but one *knows*. All boxing fans, however accustomed to the sport, however many decades have been invested in their obsession, know that boxing is sheerly madness, for all its occasional beauty. That knowledge is our common bond and sometimes—dare it be uttered?—our common shame.

To watch boxing closely, and seriously, is to risk moments of what might be called animal panic—a sense not only that something very ugly is happening but that, by watching it, one is an accomplice. This awareness, or revelation, or weakness, or hair-

line split in one's cuticle of a self can come at any instant, un-
anticipated and unbidden; though of course it tends to sweep
over the viewer when he is watching a really violent match. I
feel it as vertigo—breathlessness—a repugnance beyond language: a sheerly physical loathing. That it is also, or even primarily, self-loathing goes without saying.

For boxing really isn't metaphor, it is the thing in itself. And
my predilection for watching matches on tape, when the out-
comes are known, doesn't alter the fact that, as the matches
occurred, they occurred in the present tense, and for one time
only. The rest is subterfuge—the intellectual's uneasy "control"
of his material.

Impossible to see the old, early fights of Dempsey's and not to
feel this *frisson* of dread, despite the poor quality of the films,
the somewhat antic rhythms of the human figures. Or, I would
guess, the trilogy of Zale-Graziano fights about which people
speak in awe forty years later. For one man of my acquaintance
it was a fight of Joe Louis's, against a long-forgotten opponent.
For another, one of the "great" dirty matches of Willie Pep and
Sandy Saddler—"little white perfection / and death in red plaid
trunks" as the poet Philip Levine has written of that infamous
duo. There was Deuk Koo Kim, there was Johnny Owen, in an
earlier decade luckless Benny Paret, trapped in the ropes as referee Ruby Goldstein stood frozen, unable to interfere—

And Paret? Paret died on his feet. As he took those eighteen punches
something happened to everyone who was in psychic range of the
event. Some part of his death reached out to us. One felt it hover
in the air. He was still standing in the ropes, trapped as he had
been before, he gave some little half-smile of regret, as if he were
saying, "I didn't know I was going to die just yet," and then, his
head leaning back but still erect, his death came to breathe about
him. He began to pass away. He went down more slowly than any
fighter had ever gone down, he went down like a large ship which
turns on end and slides second by second into its grave. As he
went down, the sound of Griffith's punches echoed in the mind
like a heavy ax in the distance chopping into a wet log.

—Norman Mailer, "Ten Thousand Words a Minute"

For one friend of mine it was a bloody fight fought by the lightweight contender Bobby Chacon that filled him with horror—though, ironically, Chacon came back to win the match (as Chacon was once apt to do). For another friend, a fellow novelist, enamored of boxing since boyhood, it was the Hagler-Hearns fight of 1985—he was frightened by his own ecstatic participation in it.

At such times one thinks: What is happening? why are we here? what does this mean? can't this be stopped? My terror at seeing Floyd Patterson battered into insensibility by Sonny Liston was not assuaged by my rational understanding that the event had taken place long ago and that, in fact, Patterson is in fine health at the present time, training an adopted son to box. (Liston of course has been dead for years—he died of a heroin overdose, aged thirty-eight, in "suspicious" circumstances.) More justified, perhaps, was my sickened sense that boxing is, simply, wrong, a mistake, an outlaw activity for some reason under the protectorate of the law, when, in March 1986, I sat in the midst of a suddenly very quiet closed-circuit television audience in a suburban Trenton hall watching bantamweight Richie Sandoval as he lay flat and unmoving on his back . . . very likely dead of a savage beating the referee had not, for some reason, stopped in time. My conviction was that anything was preferable to boxing, anything was preferable to seeing another minute of it, for instance standing outside in the parking lot for the remainder of the evening and staring at the stained asphalt. . . .

A friend who is a sportswriter was horrified by the same fight. In a letter he spoke of his intermittent disgust for the sport he has been watching most of his life, and writing about for years: "It's all a bit like bad love—putting up with the pain, waiting for the sequel to the last good moment. And like bad love, there comes the point of being worn out, when the reward of the good moment doesn't seem worth all the trouble. . . ."

Yet we don't give up on boxing, it isn't that easy. Perhaps it's like tasting blood. Or, more discreetly put, love commingled with hate is more powerful than love. Or hate.

One of the paradoxes of boxing is that the viewer inhabits a consciousness so very different from that of the boxer as to suggest a counterworld. "Free" will, "sanity," "rationality"—our characteristic modes of consciousness—are irrelevant, if not detrimental, to boxing in its most extraordinary moments. Even as he disrobes himself ceremonially in the ring the great boxer must disrobe himself of both reason and instinct's caution as he prepares to fight.

———

Dustin Hoffman recalls a boxing match he had seen as a boy: As the triumphant boxer left the ring to pass up the aisle, an ecstatic fight fan, male, followed closely after him, wiping all he could of the sweat from the boxer's body onto himself.

An observer is struck by boxing's intense preoccupation with its own history; its continuous homage to a gallery of heroes—or are they saints? At Muhammad Ali's Deer Lake, Pennsylvania, training camp the names of heavyweight champions—Louis, Marciano, Liston, Patterson, et al.—were painted in white letters on massive iconographic boulders. "Jack Dempsey" named himself for the middleweight champion Jack Dempsey (1884–91, known as Dempsey "The Nonpareil" because he outboxed every man he fought). "Sugar Ray" Leonard named himself boldly after "Sugar Ray" Robinson—an act of audacity that did not prove embarrassing. If Marvin Hagler shaves his head, the image of Rubin "Hurricane" Carter comes to mind, and, beyond him, that of Jack Johnson himself—the first and very likely the greatest of defiantly *black* boxers, whom Cassius Clay/Muhammad Ali admired as well. So frequently are a few names evoked—Dempsey, Louis, Marciano, Pep, Robinson—one might think these boxers were our contemporaries and not champions of eras long past.

If boxing exhausts most of its practitioners in a Darwinian struggle for survival like virtually no other, it so honors a very few, so enshrines them in the glamour of immortality, surely the danger is justified? As in any religion, present and past are magically one; Time, even death, are defeated. The dead immortals are always with us, not only their names and the hazy outlines of careers recalled, but individual bouts, moments when decisive punches were thrown and caught, the size of a boxer's fist, the measurement of his reach, his age when he began and when he retired, his record of wins, losses, draws. The uppercut Jack Johnson used against Stanley Ketchel in 1909—the famous Fitzsimmons "shift" of 1897 (when Fitzsimmons defeated Gentleman Jim Corbett for the heavyweight title)—the wicked left hook with which Jack Dempsey caught a distracted Jack Sharkey in 1927—Rocky Marciano's several right-hand knockout punches—Cassius Clay's mystery punch in the first minute of the first round of his second match with Sonny Liston—the left hook of Joe Frazier that knocked Muhammad Ali on his back in the fifteenth round of their first fight: All are commemorated. The typical boxing writer's imagination is not so much stimulated by his subject as enflamed. Dream matches are routinely fantasized in which boxers of different eras meet one another—Marciano-Dempsey, Louis-Ali, Hagler-Robinson, the 1961 Sonny Liston and the 1973 George Foreman. Boxers of different weights are thrown together—how would Willie Pep or Benny Leonard or Roberto Durán have done against Joe Louis, equipped with the necessary poundage? Though preoccupation with past records is common to most sports there is something unusually intense about it in boxing, perhaps because, in boxing, the individual is so very alone, or seems so. Like the saint he gives the impression of having arrived at his redemption by unflagging solitary effort.

The boxing past exists in an uncannily real and vital relationship with the present. The dead are not dead, or not merely dead. When, for instance, Larry Holmes made his ill-advised attempt to equal Rocky Marciano's record (forty-nine wins, no losses) it seemed suddenly that Marciano was living again, his name and photograph in all the papers, interviews with his family published. Michael Spinks resurrected not only Billy Conn, the light-heavyweight champion who was defeated in a famous match by Joe Louis in 1941 (and again in 1946) but any number of other light-heavyweight champions who were defeated by heavyweight champions—Georges Carpentier, Tommy Loughran, Joey Maxim, the indefatigable Archie Moore. The spectacular first round of the Hagler-Hearns match provoked reminiscences of "the greatest first rounds of all time." (Number one remains Dempsey-Firpo, 1923.) *The Ring*'s Hall of Fame—to which controversial Jake LaMotta was only recently elected—corresponds to the pantheon of saints elected by the Vatican except it is in fact more

finely calibrated, its saints arranged under various groupings and subgroupings, and its balloting highly complex. (Indeed, no intellectual journal in the States is more scrupulously attentive to its history than this famous boxing magazine, founded by Nat Fleischer in 1922, in which past, present, and a hypothesized future are tirelessly examined, and in which one finds articles on such subjects as "The Greatest Disappointments in Ring History," "The Greatest Mismatches," "The Greatest Left Hooks," "When a Good Little Man *Did* Defeat a Good Big Man.")

It is as if by way of the most strenuous exigencies of the physical self a boxer can—sometimes—transcend the merely physical; he can, if he is lucky, be absolved of his mortality. The instinct is of course closely allied with the desire for fame and riches (those legendary champions with their purple Cadillacs!) but is not finally identical with it. If the boxing ring is an altar it is not an altar of sacrifice solely but one of consecration and redemption. Sometimes.